D0329182

TAKEOVER

★★

THE 100-YEAR WAR FOR THE SOUL OF THE GOP
AND HOW CONSERVATIVES CAN FINALLY WIN IT

FOREWORD BY JENNY BETH MARTIN

RICHARD A. VIGUERIE

WND Books

TAKEOVER

Published by WND Books®, Washington, D.C. WND Books is a registered trademark of WorldNetDaily.com, Inc. ("WND")

All photographs in the insert are courtesy of the author. Unless otherwise noted, all photographs in appendix 7, Rogue's Gallery, are in the public domain and courtesy of Wikimedia Commons. The photograph of Reince Priebus on page 311 © AP Photo/Susan Walsh and used with permission. The photograph of Chris Christie on page 312 © AP Photo/Julio Cortez and used with permission.

Library of Congress Cataloging-in-Publication Data

Viguerie, Richard A.
Takeover: the 100-year war for the soul of the GOP and how conservatives can finally win it / by Richard A. Viguerie. -- First edition.
pages cm
Includes index.
ISBN 978-1-936488-54-4 (hardcover)
1. Republican Party (U.S. : 1854-)--History. I. Title.
JK2356.V47 2014
324.2734--dc23

2013051143

Book designed by Mark Karis

WND Books are distributed to the trade by:
Midpoint Trade Books, 27 West 20th Street, Suite 1102, New York, New York 10011

WND Books are available at special discounts for bulk purchases. WND Books, Inc., also publishes books in electronic formats. For more information call (541) 474-1776 or visit www.wndbooks.com.

First Edition

Hardcover ISBN: 978-1-936488-54-4   eBook ISBN: 978-1-936488-64-3

Printed in the United States of America

14 15 16 17 18 19 BVG 9 8 7 6 5 4 3 2 1

DEDICATION

This book is dedicated with great appreciation to the now deceased giants of the conservative movement, most of whom were friends of mine, who did not serve in public office, but upon whose mighty shoulders the conservative movement stands today.

Among those who have passed on, but with whom God blessed us for this great work, are William F. Buckley, Jr., L. Brent Bozell, Jr., Joe Coors, Terry Dolan, Russell Kirk, Marvin Liebman, Clarence Manion, E. Victor "Vic" Milione, Frank Meyer, Howard Phillips, Henry Regnery, William Rusher, Paul Weyrich, and Cliff White.

The conservative movement has been fortunate to have had elected officials such as Barry Goldwater, Jesse Helms, John Ashbrook, and most of all, Ronald Reagan, who relied heavily upon the individuals mentioned above to lead and advance the conservative cause.

CONTENTS

FOREWORD

There is a bitter political civil war taking place that will determine whether America remains a constitutional republic. It is a timeless struggle between those who have power and those who desire to be free. The modern version of this struggle is not between Democrats and Republicans, but within the Republican Party itself.

This civil war began over one hundred years ago and not with the rise of the Tea Party movement in 2009.

It is a civil war between limited-government, constitutional conservatives and the progressive, establishment wing of the GOP. And make no mistake: the establishment wing of the Republican Party is progressive, and has been ever since conservatives stymied Teddy Roosevelt's attempt to reclaim the Republican presidential nomination in 1912 and make progressivism the governing philosophy of the Republican Party.

In the years since 1912, this civil war has been playing out, and for the majority of that time, from the Taft-Eisenhower campaign of 1952 to the Tea Party's battles to nominate and elect limited-government constitutional conservatives in 2010 and 2012, Richard Viguerie has been in the thick of the battle.

Richard's objective in writing this book is to provide a plan for conservatives to win this civil war based on the lessons he has learned—from both success and failure—in over fifty years of being active in the conservative movement at the national level.

It is a plan for constitutional conservatives to take over the GOP so that we may restore the liberty and opportunity that the Founders intended and protect that great document, the United States Constitution.

The millions of Americans who are drawn to the Tea Party movement understand that progressives in both the Democratic and Republican Parties have usurped power and overrun the Constitution. The Obama administration is the most extreme example of progressive rule, but the road to where we are today was built with the willing participation of establishment Republicans.

James Madison foresaw the likelihood of this civil war, although not within a political party, in Federalist No. 44, where he wrote, "In the last resort a remedy must be obtained from the people who can, by the election of more faithful representatives, annul the acts of the usurpers."

Madison's "remedy" must play out within the Republican Party since the Democratic Party has been completely taken over by progressives whose policies cannot succeed without ignoring and violating the Constitution.

In *TAKEOVER* Richard shows us that the ballot box of the Republican primaries is where we must begin to fulfill Madison's remedy of electing "more faithful representatives."

Time is running out, and if we fail in this task, our children, grandchildren—our posterity—will never know the America for which millions have sacrificed their labor, capital, lives, and limbs. Unless the Republican Party fulfills its promise and becomes the constitutional alternative to the progressives, I fear the "American experiment" is over.

The rise of the Tea Party citizenry and the election of young, principled constitutionalists to the Congress and in state legislatures is a sign that this war is about to turn, and in *TAKEOVER* Richard Viguerie gives us a road map to make it turn in our favor.

Where we are now is the culmination of decades of struggle, which is why the younger people in our movement especially must know what has worked and what has failed up until now.

It is to the younger generation, who has the most "skin in the game," that *TAKEOVER* is addressed. Those who join us in this civil war are fulfilling an obligation to our children, grandchildren, and generations yet to be born that I dare say is no less consequential than that of the Founders.

The goal of Richard Viguerie's *TAKEOVER* is for limited-government constitutional conservatives to take over the Republican Party and govern America in 2017. I urge you to read the book, follow the plan, and get in the fight today.

—*Jenny Beth Martin*
President and Cofounder of Tea Party Patriots

INTRODUCTION

All elections are, in some sense, about the future. Politicians may base campaigns on the past by running on their record, but voters must still decide: if they like the candidate's record, whether he can be trusted to maintain that record in the future—or if they don't like his record—if he can be expected to continue voting against their interests and should be thrown out.

Even more important than a candidate's record may be the candidate's *vision* of the future, and how he or she frames it.

Think of Winston Churchill. His record was stellar; however, having just saved Great Britain from the Nazis and helped lead the Allies to victory in the Second World War, on July 5, 1945, he lost the election to lead the country in peacetime that he had just saved in wartime. British voters were looking for a different vision of the future than the one Churchill offered.

History doesn't start or stop on Election Day, and elections don't happen in a historical vacuum. What has happened in the past informs and molds our vision of the future.

The purpose of this book is to provide limited-government constitutional conservatives and other liberty-loving voters with a vision of the future of the Republican Party as the political home of limited-government constitutional conservatives, and a plan to achieve that goal.

An equally important part of this plan is an understanding of the historical perspective on how the GOP was hijacked by an elite progressive minority who, over the past one hundred years, have taken the Republican Party far afield from its conservative platform and the interests and values of its grassroots conservative base.

Let's turn back the clock to 1952 when, as a nineteen-year-old kid too young to vote (you had to be twenty-one at that time), I sat in a polling place in Houston, Texas, from 7:00 a.m. to 7:00 p.m., trying to help "Mr. Conservative," Senator Robert Taft of Ohio, win the Republican nomination for president.

It mostly ended up being a "family values" moment, when the only people to vote that day in my precinct were my mother and father.

Republicans were rare birds in Texas in 1952, and I'm sure plenty of my college friends thought I was nuts for spending my time on politics, particularly Republican politics.

Since Reconstruction, no Republican in Texas had been elected governor or senator. Republican elected officials in Texas were few and far between, with the GOP existing largely as a patronage party to claim federal appointments during the times when there was a Republican in the White House.

From my perch out in Harris County, Texas (Houston), it looked like Taft had it wrapped up. After all, he had won the most votes in the primaries, had the most delegates going into the Republican National Convention, and despite Eisenhower's status as a war hero, Taft was the favorite of the grassroots activists of the GOP.

But Taft was not the favorite of the Eastern establishment leaders of the National Republican Party; they worked all out to hand the nomination to General Eisenhower, and when Senator Taft was defeated, I was surprised and disappointed, but I was not dissuaded from my interest in conservative politics.

Making sure that I was on the winning side wasn't what interested me; making sure the right side won did.

Fast-forward to September 11, 1960, and a meeting at the family home of William F. Buckley, Jr. in Sharon, Connecticut: The Sharon Statement, primarily drafted by author and educator M. Stanton Evans, and still one of the most compelling statements of conservative principles and values ever written, was adopted and signed by the ninety-some young attendees. You can find the full text of the Sharon Statement in appendix 1 of this book.[1]

The Sharon Statement, in its eloquent homage to liberty and limited government, has stood the test of time. With the exception of its provision regarding international Communism (for which we might today substitute radical Islam), it is still relevant. Young Americans for Freedom was launched, and with it began the modern conservative movement we know today.

Less than a year later, in August 1961, I became executive secretary of Young Americans for Freedom, and because we needed to raise money to build the organization, I began to learn how to market the conservative ideas, principles, and values for which we stood.

For those born in the Internet age or after the advent of cable TV, it may be hard to imagine how difficult the job of marketing conservatism and conservative ideas was in 1961.

To this day, the *New York Times* carries on its front page the motto "All the news that's fit to print," and in 1961, as it is today, liberals were largely in charge of deciding what was fit to print in the establishment press and what wasn't.

The conservative print media was small; *Human Events* was an eight- to twelve-page newsletter, the *National Review* was just getting started, and YAF's publication, the *New Guard*, first edited by Dr. Lee Edwards, now a senior fellow at the Heritage Foundation, had just a few thousand subscribers.

It was hard, if not impossible, to find the conservative point of view on television. Walter Cronkite of CBS and his establishment media colleagues at ABC and NBC would go on air at 6:30 p.m., and by 7:00 p.m. America would have been told what to think—and it wouldn't be that communism was evil and dangerous and that lower taxes, less government, and more freedom were good ideas.

This remained true into the 1970s and 1980s, even as Ronald Reagan rose to national prominence and won two landslide elections.

If you were a conservative on a college campus or in a suburban neighborhood reading the newspapers and watching TV, you were marooned in a world where the elite opinion makers of New York and Washington found your ideas fit to be ignored or attacked, but not printed or aired.

The one means we had to get our message out, to share ideas, and to bypass the establishment media filter, was direct mail—the first and most long-lived form of new and alternative media.

I didn't set out to change the media or the media culture by applying the techniques of commercial direct marketing to conservative politics; we simply needed money to run Young Americans for Freedom and it was my job to raise it—a job that became all the more urgent after our conservative standard-bearer, Senator Barry Goldwater of Arizona, was obliterated in the 1964 election.

Goldwater—the candidate of the New West and conservatives—had won the Republican nomination over the strong objections of the Eastern establishment Republican leaders. Once he had the nomination in hand, they did little to help him and much to hurt him, and when he went down in flames, they were quick to blame conservatives for the Party's defeat and do their best to purge Goldwater supporters from the GOP.

If things look bleak for conservatives today, trust me: conservatives were in a darkness of biblical proportions after Goldwater's defeat.

The long knives of the Republican establishment were out for anyone who had supported Goldwater or who questioned the "go-along, get-along" attitude of the Party's congressional leaders whose failure to stand for conservative principles had assigned Republicans to what appeared to be the status of a permanent minority on Capitol Hill.

Plenty of conservatives then, and throughout the early years of the rise of the modern conservative movement, thought that the only way to advance the cause of conservative governance was to form a third party.

William F. Buckley, Jr. disagreed. Buckley argued that conservatives should take over the Republican Party, while others, such as author Ayn Rand, argued for a separate movement and a third party.

Angry as we were about the criticism verging on sabotage Senator Goldwater received from the Republican establishment, and as insulted as some conservatives were over the personal attacks they received at the hands of establishment Republicans, we had a sense that even though Goldwater had lost the election, his grassroots support demonstrated that millions of Americans thought he was right on many issues.

Believe it or not, to many of us in the conservative movement, the plan to take over the Republican Party advocated by Bill Buckley made more sense than ever—even after Goldwater's defeat.

We saw the establishment leadership of the Republican Party as intellectually bankrupt, and we believed that if we could just get the message out, we could, as the late Margaret Thatcher allegedly said, "First win the argument and then win the vote."

So rather than bolt the Republican Party, most conservatives cinched up their belts; started new publications, think tanks, policy advocacy organizations, and newfangled political committees (called political action committees); and began to build a new conservative coalition around the two issues that attracted those millions of grassroots supporters to Goldwater's cause: anti-Communist national defense conservatism and economic conservatism, or what the Sharon Statement called economic liberty.

In 1961, when I became executive secretary of Young Americans for Freedom (YAF), I soon began to learn the power of fund-raising and marketing through direct mail.

As executive secretary of YAF, I came into contact with people like Bill Buckley, Bill Rusher, Frank Meyer, and other luminaries of the conservative movement. I tried to get as caught up as I could in the classics of conservative thought, but it didn't take long for me to realize I'd never really catch up.

This led me to recognize that while we conservatives had some talented thinkers, writers, candidates, and elected officials, what we didn't have were marketers. I made a conscious decision to fill that niche—that hole in the marketplace—by immersing myself in the study of marketing for the next ten years, and to this day I still spend two to three hours a day six days a week studying marketing.

In the aftermath of Barry Goldwater's 1964 defeat, I launched my own direct-mail company. With $4,000 in savings to back the venture—and a firm belief that those anti-Communist national defense conservatives and economic conservatives who had supported Goldwater could be motivated to support other conservative candidates, organizations, and causes—I formed the Richard A. Viguerie Company, Inc. and began the journey of pioneering ideological/political direct mail on behalf of the conservative movement.

My first client was Young Americans for Freedom; however, in one of the frequent upheavals typical of an organization run by a bunch of college kids, I lost the account within six weeks. But other business soon came along.

From the start, the company grew quickly, and I came to work with many of the key organizations and candidates of the New Right and the modern conservative movement, including the Conservative Caucus, the Committee for the Survival of a Free Congress, the National Conservative Political Action Committee, the National Right to Work Committee, the American Conservative Union, Senator Jesse Helms's National Congressional Club, and Gun Owners of America. We also helped market many of the early stars of the conservative movement who sought elective office, such as congressmen Phil Crane and Bob Dornan, Dr. Ron Paul, John Ashbrook, senators Jesse Helms and Strom Thurmond, California state senator H. L. "Bill" Richardson, and candidates Max Rafferty, Howard Phillips, Jeff Bell, and G. Gordon Liddy.

The coalition of national defense conservatives and economic conservatives appealed to millions of voters whom the Viguerie Company reached and energized through direct mail to create what you might call a "two-legged stool." It could, and did, win some elections, but with only two legs it wasn't yet a stable, winning national coalition.

It was Ronald Reagan who had the insight—perhaps *genius* is a better term—to create his winning political movement by starting with two legs composed of the Goldwater supporters and, by adding a third leg, creating a stable three-legged stool.

Reagan did that by welcoming social conservatives into the Republican Party.

Reagan didn't originate the idea of adding social conservatives to the existing conservative coalition. Astute observers of national politics, such as Tom Ellis of North Carolina, had already seen the unharnessed political potential of Evangelical Christians, but the idea of organizing the Religious Right into a political committee perhaps formed first in the minds of Paul Weyrich and Rev. Jerry Falwell.

Their vision came to fruition at a meeting between Bob Billings, Ed McAteer, Howard Phillips, Weyrich, and Falwell, who came together at Falwell's office in Lynchburg, Virginia, to brainstorm what eventually became the "Moral Majority."

Led by Reverend Falwell and run by Dr. Ron Godwin, the Moral Majority quickly became the largest and most effective conservative organization in the country.

Still, the combined political power of the marriage of the California free market–oriented entrepreneurs, advocates of a strong national defense, and socially conservative pastors and social commentators who led the Reagan coalition wasn't obvious in the beginning, and it certainly made establishment Republicans uncomfortable.

But it worked, and as long as Republicans hewed to the principles that held it together, they won three landslide presidential elections: 1980, 1984, and 1988.

Later, when they set those principles aside as they did in 1992,

1996, 2008, and 2012, they lost—big-time.

Many observers will be tempted to blame external factors for these election defeats, but the common thread that ran through all of these lost elections was that Republicans failed to define themselves as the party of less government. Cut through all the insider commentary and what really distinguishes the Republican establishment from conservatives is that establishment Republicans like big government and the spending, taxes, and regulations that go with it. And if the choice is between Big Government Republicans and Big Government Democrats, the Republicans almost always lose.

In 2009 a fourth leg was added to the Reagan coalition—the limited-government constitutional conservatives of the Tea Party movement, who were unfettered by ties to the old Republican establishment and represented the forgotten men and women of America whom Angelo Codevilla identified as "the Country Class" in his essay "America's Ruling Class —and the Perils of Revolution" in the July–August 2010 issue of the *American Spectator*.

As a result of adding this fourth leg to their coalition, the GOP was swept back into control of the House of Representatives, came within striking distance of a Senate majority, and a reenergized Republican Party elected thousands of down-ballot candidates.

Unfortunately, unlike the wise conservative leaders who built the Reagan coalition, men such as Nevada senator Paul Laxalt, Lyn Nofziger, Dick Allen, Ed Meese, Marty Anderson, Jeff Bell, Tom Ellis, and Judge William Clark, between 2010 and 2012 today's establishment Republican leaders did their best to alienate and marginalize the new conservative voting bloc of the Tea Party movement.

Today, in the aftermath of the disappointments of the 2012 elections, conservatives are once again at a crossroads.

We are angry at being blamed for Mitt Romney's defeat, when we argued from the beginning that he was a Big Government establishment politician and that if he ran a content-free campaign, he would lose.

We are angry at the disrespect shown to limited-government

constitutional conservatives who were delegates to the 2012 Republican National Convention. We are angrier still when members of Congress, whom we elected, who want to use the democratic process to push policies based on limited government conservative principles, are told to "get their ass in line" by Speaker of the House John Boehner, and to go along with the Republican Party leadership's betrayal of conservative principles—or else.

These frustrations among conservatives have boiled over into new calls for the formation of a third party, especially from some Tea Party movement supporters and libertarian-minded conservatives who were attracted to the presidential candidacy of Congressman Ron Paul.

However, the arguments against a third-party are the same now as they were when Bill Buckley and Ayn Rand first jousted over where conservatives should find their political home a half a century ago.

The bottom line is that while third-party movements, such as Libertarians, have gained some recognition and added to their numbers, they haven't actually been electing candidates to office. Limited-government constitutional conservatives running as Republicans win, but the same candidates, with the same ideas, running as Libertarians, lose.

Congressman Ron Paul admitted as much when he said no one would have paid any attention to him or his ideas if he had run as a Libertarian, and there is no doubt that his son Rand Paul would not be a US senator if he had run as a Libertarian, instead of as a Republican.

But there is good news and bad news in Libertarian ideas.

The good news is that, while as yet imperfectly realized, Libertarian ideas have had a powerful influence on the twenty-first-century conservative movement, and due in part to Libertarian influence, the Republican Party may truly become the party of less regulation, lower taxes, and more personal freedom—this certainly hasn't always been the case when one considers that fewer than forty years ago the EPA was established and wage and price controls were instituted under Republican president Richard Nixon.

The bad news is that many in the national and state Libertarian parties actually pride themselves on being destroyers, and when they lose a primary or otherwise don't get their way, rather than selling themselves and their ideas harder, they try to "teach Republicans a lesson" by running a third-party candidate and thereby causing the Republican candidate to lose, as happened in the November 2013 Virginia governor's race, when Ken Cuccinelli, one of the most principled limited-government constitutional conservatives ever to seek statewide office in America, was defeated because a Libertarian candidate siphoned off enough conservative votes to elect Terry McAuliffe, a radical liberal Democrat.

This is a bad way to sell your ideas in the best of times; it is dangerous to the future of the country if a splintering of the conservative coalition returns conservatives to permanent minority status in America.

Yes, Ron Paul and his delegates to the 2012 Republican Convention were treated in a ham-handed way by Reince Priebus and other establishment Republicans.

Yes, it makes all of us angry when John Boehner, who was made Speaker of the House through the efforts of millions of Tea Party movement voters and volunteers, refers to limited-government constitutional conservatives as "knuckle-draggers."

But the future of this country is more important than the personal slights and short-term wins or losses that any candidate and his adherents might suffer.

When Libertarians run their own third-party candidates, as they are certainly free to do, they all too often split the twenty-first-century conservative coalition and hand victory to Big Government Democrats—as they did in Virginia's 2013 gubernatorial election.

The greatest challenge limited-government constitutional conservatives running as Republicans will have in future elections where there is a Libertarian Party candidate on the ballot is to earn enough support from liberty-minded voters, who might be inclined to vote for a Libertarian candidate, to achieve a plurality in the election—and the only way to do that is to campaign on and deliver limited constitutional conservative government.

Movement conservatives have been steadily working the plan envisioned by "the Buckley generation" for over fifty years. Inspired by leaders and thinkers such as John Ashbrook, Morton Blackwell, L. Brent Bozell, Jr., William F. Buckley, Jr., Lee Edwards, Tom Ellis, Jerry Falwell, Ed Fuelner, Russell Kirk, Frank Meyer, Howard Phillips, Henry Regnery, Bill Rusher, Phyllis Schlafly, F. Clifton White, Paul Weyrich, and others, we have made great progress in the Republican Party, and more important, in public opinion at large.

For over twenty years polls have shown that Americans, by a two-to-one margin, self-identify as conservatives. Today, a record number of Americans—60 percent according to the Gallup Organization's governance poll—say that the federal government has too much power.[2] This follows on an earlier Gallup poll in which 64 percent of those responding said the greatest threat to freedom is Big Government—and the biggest jump in that fear is among Democrats. Conservatives and libertarian-minded voters should see that as a sign that American opinion is moving in our direction.[3]

In the wake of Mitt Romney's defeat, and the discrediting of the Republican establishment that tied the future of the Party to Romney's content-free campaign, now is not the time for conservatives to give up on the Republican Party and bolt to a third party. Now is the time to redouble our efforts to finish the job we started more than fifty years ago and complete the takeover of the GOP.

In large measure we conservatives have accomplished Baroness Thatcher's first step; we are winning the argument. Now is the time to take over the Republican Party and start winning the vote.

That's why the title of this book is *TAKEOVER*. In it you will find the history, the facts, the arguments, the vision, the goals, the strategy, and the tactics needed for conservatives to complete the takeover of the Republican Party by 2016 and govern America in 2017.

TAKEOVER

1

TEDDY ROOSEVELT THROUGH BARRY GOLDWATER

t's a cinch that you are going to lose a fight—let alone a war—that you don't even know you are in, but for the past one hundred odd years, the grassroots conservative voters of the Republican party have been under regular attack by the very people they elected to run their party—the establishment leadership of the GOP.

In 1912, at the Republican party convention in Chicago, former Republican president Teddy Roosevelt sought to hijack the Republican Party as the vehicle to advance his "progressive" philosophy. Roosevelt initially ran for the Republican nomination but failed—the convention endorsed incumbent President William Howard Taft for reelection—so TR created his own Progressive Party, also known as the Bull Moose Party, and ran anyway.

Roosevelt's egotistical third-party run split the Republican vote and ensured that he and the GOP's candidate, William Howard Taft, lost to Democrat Woodrow Wilson, who garnered less than 42 percent of the vote. Wilson turned out to be one of our most disastrous presidents, and the damage Teddy Roosevelt did to the Republican Party and brand was severe.

How is it possible that Teddy Roosevelt could be a bad guy? His face is on Mount Rushmore, for crying out loud!

Here's the damage Teddy Roosevelt did that still haunts the Republican Party to this day.

At the grassroots level, the Republican Party's strength has always been found among solidly conservative voters who opposed the kind of Big Government favored by the Democratic Party.

These conservative voters looked to the Declaration of Independence for their inspiration and to the Constitution, and the lean federal establishment it envisioned, for the kind of government they wanted.

Progressivism, or Big Government Republicanism, gained legitimacy through the cult of personality surrounding Teddy Roosevelt, and it became the governing philosophy of the establishment Republican leadership.

Suddenly, no one was sure what Republicans stood for, and the war to decide that question began.

Except the Big Government leaders of the establishment conveniently forgot to tell the average Republican voters there was a war going on.

So, while conservatives were routinely the grassroots-favorite candidates, for most of the past one hundred odd years, Big Government Republicans have held sway in the Party leadership.

During the Great Depression and the presidency of Franklin Delano Roosevelt, these party leaders finessed the nominations of Republican candidates for president, such as Alf Landon, the 1936 GOP presidential candidate who had supported Theodore Roosevelt's Progressive Party in 1912; Wendell L. Wilkie (a former Democrat who had been a pro-Roosevelt delegate at the 1932 Democratic National Convention), who was the GOP candidate in 1940; and Thomas E. Dewey, governor of New York, and the GOP presidential candidate in 1944 and 1948. These men were the candidates of Big Business and the Big Government Republican establishment.

Through the establishment media's deification of Franklin Delano Roosevelt, Americans have forgotten that the New Deal created monopolies, allowed price fixing, and brought about all kinds of anticompetitive economic regulation that went far beyond Social Security and the Civilian Conservation Corps. Senator Robert A. Taft, and other conservatives, drew a sharp contrast with FDR and the New Deal over these policies and opposed them.

Taft argued that totalitarianism and loss of freedom would be the inevitable result of the economic regulations and bureaucratic government Roosevelt pushed through Congress as part of the New Deal.

But while Wilkie and Dewey criticized the New Deal as being inefficient and wasteful, they shared FDR's internationalist ideas about foreign policy, and they certainly weren't prepared to campaign against the New Deal as unconstitutional and *wrong*.

Naturally, running as FDR-lite candidates (or "dime store Democrats" as FDR's Democratic successor President Harry Truman called such Republicans), Landon, Wilkie, and Dewey lost.

One of the most critical contests in this one hundred year battle for the soul of the Republican Party was the 1952 battle between Senator Robert A. Taft, representing the constitutionalist wing of the party, and the progressive wing's choice, General Dwight D. Eisenhower.

Prior to running for president, General Eisenhower wasn't even a registered Republican. As the architect of the Allied victory in Europe, Eisenhower's attractiveness as a presidential candidate was obvious, and going into the campaign he had been actively recruited by the Democrats and President Truman to run on the Democratic ticket.

No one really knew where Eisenhower stood politically, but that was somewhat the point. Wherever he stood, "Ike" was trusted and esteemed for his role in defeating the Nazis, and that made him the perfect vessel in which to carry the Republican establishment's political goals.

Senator Robert A. Taft was a man of towering intellect and character who was the leading conservative of that generation, and his analysis was that "if we get Eisenhower we will practically have a Republican New Deal Administration, with just as much spending and socialism as under Mr. Truman."[1]

Despite Eisenhower's status as a war hero, Taft far outpolled

Eisenhower in primary votes: 35.84 percent to 26.30 percent.

Going into the Republican National Convention, Taft was just seventy-five or so votes shy of having a majority and winning the Republican nomination for president.

However, the Republican National Committee, and the Convention process, were both controlled by establishment Republicans. Most delegates to the national convention were not allocated through primary elections; they were selected by Republican Party leaders.

Taft was right, these establishment party leaders were not conservatives or constitutionalists; they were what Democratic president Harry S. Truman derisively called "dime store Democrats." These were the same party leaders who had nominated Landon, Wilkie, and Dewey—they bought into the New Deal and its vast expansion of federal government power.

Senator Barry Goldwater saw these same tendencies in President Dwight D. Eisenhower's "Modern Republicanism," which he characterized as a "dime store New Deal."

The 1952 Republican National Convention was to be a bitter fight between conservatives and these "dime store" New Dealers.

The Republican Party's establishment leaders, with the power and money of their Big Business allies, were prepared to do anything to make sure Ike secured the nomination over Taft—who was the preferred candidate of the conservative grassroots movement.

They accused Taft, a man of almost puritanical rectitude, of "stealing" delegates and paraded through the Convention hall with signs that read "Thou Shalt Not Steal," and they promoted the line to the media that "Taft is about to win because he has stolen key delegations." They also questioned his intelligence. Taft's support began to waver under the relentless assault on his character.

Taft was tough, but he was out maneuvered by the leaders of the Republican establishment. They mounted fights over credentials at the National Convention, and duly and legally selected Taft delegates from Southern states, such as Texas, Louisiana, and Georgia, were challenged and ousted in favor of Eisenhower backers.

Once again, the conservative candidate was defeated because the progressive-leaning establishment controlled the levers of power within the Republican Party.

Eisenhower's nomination and election in 1952 marked the beginning of eight more years of Big Government Republican ascendency, but the election of 1952 also brought Barry Goldwater of Arizona into the United States Senate.

Senator Taft died six months after Eisenhower's inauguration, and conservatives lost their most recognized and esteemed spokesman and leader.

President Eisenhower wasn't about to question or attempt to roll back the New Deal; even during the years when Republicans controlled Congress and he was president, liberals and progressive Republicans set the agenda in Washington.

However, newly elected senator Barry Goldwater certainly was prepared to challenge the progressive conventional wisdom, and into the leadership vacuum left by Senator Taft's death strode Goldwater.

Barry Goldwater didn't have his roots in the old Midwest–Northeast Republican base that had fought and won the Civil War, as Senator Bob Taft did. Goldwater, from Arizona, was a successful businessman and a man of the New West; and he had new ideas about what being a conservative meant, but he didn't yet have a national reputation or following.

As Eisenhower's loyal vice president, Richard Nixon was reluctantly seen by the Republican establishment as the logical choice to carry the Republican banner in the 1960 election.

Despite rumblings from conservatives, by the time the Republican Convention opened, Nixon had no opponents for the nomination.

Nixon's reputation with conservatives, such as it was, rested entirely on his staunch anti-Communism. On domestic policy Nixon had accepted the establishment's New Deal Republicanism as the price of admission to the Eisenhower ticket in 1952. Nixon believed that the greatest threat to the party came not from defections of conservative voters on the Right, but from loss of support of progressives on the Left.

This led Nixon to get into his limo one summer evening in 1960 and drive over to sit down with New York governor Nelson Rockefeller, the leading progressive Republican, at Rockefeller's Fifth Avenue apartment, where he agreed to change the Republican Party platform to win progressive Republican support.

Conservatives were outraged, and began to refer to it as "the sellout on Fifth Avenue" or in Goldwater's words, the "Munich of the Republican Party."[2]

For conservatives, the highlight of the 1960 Republican National Convention was the speech by Senator Goldwater taking himself out of the race for the nomination, but calling upon conservatives to take back the Republican Party.

Even after he officially bowed out of the presidential sweepstakes, the delegates to the 1960 Republican National Convention gave Goldwater ten votes on the first ballot—the power and popularity of Goldwater's new brand of conservatism were beginning to show.

Goldwater, like Taft, opposed the New Deal and the welfare state.

But Taft represented the anti-interventionist "traditional foreign policy" brand of conservatism that opposed a large military establishment and found its intellectual roots in Washington's Farewell Address with its admonition against foreign entanglements.

Goldwater saw Communism and the Soviet Union as existential threats to the United States and Western civilization. To Goldwater, such threats required an aggressive foreign policy and a large and forward-leaning nuclear-armed military.

The old, anti-interventionist conservatives of Senator Taft's generation were fading away. Many younger conservative leaders and thinkers, such as William F. Buckley, Jr. and M. Stanton Evans, saw things much the same way as Goldwater did. The courtship that eventually led to the marriage of anti-Communist "national defense conservatives" and economic conservatives had begun. This led to a redefinition of conservatism and to a generational shift in the Republican Party.

Nixon lost to John F. Kennedy in 1960. While some Republicans and Nixon partisans still allege the Kennedy–Johnson ticket won through election fraud, the bottom line is that the election was close because Nixon and Kennedy were largely campaigning on the same platform.

In a campaign where the candidates were similar on the issues, Kennedy's photogenic and telegenic image and support from the liberal establishment press were difficult advantages for Nixon to overcome.

In contrast to Nixon's "me-too-ism" during the 1960 presidential campaign, Goldwater was traveling around the country as chairman of the Republican Senatorial Campaign Committee, selling his new brand of conservatism.

In 1960, with the help of L. Brent Bozell, Jr., Goldwater published the groundbreaking *The Conscience of a Conservative*. The book was intended, Senator Goldwater said, "to awaken the American people to a realization of how far we had moved from the old constitutional concepts toward the new welfare state." The book quickly went through twenty printings and sold 3.5 million copies, and it is still in print.[3]

First published by Clarence Manion's Victor Publishing, *The Conscience of a Conservative* "was our new testament," Pat Buchanan later said. "It contained the core beliefs of our political faith, it told us why we had failed, what we must do. We read it, memorized it, quoted it. . . . For those of us wandering in the arid desert of Eisenhower Republicanism, it hit like a rifle shot."[4]

The book's strong statement of the dangers of, and opposition to, world Communism helped define the conservative movement as the natural political home of first- and second-generation Eastern Europeans, Cubans, and Asians who had fled Communist revolutions in their homelands, and solidified Barry Goldwater as the premier spokesman for rolling back the Communist tide.

During the 1960 campaign, Goldwater visited almost every state and appeared at dozens of party conventions and smaller gatherings.

That experience put him in contact with grassroots Republicans all over the country. After Nixon's defeat, and more than two years before the 1964 election, "Draft Goldwater for President committees" were formed.[5]

In the haze the liberal establishment media has created in their celebration of the election of John F. Kennedy as the beginning of "Camelot," it is easy to lose sight of the fact that the election of Kennedy coincided with the rise of a new conservative movement in the United States and in the Republican Party.

- In 1960, Young Americans for Freedom (YAF) was founded, as we have noted.

- In 1960, Senator Barry Goldwater published *The Conscience of a Conservative.*

- In 1961, conservative Republican John Tower was elected in a special election to fill Lyndon Johnson's vacant Senate seat; he was the first Republican to win a Senate election in the Old South since the Reconstruction Era.

- In 1962 the New York Conservative Party was formed.

- On March 7, 1962, while I served as executive secretary of Young Americans for Freedom, YAF held a huge rally at Madison Square Garden in New York City.

The Madison Square Garden Rally would be my nomination for the day the modern-day conservative movement had its public debut. The rally was put on by youngsters: Don Shaftoe and David Franke were in their early twenties; I was the old man at twenty-eight. Marvin Liebman, whose small PR firm housed YAF, was the adult supervision.

"A Conservative Rally for World Liberation from Communism" drew a sellout crowd of 18,500 mostly young people to liberalism's East coast citadel, and gave national exposure to its featured speakers, L. Brent Bozell Jr., conservative Republican senators Barry

Goldwater, Strom Thurmond, and John Tower, and to honorees "for contributions to conservatism and the nation," such as Sen. Thomas J. Dodd (D-Conn.), novelist John Dos Passos, Herbert Hoover, Prof. Richard M. Weaver, actor John Wayne, columnist David Lawrence, newspaper publisher Eugene C. Pulliam, and editor M. Stanton Evans.[6]

Before that day what we were doing was largely out of the public eye, but when thousands were lined up around Madison Square Garden and the speeches and sellout crowd were front-page, "above the fold" news the next day in the *New York Times*, the conservative movement leapt onto the national political stage.

Far from being intimidated by the media's love affair with Kennedy, or swept away in the glamour and liberal celebrity worship surrounding "Camelot," conservatives were an energized and growing force rallying for the ideals of freedom, liberty, and limited government.

Goldwater was enthusiastic about the prospects of running against President John F. Kennedy and drawing a sharp contrast to Kennedy's policies. What's more, Goldwater understood that the problem was as much the establishment Republican Party leadership as it was the Democrats.

In 1961, F. Clifton White organized a movement to nominate a Republican conservative for president. Traveling around the country, White exhorted conservatives to seize control of their local Republican Party organizations and elect conservative delegates to the Republican National Convention.

The movement he orchestrated gave conservatives more influence over the inner workings of the Republican Party than they had had during Taft's 1952 defeat and helped persuade Goldwater to run for president.[7]

In the wake of Kennedy's assassination, Goldwater briefly considered dropping his campaign, but he was persuaded to continue by this grassroots support and a desire to wrest control of the Republican Party away from the establishment's Eastern liberals, and for what Bill Middendorf called the "noble reason" of building the conservative movement.[8]

This scared the devil out of the progressive-dominated Republican establishment, who had long embraced me-tooism and ceded the national agenda to the Democrats.

The establishment launched a desperate "Stop Goldwater" campaign in the face of which Goldwater's support began to wane, especially in those states where the progressive establishment held sway. He lost in New Hampshire to Henry Cabot Lodge, then US ambassador to Vietnam, who won as a write-in candidate, and he lost in Oregon to New York governor Nelson Rockefeller.

Goldwater won Illinois, Indiana, and Nebraska, but the pounding he was taking from the progressive Republican establishment was having some effect. However, Goldwater roared back and upset Rockefeller, who had been the favorite, in the California Republican primary, and Rockefeller dropped out of the race.

Pennsylvania's Governor William Scranton was the last-ditch hope of the "Stop Goldwater" forces, but his campaign, which launched only weeks before the Republican Convention, never really got off the ground. Goldwater won the nomination on the first ballot with 883 delegates to Scranton's 214.

One of Goldwater's key supporters and confidants in the presidential campaign, Bill Middendorf, put it this way: Goldwater "changed American politics" by bringing about "a marked shift in Republican philosophy and geography, from liberal to conservative, and from the Northeast to the South and West."[9]

Goldwater's acceptance speech at the 1964 Republican National Convention at the Cow Palace in San Francisco has become a classic of American political thought, but its most memorable line, "I would remind you that extremism in the defense of liberty is no vice. And let me remind you also that moderation in the pursuit of justice is no virtue," would be used against him.[10]

Liberal Republicans claimed to be shocked. The party they had controlled for so long had fallen into the hands of "extremists."

Political commentators were equally taken aback. After hearing the speech, one reporter expressed their collective opprobrium: "My God, he's going to run as Barry Goldwater."[11]

Goldwater's credo played into the hands of establishment Republicans eager to thwart the conservative takeover of the GOP, and Democrats eager to hold on to power in Washington, by allowing them to continue the drumbeat of criticism of him as an "extremist" that began during the Republican primaries.

After Goldwater won the nomination, the progressive Republican establishment did precious little to help him and much to hurt him—unlike Senator Bob Taft, who actually campaigned for Eisenhower, even after he lost the nomination in what was arguably the dirtiest Republican Convention ever.

The pattern set in the Eisenhower and Goldwater campaigns still holds true today. When a conservative loses, he is expected to campaign for the establishment Republican winner, as Taft did. When a conservative wins, the losing establishment candidate routinely undermines the conservative, as Rockefeller, Scranton, and Romney did to Goldwater in 1964 and Virginia's establishment Republican Lt. Governor Bill Bolling did to conservative Ken Cuccinelli in 2013.

Rockefeller, Lodge, and Scranton made no real attempt to debate Goldwater on domestic policy or national defense or refute his criticism of establishment Republican me-tooism. Instead, he was attacked on a personal level as an "extremist," a "kook," and a "crackpot" who had no hope of winning the general election.

Progressive establishment Republicans also labeled Goldwater as a racist for opposing, on principled constitutional grounds, much of President Johnson's civil rights legislation, and labeled him a warmonger for advocating a military build-up to not just counter, but to roll back the Soviets. Goldwater's blunt and often profane, off-the-cuff comments seemed to confirm such charges when he joked that he would "lob" missiles "into the men's room at the Kremlin."[12]

And the Democrats took up the attacks where establishment Republicans left off.

Conservatives, to the extent they had seized control of Republican organizations, were still political neophytes. Goldwater's criticisms of the Democrats and progressive Republican me-tooism were appealing and perceptive, but he had no real positive program to sell.

Like many conservative candidates and intellectuals since, Senator Goldwater and his inner circle seemed to believe that all they had to do was expose Americans to conservative ideas and the election would be won.

They subscribed to what Morton Blackwell, president and founder of the Leadership Institute and Virginia's long-serving Republican national committeeman, calls the "Sir Galahad Theory of Politics": "I will win because my heart is pure."

Goldwater's supporters seemed to believe that being right, in the sense of being correct, would be sufficient to win, and that if we conservatives could logically demonstrate that our candidate was of higher character and that his policies would be better for our country, somehow victory would fall into our deserving hands like a ripe fruit from a tree.

Goldwater ended up vaporized in a 486 to 52 Electoral College wipeout that saw President Lyndon Baines Johnson and the Democrats garner over fifteen million more votes than did Goldwater and the Republicans.

Senator Goldwater undertook his campaign knowing he would not be president. Goldwater thought it was unlikely that the American people would accept three presidents in the space of fourteen months, but he felt his campaign could help launch the conservative movement.[13]

And in that sense he was right—the Goldwater campaign did turn out around twenty-seven million conservative voters, and it trained thousands of grassroots volunteers in the techniques of political organizing. It proved that there was a vast market for conservative ideas and conservative candidates—if they were presented correctly.

Goldwater may have looked like he was defeated in 1964, but as George F. Will observed, those whom his ideas brought into politics believed he won; "it just took 16 years to count the votes."[14]

Goldwater's belated "victory" ultimately benefited a new actor in national politics—Ronald Reagan.

Reagan was not new to conservative or Republican politics. A staunch anti-Communist (although he was a Democrat at that time), he supported Richard Nixon over John F. Kennedy in the 1960 presidential race, and in 1961 he joined the board of advisors of Young Americans for Freedom (YAF).[15]

As executive secretary of YAF, I wrote a letter to Ronald Reagan in the spring of 1962, asking him to sign a fund-raising letter for us. After a month or so went by and I had received no response, I put the matter out of mind.

Then several months later I opened an envelope that had inside a letter with a child's crayon scribbling on it. Since it was not unusual for us to receive our fund-raising letters back telling us to go jump in a lake (or worse), I threw it away, but something made me pull it out of the trash.

I quickly realized that it was my letter to Ronald Reagan with a handwritten note in the bottom left-hand corner, saying words to the effect of, "Dear Mr. Viguerie, I'm sorry, but I just found your letter in Ronnie's toy chest. If you think my name will be of help, please feel free to use it."

Reagan traveled the country on behalf of General Electric and as a dinner speaker. He had delivered a speech titled "A Time for Choosing" to business and political groups a number of times over the course of almost two years—it was a message he believed and knew well.

On October 27, just a week before the election, Reagan delivered a version of "A Time for Choosing" to a national TV audience on behalf of Senator Barry Goldwater's faltering presidential campaign. You can find the full text of "A Time for Choosing" in appendix 2 of this book.[16]

Goldwater's inner circle initially opposed the idea of a national broadcast of "A Time for Choosing," but Houston, Texas, banker Jimmy Lyons threatened to pay for it himself, as was legal in those days.

Eventually the controversy made its way up the food chain to Senator Goldwater, who watched the video and liked it, and Goldwater's campaign staff reluctantly acquiesced to airing the ad, if for no other reason than to maintain control.

The title "A Time for Choosing" derives from a paragraph in the speech in which Reagan set before his audience a choice between self-reliance and the welfare state: "So we have come to a time for choosing. Either we accept the responsibility for our own destiny, or we abandon the American Revolution and confess that an intellectual elite in a far-distant capitol can plan our lives for us better than we can plan them ourselves."

Reagan also went straight at Goldwater's name-calling detractors in both Democrat and establishment Republican circles by saying, "Those who deplore use of the terms *'pink'* and *'Leftist'* are themselves guilty of branding all who oppose their liberalism as right-wing extremists."

But Reagan took the argument a step beyond party politics by asking, "How long can we afford the luxury of this family fight when we are at war with the most dangerous enemy ever known to man?"

Suddenly Reagan wasn't just talking to Republicans or conservatives, he was talking to all Americans—and he was selling conservative ideas about the dangers of Communism and the loss of freedom that was sure to follow the growth of the welfare state.

In some sense, for the next twenty-five years Reagan never deviated from that script.

"The Speech," as it came to be known, set forth a conservative manifesto that was certainly grounded in Goldwater's analysis of the shortcomings and dangers of the welfare state and appeasement of the Soviet Union, but was somehow deeper and more appealing than mere criticism of Great Society liberalism and the establishment elite's "softness" on Communism.

The broadcast of "A Time for Choosing," up against *Pettycoat Junction* and *Peyton Place*, raised some $6 million for Goldwater; the ad ran multiple times, but it sparked little interest or comment in the media at the time. Even in the *Los Angeles Times,* which leaned Republican in those days, Reagan's speech only made Hedda Hopper's Hollywood gossip column.[17]

A week out from what was to be an electoral defeat of epic proportions, what the media thought of that last-ditch ploy by the Goldwater campaign wasn't really important. What was important was that in its content and in Reagan's smooth and reassuring delivery, "the Speech" landed like a bombshell in the midst of the conservative movement.

2

RICHARD NIXON AND THE RISE OF RONALD REAGAN

The frustration many conservatives felt after the Republican defeats of 2006, 2008, and 2012 were nothing compared to how we felt after Goldwater's 1964 defeat.

For me it was six months before I could go directly to the front section of the newspaper. The news was so bad I had to sort of sneak up on it, starting with the comics, then the sports section, the local news, and finally the front page and editorials.

The *New York Times* opined that the only way Republicans could win was through the establishment Republican me-tooism that Goldwater had campaigned against in the primaries and conservatives abhorred. Sound familiar?

Unlike the Republican National Committee's whitewash of the Romney campaign's failures, the "I told you so" postelection autopsy of Goldwater's defeat was brutal.

The Republican establishment was on the warpath, and anyone who had been an outspoken conservative or Goldwater supporter was in danger of being scalped.

Republican governor George Romney—father of 2012 establishment Republican presidential nominee Mitt Romney—after refusing to endorse Goldwater's campaign and helping to lead a preconvention "Stop Goldwater" movement, wrote him a scathing twelve-page letter criticizing his "extremism" in the wake of his loss.

Republicans had no ability to stop or even slow down the Democratic agenda. When President Johnson took the oath of office on January 20, 1965, Democrats had more than a two to one majority in the Senate (68 to 32) and a better than two to one majority in the House of Representatives (295 to 140).

The 1964 election brought Senator Ted Kennedy to his first full six-year term in a Senate inhabited by such hard-Left liberals as Eugene McCarthy and George McGovern, and they were passing bills, creating new programs, and spending money with abandon.

Despite the prevailing gloom, some in the conservative movement, such as Ronald Reagan, found a reason to be optimistic: "Sure, we didn't expect this . . . but take a look at the figure on our side and remember every one [vote] represents a conservative we didn't have when we started out."[1]

Reagan was right; some twenty-seven million voters had voted for Goldwater in the face of the overwhelming personal attacks against him from Democrats, their enablers in the media, and from the Republican establishment.

Reagan's optimistic analysis was shared by many other conservatives who looked at Goldwater's success in spreading the conservative message and concluded that, much as we loved and respected Senator Goldwater and his blunt manner of speaking, it wasn't the message, but the messenger, that voters had rejected.

Conservatives resolved to continue the battle for control of the Republican Party that Cliff White, Neil McCaffrey of the Conservative Book Club, Stan Evans, and many others had begun to advance Goldwater's candidacy. Just a month after Goldwater's defeat, William F. Buckley Jr., William Rusher, Don Bruce, Tom Winter (the longtime editor of *Human Events*), Bob Bauman, John Ashbrook, and a few others launched the American Conservative Union, and they began to create other vehicles to advance their ideas.

And on January 3, 1965, I started my direct-mail company (an enterprise that I had planned to start on January 2, but two feet of snow got in the way) with the idea that I could mobilize the hundreds of thousands of small donors who had supported Goldwater to support other conservative causes and candidates.

In 1964 if you were a candidate for president, you had to file a list of all of your fifty-dollar-plus donors with the clerk of the US House of Representatives. To me these individuals represented an invaluable potential source of support for the growing conservative movement—and there was no prohibition against copying and using those names and addresses.

While Goldwater's campaign was floundering, I sat in the clerk's office, copying Goldwater donor names and addresses and building a list of those who would oppose Johnson's program when he was elected.

I soon realized that working by myself was getting me nowhere fast, and I hired six women, who produced 12,500 three-by-five index cards with the names and addresses of Goldwater donors. Eventually, I went around the country doing the same thing in state capitols where the rules were favorable.

My very first client was Young Americans for Freedom. Keeping the account of an organization run by a bunch of college kids dedicated as much to organizational intrigue as anything else soon proved to be a challenge—in fact, I was fired after just six weeks.

With a young wife and two babies to support, I had to hustle, but I never lacked for clients. My first political campaign client was H. L. "Bill" Richardson, a candidate for State Senate in a special election in California. Using the 12,500 Goldwater donors that I had acquired, we raised fifty thousand dollars for Bill's winning campaign. He became the leader of conservatives in California, started Gun Owners of America and Gun Owners of California, and has made a huge difference for the country and the conservative movement—and he is still active today.

After the Richardson campaign I became ever more heavily involved in the marketing necessary to launch the new organizations and energize the supporters of the new conservative movement.

I helped in a small way to win Senator John Tower's reelection in 1966. In 1968 we handled our first congressional client, a relatively unknown assistant district attorney from Poughkeepsie, New York, named G. Gordon Liddy. We handled the mail for Phil Crane's special election to Congress in 1969 for the seat Donald Rumsfeld vacated to join President Nixon's cabinet. In 1972 we worked on Senator Strom Thurmond's campaign and John Ashbrook's run against Nixon in the 1972 Republican primaries. In 1973 we helped Senator Jesse Helms retire his 1972 Senate race debt and launch his Congressional Club. In 1976 we helped a fiery California conservative named Bob Dornan win a tough primary and general election, and in 1975 to 1976 and again in 1978 we worked for a then-unknown baby doctor from Lake Jackson, Texas, named Ron Paul, and helped him win his first and second elections to Congress.

But I didn't have a crystal ball—some good candidates that I helped were defeated. Others we helped to win, like a bright young attorney named Orrin Hatch, first in the Utah Republican state convention and then in the Senate general election of 1976, disappointed conservatives by joining Washington's Big Government establishment.

In December 1976 Howard Phillips, under the auspices of the Conservative Caucus called a national meeting of conservatives to plan our activities in response to the election of Democrat Jimmy Carter. As I checked into the hotel, Jesse Helms—one of the principled giants of American politics and the conservative movement—was standing in front of me, and we began to talk. Orrin Hatch, who had just been elected to the Senate, approached.

At that moment I had the pleasure of introducing Orrin to Jesse Helms, with whom he would regularly clash in later years because while Hatch eventually abandoned the conservative movement to become part of the Republican establishment, and part of the problem in Washington, Helms, by contrast, stood fast to his conservative principles.

The point of these stories is that out of the ashes of Goldwater's defeat rose the people, the leaders, the organizations, and the tools needed to build the modern conservative movement and to elect a conservative president.

But who would that president be?

When the lights went down on the set where Ronald Reagan delivered "The Speech" on behalf of Senator Barry Goldwater's losing 1964 presidential campaign, it was by no means clear that Reagan would inherit Goldwater's mantle as the leader of the Republican conservatives.

In the immediate aftermath of Goldwater's loss, Reagan did nothing to encourage such speculation. Reagan said shortly after the election that his experience with the Goldwater campaign had not whetted his appetite for public office.

Running as a Republican candidate, he said, "has never appealed to me." When asked if he could spurn a strong Republican request to run, Reagan replied, "I hope I could turn it down."[2]

In the wake of Goldwater's defeat, it seemed as if all of the obvious candidates on the Republican side hailed from the same establishment Republican bloc that had tried to stop Goldwater and who had labeled conservatives as "extremists."

Chief among the establishment Republicans vying to be the next Republican candidate for president were Michigan governor George Romney and New York governor Nelson Rockefeller. Rockefeller's me-tooism and tangled personal life had killed his chances of defeating Goldwater for the nomination in 1964, but that did not quell his ambition to be president.

When the ultimate establishment Republican, Connecticut's Senator Prescott Bush (father of President George Herbert Walker Bush and grandfather of President George W. Bush and former Florida governor Jeb Bush), asked rhetorically, "Have we come to the point in our life as a nation where the governor of a great state—one who perhaps aspires to the nomination for president of the United States—can desert a good wife, mother of his grown children, divorce her, then persuade a young mother of four youngsters to abandon her husband and their four children and marry the governor?" At that point, Rockefeller's doom as a national candidate was sealed, but he wasn't about to admit it.[3]

Michigan governor George Romney was a much more appealing standard-bearer for establishment Republicans, and Romney emerged as the front-runner in the race to be the Republican nominee in 1968.

After Republicans did well in the 1966 off-year election, the Republican establishment had some cause to believe that the old order would be restored. Republicans picked up three Senate seats in 1966, and the winning Republican candidates; Charles H. Percy of Illinois, Mark Hatfield of Oregon, and Howard Baker of Tennessee, were all establishment-type Republicans.

Republicans also picked up forty-seven House seats. However, almost half of those seats were in the South and West and were won by candidates who, if not fire-breathing Goldwater conservatives, were at least a lot more conservative than their classmate, George H. W. Bush, of Texas House District 7.

Eight new Republican governors were also elected, many of them in the South and West as well, including the new governor of California, Ronald Reagan.

While the recruitment of Ronald Reagan to run for governor of California, and who did what to convince him to run, has entered the realm of myth, there are several key points that bear on the situation in which conservatives find themselves in the aftermath of the 2012 election.

The men who recruited Reagan were all men of the New West; they had no ties to the old Republican establishment.

Robert Tuttle, Reagan's director of White House personnel and son of Reagan "kitchen cabinet" member Holmes Tuttle, recalled that his father, Henry Salvatori, and A. C. (Cy) Rubel "were all self-made. . . . What I admired about them, especially that early group, was they didn't really want anything. . . . They all just wanted better government. And they wanted smaller government. They were all concerned about the size of government. In those days, in the '50s right after the war, the tax rate was 90 percent."

As Robert Tuttle later said, "they were concerned about the size of taxes. They saw how Communism was a real threat, a real menace, and they were concerned about that, and how we were responding to it. They loved their country and they'd all been fantastically successful. . . . It was interesting because these guys were all about ten to fifteen years older than Ronald Reagan, but he was a real hero to them. What they loved about Reagan was that he could articulate what they felt and articulate it so well."[4]

Tuttle, Salvatori, and Rubel were later joined by other successful entrepreneurs, such as Justin Dart and Joe Coors, who all recognized that to win, Republicans didn't need to become more like Democrats; what Republicans needed was someone to articulate the conservative beliefs they held, and articulate them well.

Some New Right conservatives, including me, wanted Joe Coors to put himself forward to be secretary of commerce. Coors's response was that if Reagan wanted him to serve, he knew how to get in touch with him—he wasn't looking for a job.

Joe Coors and the other early Reagan kitchen cabinet were selfless men, only interested in their country.

I will expand on this later, but these successful entrepreneurs looked at Reagan, and probably without really ever saying it, applied the same analysis they would apply if they were evaluating a new product or business idea, what I call "Viguerie's Four Horsemen of Marketing":

- Position (a hole in the marketplace)

- Differentiation

- Benefit

- Brand (it's what makes you singular or unique)

Reagan's position was that he filled the "hole" of being the national conservative leader that was left in the marketplace by Goldwater's epic defeat; he was a fresh face, different from the Old Right conservatives. Probably his greatest benefit when compared to other potential candidates was his skill as a communicator, which made him electable; and his position, differentiation, and benefit established his brand, and his days on TV and in the movies had made it trusted.

In other words, conservatives needed a salesman, and Ronald Reagan, his skills honed in Hollywood, television, and on the dinner circuit, was the best salesman for conservative ideas the self-made entrepreneurs of his early "kitchen cabinet" ever saw.

Today, the number one problem conservatives have is that we have no one leader who has all four of my four horsemen, although we have six to eight young conservative governors and members of Congress who in the next few years could easily qualify.

The notion that conservatives needed to sell their ideas marked a huge mental shift for the conservative movement. Many who supported Goldwater and who were early adherents of the movement tended to think the truth of conservative criticism of liberalism was self-evident, as illustrated with that great quote by Morton Blackwell about the "Sir Galahad Theory of Politics," Morton has often gently criticized many of our fellow conservatives who think it is sufficient to be right (as in correct) and then victory will come our way.

Aren't we conservatives in much the same position today?

Establishment Republicans today are making the same mistake of embracing me-tooism that they did back in the 1960s.

When over 60 percent of Americans think Big Government is the greatest threat to freedom, it is clear that our conservative ideas resonate with millions of voters, but the establishment Republican Party and its leaders do a terrible job of selling those ideas, or worse yet, simply run away from them.

Goldwater's defeat caused a complete reassessment of how conservatives framed the debate at that time, and Reagan's well-aimed critiques of liberal influence on government and culture, coupled with his optimistic belief that America's best days were ahead if only the shackles of government could be thrown off, showed them a way forward.

Reagan polled nearly one million more votes in the general election than his Democratic opponent, incumbent Democratic governor Pat Brown did, and he did it without the support of liberal Republicans.

Two of their groups, Republicans for Progress and the Ripon Society, pointedly refused to endorse Reagan's race for California governor even as they quite publicly enthused over the GOP moderates, such as Governors Nelson and Winthrop Rockefeller, Senator Edward Brooke of Massachusetts, Senator Charles Percy of Illinois, Governor George Romney of Michigan, and Howard Baker running for senator in Tennessee.[5]

Just four years earlier, former vice president Richard Nixon had been defeated by about 300,000 votes for the office Reagan had just won. The former vice president had been savaged by the establishment media and in an angry outburst declared that he was holding his "last press conference" after his defeat, saying, "You won't have Nixon to kick around anymore."

Nixon had not abandoned politics or his presidential aspirations. Even though he was widely distrusted by conservatives for selling out to Rockefeller in the 1960 Convention fight over the Republican platform, Nixon had worked hard for Goldwater in 1964, even making a speech at the San Francisco convention, admonishing the Senator's establishment detractors by telling them:

> Before this convention we were Goldwater Republicans, Rockefeller Republicans, Scranton Republicans, Lodge Republicans, but now that this convention has met and made its decision, we are Republicans, period, working for Barry Goldwater. . . . And to those few, if there are some, who say that they are going to sit it out or take a walk, or even go on a boat ride, I have an answer in the words of Barry Goldwater in 1960—Let's grow up, Republicans, let's go to work—and we shall win in November![6]

Nixon was no conservative, but he knew better than anyone how the Republican establishment worked, and he was prepared to help Goldwater on the theory that the favor would be repaid.

He was right. On January 22, 1965, just two days after Lyndon Johnson was sworn in for his full term as president, Goldwater and Nixon attended a meeting of the Republican National Committee.

Goldwater turned to Nixon during his remarks and to express his gratitude for the extraordinary effort Nixon made on his behalf, told him: "Dick, I will never forget it." He then added, "If there ever comes a time, I am going to do all I can."[7]

In 1966, while Reagan campaigned for governor of California, Nixon traveled the country, stumping for Republican candidates, hammering Johnson on foreign policy, and reestablishing his credibility with the leaders of the Republican Party. Nixon's political resurrection began to take shape.

In his 1966 run for governor, Reagan defeated Brown with a campaign that emphasized law and order, wasteful government, welfare, overtaxation, and dealing with student disturbances at the University of California.[8]

Having defeated Brown by almost a million votes, Reagan proved the power of what, broadly speaking, became the Republican message on the national domestic policy front from the mid-1960s through the 1970s.

Going into the 1968 presidential primary campaign season, Governor Reagan was probably the hottest political "property" on the national scene.

Reagan was the charismatic standard-bearer for the new conservative movement, and he was the spokesman for millions of Americans who were beginning to see the Democrats as the party of wasteful government, welfare, overtaxation, and the coddling of criminals and student protesters. Ronald Reagan was a contender for the Republican presidential nomination, even if he hadn't officially announced.

As "hot" and charismatic as Reagan was in 1968, the inability of conservatives to unite to control the inner workings of the

Republican Party would launch Richard Nixon into the White House first, and ultimately place political power and control of the Republican Party firmly back into the hands of the "me-too" Republican establishment.

If going into the 1966 campaign cycle it seemed that the only logical Republican candidates for president were progressive "me-too" Republicans, like Rockefeller and Romney, coming out of the 1966 Republican victories, the somewhat unanticipated resurrection of Richard Nixon suddenly put a new player on the field.

Nixon didn't fit neatly into the political landscape created by the fight between the mostly Eastern progressive Republicans and the new movement conservatives who had supported Barry Goldwater.

And that's the way Nixon wanted it.

When Nixon was running in 1967, he made a point of meeting with conservatives in DC. As introductions were made and came around to Neil McCaffery, the head of the Conservative Book Club, Nixon said he didn't know "we" had a book club.

Establishment Republicans saw Nixon as a known quantity, and they knew that even if they didn't like him, they could do business with him; the question was, would they even have to if Governor Romney continued to be the leading contender for the nomination?

Those on the inside of the conservative movement viewed Nixon with skepticism as the architect of the "Fifth Avenue Sellout" to Nelson Rockefeller on the 1960 Republican platform, and as Eisenhower's silent partner in the growth of government and the continuation of the New Deal during Ike's presidency. But to many grassroots Republicans, Nixon's strong anti-Communism, his support for Goldwater, and his tough talk on law and order made him look and sound like a conservative.

There was also a strong feeling among many Republicans that the media had conspired to defeat Nixon and that Nixon had been cheated out of the presidency in 1960 due to Democratic election fraud. These Republicans felt that somehow Nixon was owed another shot at the White House; it was, they felt, "his turn."

In one of those seemingly innocuous word choices that can change the dynamics of a political campaign—and history—on September 4, 1967, Governor Romney told Detroit television newsman Lou Gordon that he had been "brainwashed" by American generals and diplomats into supporting the Vietnam War while touring Southeast Asia in 1965.[9]

Gordon made sure the wire services got the story, and the *New York Times* and other major newspapers around the country carried the unflattering coverage. Democratic candidate Eugene McCarthy quipped that attempting to brainwash Romney might be overkill. "A light rinse would have been sufficient," he said.[10]

Romney's support dropped like a stone. The next Harris poll showed him losing sixteen points, and he went from the presumptive front-runner for the Republican nomination, with 34 percent supporting him in February 1967, to just 14 percent in November.

Suddenly, it appeared Nixon had the field by himself, or did he?

Even though the bottom fell out of George Romney's campaign, he did not withdraw from the race right away, and the Republican establishment was not about to give up the fight.

Despite all of the marks against him, when Romney dropped out of the race in February 1968, New York governor Nelson Rockefeller jumped in, and he promptly won the Massachusetts Republican primary.

Were Rockefeller to continue his winning streak in the Northeast and command the large New York delegation, he would be a formidable force at the Republican National Convention.

Conservatives began to urge Governor Reagan to run to provide Republican primary voters with a clear conservative choice in the primaries.

Ronald Reagan obliged them, in part because he "had strong views on Vietnam that distinguished him [even] from Richard Nixon. Reagan's opinion of Nixon seemed to vary depending on the circumstance. He had supported Nixon in Nixon's 1960 presidential run and again in his ill-fated 1962 governor's race in

California. But as Nixon geared up to run against Johnson in 1968, Reagan was clearly doubtful about his fellow Republican's ability. They disagreed about Vietnam, where Nixon believed "economic détente" would lead Moscow to broker a deal to end the war. The divide was so great that it was one of the factors that motivated Reagan's 1968 presidential run.[11]

While Ronald Reagan gained votes as a write-in candidate, he wasn't officially campaigning for the nomination or drawing a clear contrast between his conservative positions and the positions of Richard Nixon.

Conservatives were not yet seasoned enough in the ways of Convention politics to recognize that the admonition "to get there first'us with the most'us" applied to the political battlefield as well as the Civil War battlefield.

In contrast to the effort the progressive establishment had organized for Eisenhower to outmaneuver Senator Taft back in 1952, Reagan's write-in effort started late and produced few votes. As the Republican primary election season progressed, the stage was set for Richard Nixon to become the Republican nominee for president.

Andrew Busch, writing for the Heritage Foundation, noted that Reagan's main impediment to gaining the nomination was:

> Reagan initially ran only as a favorite son, winning the California primary and securing the state's large bloc of delegates. He received 10 percent or more of the vote in an additional three primaries without running an active campaign (21 percent in Nebraska, 20 percent in Oregon, and 10 percent in Wisconsin). At the end of the primary season, Reagan actually had accumulated more primary votes than any other Republican, leading Richard Nixon by nearly 17,000, though this advantage was due to his uncontested victory in California.[12]

After the passage of forty-six years, it is not easy to capture the mood of the American electorate in 1968.

The country was in chaos in many respects; the assassinations of

Dr. Martin Luther King Jr. and Bobby Kennedy, antiwar riots, race riots, and the public rejection of traditional values by the cultural elite in Hollywood and on college campuses made millions of voters wonder if the country wasn't falling apart.

Yet, what appeared to be chaos had behind it a potent liberal political force; thousands of young people opposed to the war in Vietnam campaigned for "Clean Gene," Minnesota senator Eugene McCarthy. Even though President Johnson actually won the New Hampshire Democratic Primary, McCarthy's close second-place finish convinced Johnson to drop out.

Four days after Johnson dropped out, Senator Bobby Kennedy, the fallen president's charismatic younger brother, got in. Kennedy, a celebrity in his own right, also benefited from a unique coalition of Hollywood celebrities and African-American athletes who were attracted to his candidacy by his outspoken support for the civil rights movement.

Among the Hollywood and celebrity supporters working for Kennedy were: Warren Beatty, Bill Cosby, Tony Curtis, Bobby Darin, Henry Fonda, Jack Lemmon, Shirley MacLaine, Malina Mercouri, Jack Parr, David Suskind, Nancy Wilson, Gene Kelly, Gregory Peck, Rod Steiger, and Sammy Davis Jr.

McCarthy also had Hollywood on his side, but some of his early Hollywood supporters, such as Lauren Bacall, Kirk Douglas, Sammy Davis Jr., Candice Bergen, Rosemary Clooney, Andy Williams, and the rock 'n roll group Jefferson Airplane, jumped to Kennedy as soon as he got in the race.[13]

Kennedy's assassination on the very night he won the California Democratic Primary sent the Democrats into a tailspin and appeared to make the remaining primaries a mano a mano contest between McCarthy and Johnson's vice president, Hubert Humphrey, the establishment Democrats' choice.

A watershed moment in the rise of the conservative movement was lost to history due to the Kennedy assassination: the defeat of California's liberal Republican US senator Tommy Kuchel, the

US Senate's Republican minority whip, by the relatively unknown Max Rafferty.

Rafferty, California's nonpartisan elected superintendent of public instruction had written several books attacking the radical liberal ideas and policies of the education establishment and wrote a well-regarded syndicated column on education. He chose my firm, and our expertise in the new and alternative media of direct mail, to get his conservative message out to California's Republican primary voters.

We mailed some 6 million letters to national conservative donors to finance Max Rafferty's California campaign. We then mailed twice to 2 million Republican households in California. I'm confident that the over 4 million letters that twice reached some 3.5 million registered Republican voters was the major reason a relatively unknown state superintendent of public education with little campaign money was able to beat one of California's best-known and most powerful politicians by 67,000 votes.

In the November general election, Rafferty's people decided they didn't want a big direct-mail effort; they asked us to mail only to the approximately sixty thousand Rafferty contributors we had developed and used the money our letters raised mostly to buy TV ads. While that wasn't the only reason Rafferty lost badly in November, I have no doubt it certainly was one of the principle reasons.

How the professional political class of Republican consultants loots the Party and runs campaigns into the ground—while getting paid millions of dollars—is such an important topic that I will cover it in more detail later in this book.

After Kennedy's assassination, McCarthy's antiwar base was split with the late entrance of Senator George McGovern of South Dakota just ahead of the Democratic National Convention. McGovern's spoiler act set the stage for Vice President Humphrey to be the Democratic nominee. Despite winning the popular vote, McCarthy lost to Humphrey at a Chicago Democratic Convention marred by protests and riots.

The Democratic establishment got their preferred candidate in 1968; now the question was, what would Republicans do?

The Republican establishment's preferred candidate, Romney, had imploded, but New York's liberal Republican governor Nelson Rockefeller—the bête noire of conservatives—was still in the race. According to Heritage senior scholar Dr. Lee Edwards:

> [William F.] Buckley and *National Review* carefully considered the 1968 presidential campaign, focusing on a practical question: Who was the most viable conservative candidate? Barry Goldwater had already endorsed Richard Nixon. Ronald Reagan had been governor of California for little more than a year. Nelson Rockefeller was an impossibility for any right-thinking conservative. That left Nixon, whom Buckley admired as the man who had stoutly defended Whittaker Chambers against the liberal establishment and ensured that Alger Hiss went to jail.[14]

Buckley and many other leading conservatives decided they could support Nixon as "an anti-Communist moderate open to conservative ideas and influence," viewing him as a "competent, intelligent, experienced, professional politician" known for his "election-machine style of politics," as the *National Review*'s endorsement put it.

Coming into the National Convention, Richard Nixon led but did not have the nomination sewn up. Not until the Convention opened did Reagan announce he was a full-fledged candidate. His chief immediate objective was to prevent Nixon from gaining a majority of delegates on the first ballot.

It was Reagan's hope—and there was some reason for him to be hopeful—that many delegates who backed Nixon on the first ballot out of obligation would subsequently shift to him out of philosophical conviction.

Reagan's 1968 effort was blunted by the fact that Nixon had already lined up a formidable group of conservative elected officials to support him, including Barry Goldwater, Texas senator John

Tower, and South Carolina's senator Strom Thurmond, who had moved from the Democratic to the Republican Party in 1964 and worked hard for Goldwater in his unsuccessful bid for the presidency against Lyndon Johnson. On the first ballot, Nixon assembled a majority—with only twenty-five votes to spare. Reagan then released his delegates and urged the Convention to support Nixon unanimously.

Of course, no one will ever know whether or not Reagan could have defeated Nixon in 1968 if he had gone all out in the primaries, or if conservatives had been more seasoned in the ways of Republican Convention politics and mounted a more effective write-in campaign for him, or if conservative leaders hadn't concluded that Nixon was "open to conservative ideas and influence" and accepted his candidacy without a real fight.

The day after the 1964 election, and Goldwater's epic defeat, it looked to many in the media as if the new conservative movement was dead.

Four years later, to claim the nomination, Richard Nixon needed to campaign as a conservative to win.

Nixon shared none of Goldwater's fire for individual liberty and a smaller government, and he was by no means a movement conservative on domestic policy, having silently gone along with Eisenhower's New Deal Republicanism.

However, the media decided Nixon was a "conservative," equating Nixon's law-and-order campaign and anti-Communist rhetoric with conservatism, and that, along with the endorsements of leading conservatives, was probably enough to convince most delegates to the 1968 Republican National Convention in Miami that Nixon was the right candidate for the nomination.

Boy, were they ever taken to the cleaners!

Nixon chose Maryland's obscure governor, Spiro T. Agnew, as his running mate. Agnew was a Rockefeller supporter whose nomination was seconded by New York mayor John Lindsay, the new liberal Republican icon of the Eastern establishment.

Politically, Agnew was a nonentity with no national following, and that was exactly the point. Nixon was famously insecure, in much the same way as was George H. W. Bush. Just as Bush and his team knew that Indiana's junior senator, Dan Quayle, would offer no criticism or pushback against their plans to dismantle Reaganism and eliminate any Reagan influence in the new Bush administration, Nixon knew Agnew would do what he was told and not bring anyone to Washington who might challenge his campaign team or his policy team.

And that included Senator Strom Thurmond, who was very instrumental in Nixon getting the nomination.

Thurmond and Bill Middendorf had an 8:00 a.m. breakfast meeting set with Nixon the morning following the election.

They entered the Pierre Hotel, where Nixon was staying, excited about the prospect of having a conservative administration and getting strong conservatives appointed to key positions in the new administration.

When they arrived at the Pierre at 7:50 a.m., coming out of Nixon's suite were Nelson Rockefeller and Henry Kissinger, and they recognized that conservatives had, once again, been beaten to the punch.

As Lee Edwards later wrote,

> Nothing equals the anger of a woman scorned except, perhaps, the anger of a conservative who feels he has been betrayed. In 1971, Henry Kissinger's secret trips to Communist China were revealed, and Nixon unveiled his New Economic Plan featuring wage and price controls. "We are all Keynesians now," Nixon said in a bit of bombast sharply challenged by conservatives.[15]

Nixon's strategies of détente, his version of "triangulation" with Red China, and his economic policies destroyed any pretense that Richard Nixon was a conservative.

In 1971 twelve leaders of the Right, with William F. Buckley

Jr. at the top of the list, announced that they were suspending "our support of the Administration."

In December of that year, Congressman John Ashbrook, one of the leading conservatives on Capitol Hill, broke with the Nixon administration, criticizing "the presentation of liberal policies in the verbal trappings of conservatism." He especially opposed the president's budget deficits, wage and price controls, and recent rapprochement with China. New Deal policies, he claimed, "have not been changed but extended and refined" under the Nixon presidency.

Ashbrook soon announced his intention to oppose Nixon's re-nomination in a number of Republican primaries. Justifying his candidacy, he denounced the Nixon administration for squandering an opportunity to build a conservative coalition to govern the country; "The result of such leadership could well have been a period of conservative and Republican ascendancy to match the Democratic era that followed upon the victory of Franklin Roosevelt. Instead, the net result of this administration may be to frustrate for years to come the emergence of the conservative majority."

Boy was he ever right.

In December 1971, as Nixon moved left, Tom Winter, the longtime editor of the influential conservative weekly *Human Events*, called me on behalf of John Ashbrook and asked me to raise money for his presidential campaign, and I enthusiastically agreed, even though it ended up costing me a lot of money.

Ashbrook ran on the slogan "No Left Turn," and called his campaign in New Hampshire "a small Paul Revere ride." Although he received only 9.6 percent of the vote in the Republican primary in New Hampshire, he pushed on to Florida, where he got less than 9 percent. The campaign was chaotically run, and his 10 percent showing in California persuaded him to withdraw from the presidential contest.

John Ashbrook ended up supporting Nixon's reelection campaign in 1972 "with great reluctance" and I was frustrated with the lack of leadership in the conservative movement, and we were something like $250,000 in the hole on the work we did for Ash-brook's campaign.[16]

And then there was Watergate.

It is important to remember that Nixon's opponents on the Left had little to complain about as far as policy went.

Nixon ended the war in Vietnam, he readily instituted wage and price controls, he followed a policy of détente with the Soviet Union and opened the door to Red China, he established the Environmental Protection Agency (EPA), supported the creation of the Legal Services Corporation, expanded welfare through his Family Assistance Plan welfare "reform," signed the Occupational Health and Safety Act of 1970, and he signed an Emergency Employment Act creating government jobs to stimulate the economy—in short, he followed exactly the policies the Washington establishment supported at the time.

If Lyndon Johnson created the modern welfare state that conservatives despise by passing "the Great Society" programs, Richard Nixon funded it, and added a lot of government on his own.

Nixon's opponents on the Left hated Nixon for being Nixon, not for his policies.

They resented his defeat of Eleanor Roosevelt's friend, hard-Left Democrat Congresswoman Helen Gahagen Douglas, in the 1950 California Senate campaign. They hated him for giving credence to the idea that the establishment elite was infiltrated by Communists by helping to bring down Alger Hiss and defending Whittaker Chambers. Nixon obliged them in this hatred by abusing his power, engaging in the infamous Watergate cover-up, and being as bad or worse in reality than his opponents fanaticized he was.

When Agnew was forced out of the vice presidency, Watergate was already percolating strongly. Nixon looked to the establishment Republicans on Capitol Hill for help to save his presidency and chose House Minority Leader Gerald R. Ford of Michigan as his new vice president.

Not only did this advance one of the Republican establishment's leading figures to the vice presidency, but Nixon undercut his own position by putting Ford next in line to the presidency.

When Ford was sworn in, the Capitol Hill Democrats' favorite Republican was next in line for the Oval Office, and any remaining hesitation they had about forcing Nixon out was removed.

Ford served as vice president for only nine months; November 27, 1973, to August 9, 1974, when he became president after Nixon's resignation. When Ford chose Nelson Rockefeller to be his vice president and Rockefeller was confirmed by Congress, it seemed that the craziest conspiracy theories on both the Right and the Left had been brought to fruition.

During the darkest days of Watergate, I hosted a dinner at the Capitol Hill Club, where around twenty-five conservative leaders, including ten to twelve members of Congress, met to try to figure out how to get conservatives out of the mess Nixon had gotten us into. While there was much agreement on the problem, no one offered a path forward; it became clear to me that a big problem, maybe the biggest problem, we conservatives were facing was lack of leadership.

When Rockefeller's name was floated for vice president, I called together a group of about fourteen national conservative leaders for a dinner meeting at my then office at 7777 Route 7 in Tyson's Corner, Virginia, including Bill Rusher, Tom Winter, Stan Evans, Dick Obenshain, and others, who met to try to figure out how to derail Rockefeller's nomination.

It quickly became apparent that we really didn't have a strategy. The ideas kicked around included things like having conservative journalists attend Ford's press conference, which of them was going to ask what question, and who would follow up with another question.

Clearly, asking a few questions at a press conference was not a strategy to defeat Rockefeller's nomination. After the frustration of that four-hour meeting, I decided to play a more active and public leadership role and began to organize meetings, often at my home or office, to help develop and plan strategy.

In January 1977, a few weeks away from Rockefeller's leaving the office of vice president, an interviewer asked Rockefeller to reflect on his political life by noting that he had spent a lifetime preparing for the presidency, yet he had fallen short.

Why, the interviewer asked, did you fall short of achieving your goal, given your talent and practically unlimited resources? Rockefeller's reply was yes, he had spent his adult life preparing for the presidency, but he had forgotten to prepare for the nomination.

Rockefeller's somber introspection reminds me of the old Cajun recipe for rabbit stew—which begins, "To make rabbit stew, first catch a rabbit."

His ambition to be president, he finally recognized, had been thwarted by his habit of gratuitously picking fights with conservatives. Too late he recognized that conservatives might not always be able to win the nomination, but they had become strong enough to claim veto rights over who would.

In the 1974 congressional elections, Republicans were again trounced, losing four seats in the Senate and forty-nine seats in the House. Democrats once again had a better than two to one advantage in the House and held sixty seats in the Senate. The only two bright spots for Republicans in the election were Paul Laxalt's election as senator from Nevada and a young Bill Clinton's defeat by Republican John P. Hammerschmidt in the campaign to represent Arkansas's Third Congressional District.

Even if the Republican brand was practically destroyed by Watergate, the conservative brand was not.

Laxalt ran as an unabashed conservative; although his margin of victory was narrow, Laxalt showed that a principled conservative could win even under the trying circumstances of the 1974 election.

The stage was set for a conservative challenge to the establishment's plan to field a Republican ticket with Ford as the presidential candidate and Nelson Rockefeller as the vice presidential nominee in 1976.

While it is difficult to put a specific date on the beginning of the rise of the New Right, I began to meet with a group of then-young conservative political operatives and thinkers, such as Paul Weyrich, Morton Blackwell, Howard Phillips, Terry Dolan, Ed Feulner, Dick Obenshain, Bill Richardson, Lee Edwards and others, such as Tom Ellis, Joe Coors, Bob Walker (an early Reagan aide, not the congressman) as early as 1972 to strategize opposition to Nixon's leftward turn and to try to figure out how we could turn the intellectual conservative movement into a practical political movement.

Although he opposed Nixon's plan for a guaranteed wage, Reagan had mostly held his fire while Nixon was president, and even made a trip to Asia on Nixon's behalf; however, once Nixon resigned, "Reagan no longer felt compelled to remain quiet in deference to the White House."

Reagan "openly criticized the ABM treaty and the SALT I agreement, declaring that America was falling behind the Soviets in the arms race (an opinion shared in Moscow). He also rebuked the very notion of détente, saying, "Nothing proves the failure of Marxism more than the Soviet Union's inability to produce weapons for its military ambitions and at the same time provide for their people's everyday needs."[17]

This time there would be no coyness or write-in campaign; at sixty-four years of age, Reagan decided that if he wanted to actually be president, now was the time to do it.

Reagan didn't pull any punches and launched his campaign with a direct frontal assault on the entire range of establishment Republican domestic policies pursued by Nixon and Ford, especially their economic policies and failure to deal with inflation, but he reserved his strongest and toughest attacks for Ford's foreign policy.[18]

Reagan gained much-needed momentum by attacking the whole idea of détente and the weakness of Ford's foreign policy.

However, Ford attacked Reagan for being "too extreme" and used the powers of his incumbency to the fullest extent.

Essentially, Ford ran the old establishment Republican playbook from the 1964 "Stop Goldwater" campaign, and backed by the power of incumbency, and some missteps on Reagan's part, it worked.

The battle seesawed back and forth during the primaries, with Ford winning New Hampshire and Florida, Reagan winning North Carolina, Indiana, and Texas, then Ford winning Oregon, Reagan winning California and Ford winning Ohio.

Reagan's base was the conservative movement. By this point in the development of the conservative movement, all of the major movement organizations raised money, recruited members and subscribers, and educated voters through the alternative medium of direct mail; these included the *Conservative Digest*, Heritage Foundation, *Human Events, National Review*, American Conservative Union, Phyllis Schlafly's Eagle Forum, and Jesse Helms's Congressional Club, among others.

Unlike President Ford, whose base was the big donors of the Republican establishment; Reagan remained competitive because he had 250,000 small donors acquired through direct mail.

The new and alternative medium of direct mail played a key role in keeping the Reagan campaign alive, as Reagan would regularly send out an appeal for money to his small donors, and then use it to go on TV to make a pitch and raise more money.

Ford won sixteen of twenty-seven primaries and 53 percent of the total primary vote. In the caucus states, there was "hand-to-hand combat" for every delegate. Reagan ultimately won 56 percent of the caucus state delegates.[19]

When the Republican National Convention opened in Kansas City, neither candidate had a majority of delegates. In a bid to attract moderate support, Reagan announced that if nominated, he would ask moderate senator Richard Schweiker of Pennsylvania to serve as his running mate. Reagan's attempt to unify the party seemed to backfire; liberals and the Republican establishment remained opposed to his candidacy, and many conservatives were irritated.

Senator Jesse Helms went so far as to encourage a "Draft Buckley" movement, to draft New York's conservative senator James Buckley for president on the theory that Schweiker was too liberal to be one heartbeat away from the presidency.

Various conservative leaders were called upon to calm the waters. I got a call from Bill Buckley urging me to stay on the reservation, and others got similar calls from other leading conservatives who were close to Reagan.

Despite the dissension among conservatives over the Schweiker gambit, the nomination was still within Reagan's grasp until Clarke Reed, the chairman of the Mississippi Republican Party, betrayed him and handed the Republican presidential nomination to Ford. Once again, the nomination slipped away from Reagan, as Ford won on the first ballot by a slim seventy-vote margin.[20]

Reagan's analysis of the defects and shortcomings of Ford's policies wasn't disputed by a majority of Republican voters, and it wasn't what defeated him—he was once again outmaneuvered by the establishment Republicans who controlled the machinery of the party at the Republican National Convention, and beaten by the power of the incumbency.

But Ronald Reagan made another error that contributed to his defeat—he thought that establishment Republicans actually wanted a unified party going into an election where the GOP was handicapped by Watergate, and he was prepared to add Schweiker to the ticket if that would unify the party.

The Republican establishment saw things quite differently.

Far from unifying the Republican Party, and bringing in new votes from the Right, in 1976 the Republican establishment refused to reach out to conservatives in any meaningful way.

Their answer to the conservative challenge to Nelson Rockefeller was to put Big Government Republican senator Bob Dole of Kansas on the ballot as the GOP vice presidential nominee. With Dole on the ticket, Rockefeller, the long time antagonist of conservatives, would be gone, but power would remain firmly in the hands of the GOP's "dime store New Dealers" and Great Society–lite Capitol Hill establishment.

In 1976 Ronald Reagan may not have realized that he wasn't merely competing for the Party's presidential nomination; he was engaged in an all-out war for the soul of the GOP.

The Republican establishment understood the game, and just like in 1964, they had already decided they would rather lose than put a conservative in, or anywhere near, the Oval Office.

3

THE NEW RIGHT AND REAGAN'S 1980 VICTORY

We had come tantalizingly close to getting a conservative candidate for president—Ronald Reagan—nominated in 1976.

When Ronald Reagan lost at the 1976 Republican National Convention, we conservatives understood that Reagan didn't lose because the delegates rejected conservative ideas—he lost because once again conservatives were outfoxed and outgunned in Republican Convention politics.

Far from being out of favor or declining in political support, we knew conservative ideas, especially those advocated by what came to be known as the "New Right," were gaining in political and cultural influence.

Reagan campaigned for President Ford in more than twenty states, but he also took $1 million of his remaining campaign funds and established an organization called Citizens for the Republic, "to speak out for Republicanism and how we had strayed from the visions of our founding fathers."[1]

Ronald Reagan's creation of Citizens for the Republic was very much in keeping with the spirit of the times, and the feeling among many conservatives that the old ways and old vehicles for transmitting our ideas needed a serious update—as did the Republican Party.

There were many reasons for the rise of the New Right, but one of the most important (and one that gets little treatment in the popular history of the political forces that ultimately put Ronald Reagan in the White House) was conservative disillusionment with the leadership of the Old Right and the establishment Republican Party.

The rise of the New Right was as much a rebellion against the ineffectiveness and go-along-get-along policies of the Republican establishment, particularly on détente with the Soviet Union and social spending, as it was a fight against the Democrats. Our disillusionment with the Republican establishment ran deep, and was comparable to the disillusionment supporters of the Tea Party feel today with the failures of the establishment Republican Party.

In 1972 Lee Edwards invited me to lunch at the Mayflower Hotel to meet Morton Blackwell, who was then at the American Enterprise Institute. A week or so later Morton and I got back together for lunch at the Mayflower, and Morton later said I spoke "magic words" to him—I invited him to come to work for me at the Viguerie Company to help me build the conservative movement. Morton also later admitted that even though the job involved a small pay increase, he would have taken it with a pay cut.

Morton, and his wife, Helen, soon became close friends. Morton went on to found the Leadership Institute, train thousands of young conservatives in the art and science of politics, and is now one of the key players in the conservative movement. He has also been my friend, advisor, and wise counselor for over forty years. (See appendix 3 for Morton Blackwell's Laws of the Public Policy Process.)

After Morton had been in Washington for a year or two, he expressed his amazement and disappointment that Senators Goldwater, Thurmond, Tower, and the other conservatives on Capitol Hill didn't meet every day, or every week, or every month, or even once a year to plan strategy and coordinate conservative action on issues.

What Morton and I saw was that the longtime conservative members of Congress would show up on Tuesday, get beat two to one, and say,

"When's the next vote? Thursday? Okay, I'll be back then."

In 1975 I spent several days with about thirty others at the John F. Kennedy School of Government at Harvard University; one of the other people there was one of Washington's most respected and insightful political observers, columnist David Broder. Broder was still at the old *Washington Star*, and at an afternoon session of the group, he mentioned that his colleague at the *Star*, John Filka, had written an article that day featuring me and discussing the rise of a new group within the conservative movement he termed the "New Right."

We of what John Filka called the "New Right" believed that having a plan and coordinating our efforts on the conservative agenda was the only way to achieve success. We soon formalized a breakfast meeting every Wednesday from 8:00 a.m. to 10:00 a.m. To the extent that Hillary Clinton's vast right-wing conspiracy ever existed, it met at Elaine's and my home in McLean from 1975 until 1984.

The regulars at the breakfast included Ed Feulner of the Heritage Foundation, Terry Dolan of the National Conservative Political Action Committee, Paul Weyrich of the Free Congress Foundation, Morton Blackwell of the Leadership Institute, Ron Godwin of the Moral Majority, and Howard Phillips of the Conservative Caucus. We also made it a point to invite any conservative leaders who might be visiting Washington from around the country.

In order to grow the conservative movement, and build the connections between conservatives then scattered across the country (and isolated in a way that is hard to appreciate in our present Internet-connected age), we also opened our home to receptions, meetings, and fund-raisers, and made it the unofficial gathering spot for conservatives in the Washington, DC, area and for conservatives from around the country when they visited Washington, DC.

Those of us on the outside of government later realized we needed to add an inside-the-government element to our meetings if we were to more effectively advance our cause.

Conservatives who were then backbenchers in Congress, such as Newt Gingrich, Vin Weber, Hal Dobbs, Bob Walker, Bill Dannemeyer, and others, began joining us for an evening dinner meeting.

The evening meeting included the same group as our breakfast meeting, plus members of Congress. But these evening dinner meetings weren't the usual Washington "grip and grin" receptions or wonky policy seminars. Everyone was expected to contribute practical ideas and take action to advance our goals. Everyone left with assignments and follow-ups and made a commitment to report back to the group—and it worked.

In March 1977, President Carter announced that he wanted to make four changes to the election laws. He wanted to abolish the Electoral College, mandate Election Day voter registration, abolish the Hatch Act, and have federal funding of congressional elections—any of this sound familiar?

A few days later, about 10:15 one evening, Paul Weyrich called me and said he had just come from a meeting of Republican members of Congress, who agreed it was bad for the Republican Party, and the country; but it would be difficult if not impossible to stop it.

I said, "Paul, I don't agree. I think we can develop a plan to sidetrack Carter's proposed changes in elections laws, but it is late. Now, let me get back to sleep, and I'll call you in the morning."

I called Paul back, and we began to meet regularly once or twice a week to develop a strategy and plan to defeat Carter's proposed election law changes that would put the Republicans out of business and make sure Democrats had a lock on elections going forward.

In an early meeting, Dick Dingman from Paul Weyrich's Free Congress Foundation told us that he had a copy of a San Francisco underground newspaper that was carrying an advertisement for a firm that, for five dollars, would send you an official-looking ID—no questions asked.

Congressmen Steve Symms and Robert Dornan got national coverage in July 1977 with dummy ID cards obtained to demonstrate the possibilities for fraud in Carter's instant voter registration plan. The ID cards each had the photo of either Symms or Dornan, but the names of liberal Democrats on the House Administration

Committee who supported Carter's plan.

The reporters and photographers loved it, particularly when liberal committee chairman Frank Thompson blew his top in public over the IDs. The *Washington Star* published an enormous five-column photo of the phony IDs on page one, which had been blown up to poster size for a news conference, and the Carter plan died that day. That September a group of conservatives hosted a dinner recognizing Senator Laxalt and me for helping to lead the effort to defeat Carter's plan, with me representing our coalition on the outside and Laxalt representing the inside of our coalition.

The advice I gave to my conservative colleagues then is something conservatives should continue to take to heart today, and that is that we can't kick all barking dogs.

The first battles it was necessary to fight were those battles that would grow the movement; school prayer, for example, may not be the most important issue, but it would grow the movement. The Panama Canal giveaway would grow the movement.

There were also those issues that weren't as exciting to a lot of people, but would make it more difficult to elect conservatives and might even put us out of business. Clearly, Carter's plan had the potential to put conservatives out of business, so we had to develop a strategy to defeat Carter's ideas.

As Carter's effort to return the Panama Canal to Panama moved forward, the Republican National Committee was mailing out millions of letters signed by Ronald Reagan asking people to contribute to the RNC in an effort to defeat the Panama Canal treaties. Approximately $700,000 was raised.

But when Paul Laxalt asked RNC chairman Bill Brock for $50,000 to help underwrite the cost of a "Truth Squad" media tour, the RNC chairman refused. The outrageous fact is that Brock refused to spend any of the money raised by Reagan's anti-treaty letter on any anti-treaty activities.

At their insistence, Laxalt and Reagan talked with Brock on December 15, 1977, via a joint telephone call—and came away very angry. Someone present during this conversation said he heard Reagan use words that he didn't know Reagan knew.

But Brock would not budge.

Of course, many suspected that Brock's refusal had something to do with the fact that he was from Tennessee, and establishment Republican Senate Minority Leader Howard Baker of Tennessee was prepared to go along with Carter and ratify the treaty giving away control of the canal.

I was asked to raise the $50,000 Laxalt and Reagan needed to help fund the "Truth Squad," but instead of raising $50,000, The Viguerie Company, on a pro bono basis, raised over $110,000—one more demonstration of the reduced importance of political parties and proof of the New Right's ability to engage in and finance important political activity outside of the Republican Party.

Naturally, critics will argue that we *lost* the Panama Canal Treaty fight.

My answer to that was (and it applies to the Tea Party movement today), what made the New Right different from the Old Right was not ideology; what distinguished the New Right from the Old Right was that we were operationally different.

The Old Right had become defeatist; they were used to showing up and getting beat two to one and then retiring from the fight until the next vote.

However, in the same situation, those in the New Right would cinch up their belts, organize, call meetings, develop plans, and send out a couple million letters explaining why the way to win the next battle was to defeat those who voted wrong—be they Democrats or Republicans—and keep pushing forward toward our goal of having conservatives govern America.

That was really the defining difference between Old Right and New Right—we weren't afraid to try, even if there was only a small to no chance of success. We were interested in building a movement and getting grassroots conservatives engaged in that movement. In the waging of the Panama Canal Treaty battle, over one hundred thousand people got involved as activists or donors, and thousands had the opportunity to develop leadership skills.

In 1977 and 1978 Howard Phillips visited every congressional district in America. During a trip to New Hampshire in 1977, only five people showed up for a meeting. One of them was an Allegheny Airlines copilot named Gordon Humphrey, who volunteered to run against Democrat Thomas J. McIntyre. Gordon Humphrey became one of three New Right senators elected in 1978.

In 1977 my wife and I had spent a month in Taiwan as guests of the Eisenhower Chinese Fellowship Program at the recommendation of Lee Edwards. Through that trip I had established relationships with a number of government, business, and political leaders, so in December 1978, when Carter announced the new "relationship" with Taiwan, which was weaker and less formal than what Nixon and Kissinger had agreed to, I organized a trip for about thirty conservative leaders to go to Taiwan.

Newly elected New Hampshire senator Gordon Humphrey was one of those leaders;

We of the New Right understood the lesson of Babe Ruth's 1927 season. That year the Bambino led the major leagues with sixty home runs, but he also led in strikeouts with eighty-nine.

We weren't worried about how the establishment, the press, and others would view us if we lost. We knew if you expected to hit a lot of home runs, you had to expect to strike out a lot.

One would think that the Republican "leadership" on Capitol Hill and at the Republican National Committee would have understood this and exercised the leadership necessary to rally opposition to Carter's Big Government liberal agenda, but they didn't.

Politically, in 1975 things were looking very dark for Republicans, and it seemed to those attending my Wednesday breakfasts that it was like being on an airplane, that was bouncing around in the sky. Figuratively, those who attended the breakfasts were in the back of the airplane, and we thought we had some better ideas about how to fly the plane.

We didn't want to be the pilots and fly the plane; we just wanted to offer some advice. So we walked up to the front of the plane, which represented the Republican Party, and knocked on the cockpit door (you could do that in those days). No one answered, so we opened the door, and lo and behold, we found no one flying the Republican plane! So we all sat down at the controls, and for five or six years we were the main leaders of the opposition to the Democrats and President Carter. Most of the national media, as well as the country's political pros, also saw the New Right, not the Republican National Committee, as the main opposition to the Democrats.

One afternoon in 1979, influential Washington journalist David Broder came to my office and said he was very perplexed about the lack of progress on the Democratic agenda, given that Democrats had strong majorities in the House and Senate. He had been to Vice President Walter Mondale's office and he had been to the White House and other places, and no one could explain why with the Democrats' overwhelming majorities on Capitol Hill, Carter's agenda was not moving. Election law changes, consumer protection agency, and other items—it was all in paralysis; nothing was happening.

I told him, "I don't know if I can be of help, but let me tell you what we're doing at The Viguerie Company." We were mailing one hundred million letters a year, urging grassroots conservatives to speak out, write, and call their members of Congress to oppose President Jimmy Carter and the Democrats on all of the important items on Carter's agenda. What we were doing was also being done by other conservatives. This was an early example of the successful use of the new and alternative medium of direct mail to engage people politically.

Carter and the Democrats were stymied because the New Right was coordinating the opposition to their liberal policies; we were meeting multiple times a week to plan strategy, rallying millions of grassroots conservatives to our cause through direct mail, and all of this was happening under the political establishment's radar.

It was by now apparent to most observers that the most effective opposition to Carter's policies was coming out of the New Right, not the Republican National Committee.

What establishment Republicans had not grasped was that all through the Nixon, Ford, and Carter administrations, every time they abandoned conservative principles, a group of conservative thinkers and grassroots activists would meet and organize to oppose their progressive policies; be they giving away the Panama Canal, destructive energy and economic policies (which cost America millions of jobs by accelerating the contraction of the domestic auto and oil industries), creating the Legal Services Corporation, asking Congress for a tariff on imported oil, raising taxes to "Whip Inflation Now," the ABM Treaty, the first SALT Treaty, abandoning Taiwan, or the loss of US nuclear superiority to the Soviets.[2]

We had learned that the only time you are guaranteed to lose is when you fail to fight. Conservatives need more of that same kind of outside, bottom-up leadership today to replace the establishment and take over the Republican Party and make it the effective conservative opposition to progressive policies. Senators Ted Cruz and Mike Lee, and their supporters in the Tea Party movement, understand this—that's why they undertook their October 2013 fight to defund Obamacare, for example.

The New Right organizations used the alternative media of direct mail to identify and motivate millions of grassroots conservatives who opposed policies that they thought showed a lack of American political resolve, and a weakness that endangered not just America, but the entire free world.

The millions of Americans who supported these groups financially, signed their petitions, and wrote letters to the editor and to Congress, and called and visited members of Congress, thought that most of the choices the Democratic and Republican establishments were making with respect to the Soviet Union were the wrong choices, and so did Ronald Reagan.

This was one of the secrets of Reagan's ability to peel off ethnic blue-collar Democrats from their traditional allegiance to the Democratic Party. They understood—because they or their parents had fled Communism—exactly where weakness in the face of Communism led, and they also grasped better than native-born liberals that a strong and free America really was "the last best hope of man on earth," as Reagan so eloquently put it.

This became particularly relevant after President Jimmy Carter was conspicuously late with the annual proclamation of "Captive Nations Week" in 1977. Captive Nations Week was an annual proclamation expressing solidarity with Eastern Europeans and other peoples who were behind the "Iron Curtain" or otherwise under Communist domination. Carter didn't issue the proclamation until mid-week—which raised much ire within the National Captive Nations Committee. Reagan, on the other hand, was actively supported by anti-Communist intellectuals, such as Dr. Lev Dobriansky, chairman of the National Captive Nations Committee.

Because of the weakness of the Republican National Committee and the GOP leadership on Capitol Hill, plenty of conservatives then, as now, were inclined to leave the Republican Party, at least for a while. Every time the establishment GOP would "me-too" the Democrats, or strong-arm conservatives in Congress or Republican Party politics, some conservatives would contemplate forming a third party.

This conservative disillusionment with the GOP wasn't new, as I've mentioned before; it went back at least to the 1950s and early 1960s, when a vehement group of libertarian-minded thinkers, such as author Ayn Rand, argued for a separate movement, while William F. Buckley Jr. argued for a conservative takeover of the Republican Party.

Goldwater had to swat down the idea of a third party, telling conservatives at the 1960 Republican National Convention to grow up and concentrate on taking over the Republican Party.

Some conservatives had even urged Ronald Reagan to run as a third-party conservative candidate. During the 1970s I found plenty of reason to support these efforts, and I was certainly fed up enough with the failures of the Republican establishment to bolt the Republican Party myself.

This effort gathered so much steam that a group of conservatives convened a meeting in Washington to urge Reagan to leave the Republican Party, launch "a full-blown national conservative movement," and run as a third-party candidate.

To his great credit, Reagan chose not to pursue that path.

Reagan's answer to those, including some of his good political supporters, who wanted him to head this new conservative party, was to tell them "they were out of their minds."

As Reagan saw it then (and he was right) the bulk of conservative voters in America are Republicans—and they won't desert the Republican Party for a third party.[3]

Reagan understood that if he was ever going to make progress in accomplishing the things he believed in, it would have to be within the Republican Party. This is why, while I considered myself to be first and foremost a limited-government constitutional conservative, I operate, then and now, within the Republican Party.

Although dealing with the "dime store Democrat" leadership of the national Republican Party was often a hard pill for those associated with the New Right to swallow, we concluded that the path to electing conservative candidates was not to form a third party; it was to become a "third force" to conceive and advance conservative ideas, and elect conservative candidates *through* the Republican Party.

We thought of ourselves—not the establishment Republican Party—as the alternative to the Left and the Democrats. Today the Tea Party does a good job of this on some issues, but we conservatives need to focus more on starting and operating thousands of new "third force" organizations.

The Left has long been far better at this than we are. If President Obama called a meeting in the White House of all the specialized environmental organizations, there would probably be over three hundred represented, each with its own area of expertise, agenda, supporters, and donor base.

There are probably between ten and twenty thousand left-wing single-issue third-force groups. Think of the thousands of unions just at the local level (teachers, college professors, public-sector unions, service employees, electricians, plumbers, carpenters, pipe fitters, auto workers, teamsters, coal miners, nurses, etc.). Those are just a sampling of the unions, but the Left also has thousands of race-based organizations, antitraditional family organizations, radical feminists and pro-abortion advocates, and of course radical environmentalists.

The only right-of-center organizations that come close to this are the right-to-life organizations. They are among the most successful conservative third-force organizations at the local, state, and national level. They work tirelessly to get more people involved in the right-to-life cause through measures like staffing pregnancy crisis centers, holding vigils and protests, and in the process, creating more opportunities for leaders to rise to the top.

The influence of third-force groups on individuals cannot be overestimated. Hillary Rodham Clinton moved from being a Goldwater girl in 1964 to being a hard-core liberal by the late 1960s by becoming involved in a single-issue cause: opposition to the Vietnam War.

It is important to recognize that there are a relatively small number of people in your community who are interested in politics and will join and work in a political campaign or committee.

However, almost everyone you know is interested in one, two, or three local issues. Maybe it is schools, taxes, overregulation of land use and property rights, immigration, crime and public safety, or something else. By getting your family, friends, neighbors, church members, and others in your circle of influence involved in dealing with one of these causes, at some point you can help them see that the problem is caused by, or made worse by, the heavy hand of government. That is a proven way to get people to become politically active, including becoming educated and informed by focusing on a single issue of personal importance to them.

Not only that, but for each new organization that is started, new leadership positions open up; a president; vice president; secretary; treasurer; membership, media relations, and Internet coordinators; and a fund-raising chairman are needed for every organization. It greatly expands the leadership inventory of the conservative movement when new organizations are formed and people become leaders by assuming leadership duties and fulfilling the responsibilities of those jobs.

To those naysayers who still argue for a third party instead of a third force, let me say simply that I've been there out of the same frustration you have, and with that experience I can prove that what I'm advocating can work—and did work—to elect Ronald Reagan.

We of the New Right shared the conservative ideas of the "Old Right," but, as I've described, we were operationally different.

We began by having a new attitude toward politics. We understood the premise that "successful politicians do not bore the voters."

We used the new and alternative media to bypass the establishment media, get our message out, and excite voters with our ideas.

Gone was the notion that conservative ideas were or should be self-evident to voters.

Gone, too, was the perennial losers' attitude held by many old-time conservatives, and especially by Republicans on Capitol Hill and in the state capitols.

We got up every morning thinking, *What are the two, three, or four things we can do today to defeat the Democrats and put liberals out of business?*

Newt Gingrich was a key but controversial figure in our efforts, and he remains one today. However you may see Newt today, his great redeeming quality is that he is an excellent strategist and a fierce partisan, even if he does not always subscribe to limited-government constitutional conservative principles.

Unlike the old-establishment Capitol Hill Republicans, like then House minority leader Bob Michel, Newt was prepared to work tirelessly to defeat the Democrats and bring Republicans to power.

After two failed attempts, Newt Gingrich was first elected to

Congress in 1978; in early 1979 Gingrich went to the House leadership and asked, "Who is in charge of making us the majority in the House?" The response from the House Republican leadership was, "Majority?"

When Gingrich found out no one was in charge of making Republicans the majority in the House, his response was, "Okay, then I'll be in charge."

In addition to being one of the key "inside" leaders of the New Right, Newt also became a leader in the House Republican Conference, and eventually Speaker of the House, in large measure because he didn't wait around for someone else to tell him what to do—he showed leadership and put himself in charge of making Republicans the majority in the House.

Subscribing to the theory that even important and busy people will show up for good food, we began to meet regularly at my home for breakfast and dinner to develop new ways of promoting our conservative ideas and causes. I had already successfully pioneered political direct mail—and had a successful direct marketing company with more than 250 employees to communicate with conservatives, raise money, and to bypass the establishment media to get our message out. It was here that we began to refine and target our message.

We received a good bit of criticism from the Old Right, who operated on the assumption that the pot of donors was limited, and that the more we segmented the marketplace of ideas, the less there would be to go around.

In the summer of 1975, I received a visit from a friend, a conservative stalwart who shall remain unnamed—coming as the spokesman for a group of Old Right leaders—who suggested that there were only 100,000 to 125,000 conservative donors in America, and all I was doing by helping start all these new conservative organizations and publications was slicing the pie thinner and thinner, and that I should cease and desist because I was hurting the *established* conservative organizations with my efforts.

Some of this angst was simply misguided, and some came from

individuals who had grown comfortable with the way things were and didn't really want to put in the hard work to make their organizations more appealing and effective than other conservative organizations.

I listened politely, but thought to myself that if there were only 125,000 people in America that would contribute to conservative causes, then the cause of liberty didn't have long to survive, and maybe I should take what time was left to spend more time with my family and play more golf. What's more, I knew it wasn't true and far from ceasing and desisting, we redoubled our efforts.

As if to prove that I was right, two of our company's executives, Wyatt Stewart and Steve Winchell, left the company in 1977–1978 and started working for the Republican Congressional Committee, which at that time had only about 20,000 donors. By the time of Ronald Reagan's election as president in November 1980, the major GOP national committees, under Wyatt and Steve's leadership, had some two million donors. This was just another example of the Old Right's thinking proven wrong.

A good bit of the discomfort was, as I noted earlier, because the Old Right was very defeatist. They were fully invested in the "Sir Galahad" way of expressing conservative ideas, and when logic and the pureness of their hearts didn't win elections, they blamed everything but their own poor communication and organizational skills.

We didn't stop trying to broaden the New Right coalition, because we believed right down to the soles of our shoes that conservative ideas were—and are—the majority opinion in this country. All we had to do was punch through the establishment's filter to let voters know there were organizations and candidates who shared their views, values, and principles, and the support would be there.

We were not so much interested in the short-term "optics" or how things look that obsess establishment politicians—we were building a movement and were willing to fight on every street corner and invest in the movement for the long term.

One success story this strategic thinking engendered was a campaign we conducted on "common situs picketing" for the National

Right to Work Committee.

Common situs picketing, which was and is illegal, would allow a disagreement with a small union to shut down an entire construction site—it was a long-sought goal of Big Labor.

In 1975 establishment Republican president Gerald R. Ford promised George Usery, his secretary of labor, and George Meany, head of the AFL-CIO, that if Congress sent him the bill, he would sign it. The National Right to Work Committee resolved to fight the bill and pressure President Ford to reverse course on signing the bill.

They hired our company to mount the campaign, and at $0.25 each, we mailed four million letters for $1 million.

National Right to Work got back $700,000 in contributions— which meant that they lost $300,000 on the mailing, which was, and is, a substantial sum of money—but a friend of mine, John Carlson, who worked in President Ford's press operation, later told me Ford got seven hundred thousand–plus cards, letters, and phone calls demanding that he veto the common situs picketing bill.

In a move that shocked Big Labor to its core, Ford broke his promise and vetoed the bill.

Reed Larson, who headed National Right to Work at the time, understood he was building and leading a movement, not just trying to raise money for next quarter's budget. National Right to Work also added ninety thousand new donors to their file that, over time, probably gave tens of millions of dollars to the organization and more than repaid the $300,000 investment in the common situs mailing.

I received a lot of establishment media criticism back in the 1970s by those who saw political direct mail as having only one purpose—to raise money. I was regularly attacked in the national media if a mailing didn't make a profit for the client. What these critics didn't understand was that direct mail is advertising, and that it is a form of alternative media that educates voters, organizes activists to pass or defeat legislation, and identifies favorable voters and supporters—and raises money too.

However, all of the criticism I was subjected to stopped in a few hours on Election Night November 1980. I could almost hear our critics in the political community and the media collectively saying, "Aha! That's what Viguerie and his friends have been up to."

When I started in 1961, direct mail was the second-largest form of advertising, second only to television. Today in 2014, direct mail is still the second-largest form of advertising.

Of course, the Left quickly began the process of trying to catch up with us conservatives!

I wasn't initially worried because it had taken me more than fifteen years to do what I had done, and I thought it would take the liberals at least that long—but boy was I wrong.

Within three to four years, the Left had caught up and passed us in terms of using direct mail/direct marketing to advance their political-ideological agenda. It is my opinion today that the Left continues to be far better at using direct mail/direct marketing to advance their agenda than are conservatives.

In 2008, Barack Obama's campaign had three million donors, and it had over four million donors in 2012; Mitt Romney had only a fraction of that number. As a general rule, the Democratic Committees are now far more professional in their direct-marketing campaigns than are the Republicans.

To fuel the rise of the New Right, we made a conscious effort to market our ideas and to bring new voters and new supporters, such as social conservatives, into the conservative movement. We worked to expand the number of voters who would support the candidates we backed and in particular to reach those conservative voters and potential supporters who were outside of the establishment Republican Party.

Many of the voters who backed New Right candidates and supported New Right organizations didn't fit into the stereotypical picture of a Republican Party supporter as a white, suburban, or small-town middle-class businessman or corporate-type.

Our recruits were anti-Communist Eastern European immigrants; pro-life Catholic blue-collar workers; Evangelical Christians concerned about the erosion of values and lack of morality in popular culture—in short, they were the voters who had been ignored and disenfranchised by the Left and its me-too establishment Republican facilitators.

Contrast our efforts to expand the base of support for conservative candidates with today's Republican Party that seems to go out of its way to exclude potential voters and supporters who don't agree with the GOP establishment and especially its leadership on Capitol Hill.

Rather than work to bring new voters and supporters into the party, Speaker of the House John Boehner refers to conservatives as "knuckle-draggers" and Republican National Committee chairman Reince Preibus cravenly caved in to demands from the Mitt Romney campaign to strip Ron Paul supporters and Tea Party–leaning delegates of their credentials and exclude them from participating in the 2012 Republican National Convention. The damage done to the Republican brand by the disgraceful and disrespectful treatment conservative and libertarian-leaning delegates received at the 2012 convention will continue to dog the national GOP for a long time.

Of course Romney is now a nonfactor after he gave away the presidency by running a content-free campaign, but the rules changes that his supporters engineered have been maintained to provide an advantage to the next Republican presidential candidate the Republican establishment chooses to anoint.

And there's the lesson for today's Tea Partiers and libertarian-leaning conservatives. During the late 1970s and early 1980s we of the New Right weren't operating as an appendage of the GOP; we were working through it in the spirit of the biblical injunction in the book of Romans to be in the world, but not of the world.

We weren't even operating as supporters of any individual candidate, even though eventually all of us who were active in the New Right came to support Ronald Reagan for president.

We saw ourselves as separate from the established Republican Party. Our goal was to promote a set of conservative principles and values and to back candidates who would stand for those values and principles—if that meant opposing the established leaders of the Republican Party, and supporting conservative Democrats such as the late congressman Larry McDonald, former congressman and senator Phil Gramm when he was a Democrat, or Democratic state representative Woody Jenkins in Louisiana, so be it.

As I said earlier, conservative "third force" groups were a key part of Reagan's victory and the building of the 1980 Reagan coalition.

The individuals associated with the rise of the New Right—Bill Armstrong, Morton Blackwell, Joe Coors, Phil Crane, Terry Dolan, Bob Dornan, Tom Ellis, Jerry Falwell, Ed Feulner, Newt Gingrich, Ron Godwin, Jesse Helms, Gordon Humphrey, Woody Jenkins, Roger Jepson, Tim and Beverley LaHaye, Ed McAteer, Connie Marshner, Larry McDonald, Larry Pratt, Howard Phillips, H. L. "Bill" Richardson, Pat Robertson, James Robison, Phyllis Schlafly, Mike Valerio, Bob Walker (both the congressman and the former Reagan aide), Jim Watt, Vin Weber, Paul Weyrich, Carter Wren, and the groups they developed to educate, activate, and energize voters—weren't mere appendages of the national Republican Party or the Washington political establishment.

Every time Jimmy Carter proposed a new policy with which we disagreed, such as giving away the Panama Canal, cancelling the B-1 bomber, or expanding the welfare state, even when we lost the fight, it added new supporters to the conservative movement and helped create the Reagan coalition.

However, it is vital to recognize that the conservative voters who opposed giving away the Panama Canal were just as mad at establishment Republican senator Howard Baker for backing the Panama Canal Treaty as they were at Jimmy Carter for signing it.

The strategy of acting as a third force (not a third party!) in politics is still valid today; the problem is that too many conservative coalitions and organizations—including some we created back in the 1960s, 1970s, and 1980s—have become captive to the Republican establishment.

During the administration of President George W. Bush, the

leaders of some of these organizations would get all aflutter if they got a call from Karl Rove; however if they got a call that President Bush was on the line, they would wet their pants even as Rove and his boss, President Bush, were betraying them and supporting policies that went against the conservative ideas they supposedly stood for.

The Democrats who long for days when Republicans like Howard Baker and Bob Michael were running the show and the parties could "work together" remind me of the old segregationists who would say, "Don't get me wrong: I like blacks; some of them, like old Uncle Tom down the road, are like a member of our family. It is these new young radicals, such as Martin Luther King Jr., Jesse Jackson, and Andrew Young that make me nervous."

In other words, the segregationist knew his place and old Uncle Tom knew his place, and the discomfort came when the new young activists rightly wanted to change that arrangement. This same concept applies to the civil war for the soul of the Republican Party.

The progressive establishment longs to return to the day when everyone knew their place and the new young radicals of thirty or forty years ago, like Paul Weyrich, Howard Phillips, Newt Gingrich, and now Tony Perkins, Jenny Beth Martin, Tim Huelskamp, Justin Amash, Mike Lee, Rand Paul, and Ted Cruz, were not rocking the boat and effectively opposing the growth of government.

There's an old saying that the fight starts when someone strikes the second blow—there was no fight as long as establishment Republicans did not oppose the liberals' Big Government agenda.

Once conservatives started fighting back, the Left began to scream bloody murder, but it was not a fight until conservatives fought back—and it is the same today.

So as long as conservatives didn't push back against the betrayal of our principles by Republicans, like the two Presidents Bush, there was no fight—Ted Cruz, Mike Lee, and Rand Paul have struck the second blow and are fighting back, and as soon as they and their grassroots limited-government constitutional conservative supporters *did* push back, we were accused of starting an intraparty brawl.

Ronald Reagan and his key advisors understood this.

When Reagan ran for president in 1976, he ran against the entire Republican establishment; and when he remarked that we need new leaders, leaders unfettered by old ties and old relationships, he was talking about the establishment Republican Party and its "dime store Democrat" leadership, such as Ford, Nixon, Rockefeller, and their big business supporters.

The Tea Party is now the fourth leg of the conservative stool precisely because it is "unfettered."

In January 2010 I was the Friday night keynote speaker in Dallas, Texas, for a weekend of training for about 125 Tea Party leaders from around the country. I met with a dozen or so Tea Party leaders before my speech and about the same number after my speech; among them was a lady from Corpus Christi, Texas, who was a leader of a Tea Party group with about three thousand members.

Republican politicians would frequently call, asking to attend their meetings, and she would say they were welcome to attend and would be introduced, but admonished them, "You don't speak; you listen to us." I don't know a conservative leader at the national level who would talk to a Republican politician that way, and that is one reason why I say the Tea Party is a new, separate leg of the conservative coalition, unfettered by old ties and old relationships to the Republican Party.

Reagan's campaign against the establishment Republicans was every bit as tough, or tougher, than his campaign against Jimmy Carter. Reagan won because he charted a new course and campaigned as a conservative; he did not allow himself to become "fettered" to the old leaders and the old weaknesses of the establishment Republican Party.

The Republican establishment likes to hide behind what they call Reagan's eleventh commandment—thou shall not speak ill of a fellow Republican. This of course conveniently glosses over the fact that Reagan was a tough campaigner and a vigorous advocate of conservative principles.

In 1976 Reagan had lost several primaries and was in danger of being knocked out of the presidential race. As the North Carolina primary approached, Senator Jesse Helms and Tom Ellis urged him to stay away from the state and let them handle the campaign unless he would do four things: attack President Ford; attack Henry Kissinger; attack the giveaway of the Panama Canal, and attack détente. Reagan agreed and attacked Ford and Kissinger and their weak foreign policy; he won the North Carolina Republican primary in an upset and kept his campaign alive.

In 1980 Reagan was equally tough on George H. W. Bush, famously reminding him, "I paid for this microphone" in a New Hampshire debate and showing Bush to be thin-skinned and petulant.

The bottom line is that the front-runner always wants a truce on negative ads.

Establishment Republicans also like to quote William F. Buckley Jr.'s dictum about supporting the most conservative candidate "who can be elected." The problem is that so many establishment Republicans have become addicted to Big Government that they no longer qualify as conservatives. Supporting them as "conservatives" confuses voters and seriously weakens the Republican brand.

Conservatives today face a challenge that has periodically vexed the conservative movement for over fifty years: there are plenty of small-government constitutional conservatives who are ready to bolt the Republican Party for the Libertarian Party.

I sympathize with their frustration, and I share their anger, but in conversations with national Libertarian Party leaders, when I say that I share their anger and frustration with the Republican Party and ask what their strategy and plan is for winning the presidency, or even a House or Senate seat, their answer is always some form of, "Uh, I'll get back to you on that."

Too many conservative Republican candidates for senator and governor, particularly out west, have been defeated because Libertarians siphoned off a few percent of the vote and handed the race to the Democrats. Libertarians are very good at tearing down, but they have no serious plan for building a national political majority or plurality.

When Libertarians are operating in think tanks and lobbying for public policy, such as school vouchers, they have much to contribute, but when they try to operate politically, they set back the cause of liberty. They don't have a practical plan for electing their candidates to take control of the government and implement their ideas as government policy—and let's face it: that's what elections are all about.

Reagan, on the other hand, had a practical plan for running as a conservative, winning the Republican nomination for president, winning the general election, and governing.

Naturally, thirty-four years after the fact, everyone in the Republican Party and conservative politics claims they were for Reagan, but in reality, in 1980, there were plenty of conservatives who thought maybe he was too old, and backed young and dynamic congressman Phil Crane of Illinois, as I did initially. Texas governor John Connally had many conservative supporters, particularly among his fellow Texans, and of course Reagan was vehemently opposed by the Republican establishment, just as he had been in 1976.

With six other candidates in the race and others talking about running for president, when the 1980 Republican primary election season began, even though the polls made him look like the odds-on favorite, it wasn't at all clear that Ronald Reagan would be the nominee or even the horse conservatives would choose to ride in the race.

For decades I've heard that the GOP could really do well if they would just forget about the social issues. Let me remind you, as I've said before, in Goldwater's day the conservative movement rested on a two-legged stool—national defense and economic conservatives. It was only when we added the third leg of social conservatives in the late 1970s that we went from getting 40 to 45 percent of the vote, to getting over 50 percent and regularly winning elections. When we had all three legs, we were competitive, but we were not governing America. Now with the addition of the constitutional conservatives of the Tea Party movement, we've added a fourth leg to the stool, and our opportunity to build a permanent governing majority has risen dramatically. What gave Reagan the edge in the Republican primaries and ultimately paved the way for him to defeat Jimmy Carter in the fall was the creation of the "Reagan coalition" of national defense conservatives, economic conservatives, and social conservatives.

At the beginning of the rise of the New Right and the election of Jimmy Carter, Evangelical Christians were not particularly active in politics. If anything, the "religious Left," that opposed the war in Vietnam and supported the liberal social agenda was the dominant religious force in American politics.

That all changed when the Supreme Court legalized abortion in the 1973 *Roe v. Wade* decision, and when President Carter's IRS administrator issued an order stating that any religious school founded after the 1952 *Brown v. Board of Education* Supreme Court school integration ruling was presumed to be created to circumvent the ruling, and integration.

This meant that any religious school founded after *Brown* would lose its tax-exempt status as an educational institution, unless it could in essence prove a negative through an arduous and expensive bureaucratic process at the IRS.

The response to the IRS order from religious educators of all faiths was swift opposition; but it set off what amounted to an atomic bomb in the middle of the hitherto apolitical Evangelical community and set the stage for the rise of the so-called Religious Right.

Although to my knowledge no scientific study is available to confirm this, a reliable analysis of the votes in the 1976 election indicates that millions of Evangelicals supported their fellow Southern Baptist Jimmy Carter—perhaps 5 to 7.5 million who had voted for Nixon in 1972 voted for Carter in 1976.

Jimmy Carter's unprovoked attack on Evangelical schools politicized these millions of conservative Christian voters into a new force in American politics. Carter forced Evangelical Christians to confront the fact that to protect their children from state-sponsored secularism, and their institutions from an increasingly intrusive state, they were going to have to get involved in politics.

They realized that to undo the damage Carter wrought, and make sure it never happened again, the moral leadership that the clergy offered in their day-to-day ministries and Sunday morning sermons was needed.

As part of the campaign to preserve religious freedom, led in large measure by Evangelical pastors, more than five hundred thousand cards and letters opposing the IRS rule were received by the Carter White House. Unlike the Panama Canal fight, this is one where conservatives prevailed and Carter was forced to withdraw the IRS order.

Reverend Jerry Falwell, a well-known Southern Baptist preacher, used paid television and paid radio in his ministry. At one time his *Old Time Gospel Hour* was broadcast over as many as five hundred radio stations across the nation. But its message was entirely non-political until the 1973 *Roe v. Wade* decision. Falwell determined that conservative and independent Christians had to get involved in politics—something most of them had previously shunned, or at least kept separate from their religious witness.

In a meeting in Lynchburg, Virginia, with Reverend Falwell, conservative leaders Paul Weyrich, Bob Billings, Howard Phillips, and Ed McAteer recognized that there was a natural synergy between the newly politicized Evangelical Christians and the national defense and economic conservatives that were the traditional conservative Republican base.

In that meeting, Weyrich made the case that there was "a moral majority" in American that opposed the social and political agenda of the Democratic Party and their secular liberal allies.

When Falwell heard the phrase "moral majority," he said, "That's it!" and in 1979 Reverend Falwell formed the Moral Majority to create a vehicle for translating the political energy of Evangelical Christians into political action at the ballot box.

As I noted before, and will say again throughout this book, Ronald Reagan and the wise party leaders who built the Reagan coalition, men such as Nevada senator Paul Laxalt, Lyn Nofziger,

Dick Allen, Ed Meese, Marty Anderson, Jeff Bell, Tom Ellis, and Judge William Clark, had the insight—perhaps *genius* is a better term—to welcome these newly politicized social conservatives into the Republican Party.

It also helped that Ronald Reagan actually shared the beliefs and concerns of social conservatives—most people have long forgotten that Ronald Reagan actually wrote and published a pro-life book while he was president: *Abortion and the Conscience of the Nation*, the only book to be published by a US president while he held office.

In welcoming social conservatives into the Reagan coalition, Reagan took the existing wobbly (and not politically effective) two legs of the conservative Republican base, added social conservatives, and created the more stable three-legged stool of economic conservatism, national defense conservatism, and social conservatism.

The importance of Reagan's addition of social conservatives to the GOP coalition cannot be overstated. It took, as Jeff Bell insightfully put it in his book *The Case for Polarized Politics: Why America Needs Social Conservatism*, all three of the legs of the new conservative coalition to create a stable platform for victory: "When social issues came into the mix—I would date it from the 1968 election . . . the Republican Party won seven out of 11 presidential elections."[4]

Although Democrats went after liberal social issues hard in 2012 and 2013, the Democrats who won from 1968 to 2010, including even Barack Obama in 2008, did not play up social liberalism in their campaigns.

In 1992, Bill Clinton was a death-penalty advocate who promised to "end welfare as we know it" and make abortion "safe, legal, and rare." Social issues have come to the fore on the GOP side in two of the past six presidential elections—in 1988 (prison furloughs, the Pledge of Allegiance, the ACLU) and 2004 (same-sex marriage). "Those are the only two elections since Reagan where the Republican Party has won a popular majority," Bell says. "It isn't coincidental."

No one really knew if this marriage would work. The political power of a coalition of California free-market-oriented entrepreneurs, anti-Communists, conservative defense intellectuals, and the socially conservative pastors and social commentators who led the Reagan coalition wasn't obvious in the beginning.

Indeed, a few days after the 1980 election, I was invited to a press breakfast hosted by the late Godfrey Sperling, the chief Washington correspondent for the *Christian Science Monitor* and at that time one of the grand old men of the Washington press corps.

"Mr. Viguerie," Sperling began, "Ronald Reagan was elected in a landslide last Tuesday, beating an incumbent president. Republicans took control of the Senate and had big pick ups in the House, in governors' seats, and in the state legislatures. We had a political earthquake last Tuesday. No one saw it coming. What happened?"

My response was to tell the assembled inside-the-Beltway print journalists that they didn't see it coming because they had zero interest in covering what conservatives, especially social conservatives, were doing. I then asked to see the hands of the reporters present who had ever heard of Rev. Pat Robertson. Only two or three of the twenty-five or so reporters assembled had ever heard of Rev. Pat Robertson, who hosted the *700 Club* on religious television and was an eight-hundred-pound political gorilla. Point made.

Looking back at the rise of the New Right—compared to, say, the gallons of ink and hours of TV time devoted to Occupy Wall Street (which had zero effect on public policy, I might add) seldom had a major political movement had such impact as the New Right, but been ignored by the elite media.

Naturally, the addition of social conservatives to the conservative coalition wasn't welcomed by the Republican establishment—who are still quick to blame conservatives, and particularly social conservatives, every time a Republican candidate loses.

Of course, had it been up to the Republican establishment, Reagan would never have been chosen as the Republican nominee in 1980.

They were mostly for Senator Howard Baker of Tennessee (whose campaign was chaired by fellow establishment Republican senator Richard Lugar) or for former congressman and CIA director

George H. W. Bush, son of the old-time Eastern establishment Republican senator Prescott Bush; or Senator Bob Dole; or Congressman John Anderson.

Indeed Baker was held in such low regard by conservatives that my magazine, *Conservative Digest*, put out a special issue for the Republican National Convention with a picture of Senator Baker in a dunce cap on the cover—a clear signal that Baker would be unacceptable to conservatives as Reagan's vice president.

The Republican establishment wanted nothing to do with the social issues that were and are important to social conservatives, even though the damage that is being done to our society by liberal social engineering was obvious even at that early date.

Establishment Republican candidates in the 1980 primaries, notably George H. W. Bush and John Anderson, did their best to distance themselves from social and economic conservatives.

Bush and Anderson ran as pro-choice candidates and were supportive of the *Roe v. Wade* Supreme Court case that legalized abortion on demand. They also opposed the idea of supply-side economics, with Bush famously referring to Reagan's idea that cutting taxes would increase revenues as "voodoo economics" and Howard Baker ridiculing the 1981 tax cut as "a riverboat gamble."[5]

George H. W. Bush, John Anderson, Howard Baker, Bob Dole, and other establishment Republicans all had one thing in common—they were creatures of the old ways Republicans did things in Washington.

They were perfectly content to "me-too" the Democrats on the social issues, to argue for a little less spending, but not to attack the reasons for spending, and to support the continuation of Nixon's accommodationist policy with the Soviet Union.

In short, they were all for the policies that got Jerry Ford tossed out of the White House and Republicans on Capitol Hill consigned to "permanent" minority status.

Reagan took all the discontents *within the Republican Party* and molded them into a coherent conservative ideology and a winning coalition that defeated the Republican establishment in the primaries and beat Jimmy Carter and John Anderson's third-party run in a landslide carrying forty-four out of fifty states.

It is worth noting that this is exactly the opposite of what Mitt Romney and the Republican establishment did in 2012.

To the extent that Romney had an ideology, it was the same Big Government Republicanism that cost the Republicans control of the House in 2006 and left them neutered until the Tea Party came roaring to life in 2009 and ran against the Republican establishment and Obama in 2010.

Going into the 1980 Republican National Convention in Detroit, Reagan had the nomination sewed up, but the Republican establishment was not going to go quietly.

As the convention approached, there was a steady drumbeat of criticism of Reagan from the Republican establishment to the effect that Reagan's nomination would split the Republican Party and that many establishment Republicans might stay home or bolt and support John Anderson's third-party run.

This whispering campaign (in some cases it was the loudly-complaining-to-the-liberal-media campaign) wasn't as harsh as the "Stop Goldwater" campaign had been in 1964, or as devious as the campaign to defeat Senator Bob Taft had been in 1952, but the objective was still the same—to make sure control of the Republican Party remained in the hands of the progressive-oriented Republican establishment.

Even before the Convention opened, many establishment Republicans were talking up the idea of "uniting the Party" by having former president Ford join Reagan on the ticket as vice president.

There was really no doubt that what they had in mind was not Ford playing second fiddle as Reagan's vice president, but Ford taking the role of "copresident" and neutering the conservative agenda by usurping many of the responsibilities of the presidency.

The idea of Ford as "copresident" was destined to fail, but it came surprisingly close to putting Ford on the ticket with Reagan because many of Reagan's closest advisors became convinced that the establishment wouldn't support him if they didn't have one of their own on the ticket as vice president.

And thus the stage was set for Reagan to choose an establishment progressive Republican, who was opposed to practically everything he had campaigned for, to be his running mate.

The question was, which establishment Republican would it be?

Conservatives were dead set against establishment Republican senator Howard Baker, who was the face of the go-along, get-along Republican establishment on Capitol Hill and its many defeats and cave-ins to the liberal Democrats.

Conservatives had no enthusiasm for George H. W. Bush either, given his attacks on Reagan's economic policies during the primaries and his family ties to the old Eastern Republican establishment. His pro-choice stance also alienated the newly energized social conservatives, but Bush had the second most delegates, and for many in Reagan's inner circle, choosing Bush seemed like the best way to unite the party for what was expected to be a tough campaign against Carter and Mondale.

With the benefit of hindsight, Reagan's first decision after claiming the GOP nomination may have been his worst, because the choice of George H. W. Bush as vice president proved to be a decision that would have a profound effect on the conservative movement, Republican Party, and American history to the present day—and not in a good way.

4

THWARTING the REAGAN REVOLUTION

Election night, 1980. It seemed as though all of our efforts to build the conservative movement and our long fight to nominate and elect a conservative presidential candidate had finally been rewarded.

We had a big election night party at our office in Tyson's Corner, Virginia, at 7777 Route 7, that included several hundred happy conservatives, network TV cameras, and a bevy of national radio and print journalists to cover the celebration. It was an exciting night for all conservatives.

Ronald Reagan was elected president, not just by a whisker, but in a landslide, defeating incumbent President Jimmy Carter by over 8.4 million votes.

Conservatives, under the leadership of Terry Dolan's National Conservative Political Action Committee (NCPAC), had targeted six liberal senators and defeated five of them: George McGovern of South Dakota, Birch Bayh of Indiana, Frank Church of Idaho, John Culver of Iowa, and Gaylord Nelson of Wisconsin.

We had also defeated liberal Republican senator Jacob Javits of New York in the Republican primary.

Republicans gained twelve seats in the Senate, and for the

first time since the 1950s, Republicans controlled the Senate. In the House of Representatives, Democrats still held a substantial majority, but we defeated the Democratic House majority whip, John Brademas of Indiana, with a bright young conservative, John Hiler.

It was especially gratifying when Dan Rather was forced to retract an early call of the race for Brademas and announce the defeat of the House Democrats' third-ranking leader on national TV.

In all, some thirty-five new Republicans were elected to the House in 1980, including conservatives like Vin Weber of Minnesota, and Hiler. Coupled with a block of Southern Democrats, known disparagingly as the "Boll Weevils," it looked as though Reagan might have a conservative ideological, if not a partisan Republican, majority in the House for much of his agenda— particularly rebuilding our military and reining in the intrusiveness of the federal government.

Looking at the election results, conservatives went to bed Election Night believing that the success of the "Reagan Revolution" was a foregone conclusion.

Or was it?

Yes, we had elected a number of new conservatives to Congress, and we had a conservative president, but conservatives did not necessarily control the levers of power in the government.

Personnel is policy, and conservatives did not dominate the executive branch of the federal government or run Capitol Hill. These areas remained largely the province of liberals in the civil service and the "me-too," Big Government progressives of the establishment Republican Party.

Vice President George H. W. Bush came to the White House with an extensive Rolodex of progressive establishment Republican friends and contacts whom he worked hard to place in key positions in the government—starting with his campaign manager and fellow Texan, James Baker, as chief of staff at the White House. With Jim Baker in that key role, it became that much harder to place movement conservatives in other policy-making positions in the government.

The new Republican majority in the Senate was run by Senator Howard Baker of Tennessee, who had run against Reagan in the Iowa caucuses and New Hampshire primary before dropping his bid for president.

Senator Baker was known as "the Great Conciliator" and was well liked by progressive senators on both sides of the aisle for his ability to finesse compromises and get his fellow Republicans to support policies that grew government, not for his unswerving commitment to conservative principles—this was the same Baker who had called Reagan's economic plan "a riverboat gamble" during the primaries and had no enthusiasm for cutting the programs he'd helped Democrats pass.

In the House, Reagan could expect little help from Republican minority leader Bob Michel of Illinois.

Michel, a World War II hero, was a longtime member of the House Appropriations Committee. Noted for his bipartisanship in striking bargains with the Democrats, while a good and honorable man, he was not one to fight for conservative principles, particularly on spending and other matters within the purview of the House appropriators.

On the Democratic side, even though conservative Democrats from the South and West might be in ideological sympathy with Reagan, and occasionally support him on national defense or on cutting back the growth of government, they paid a heavy price for not toeing the line Massachusetts liberal Speaker Tip O'Neill laid down.

Texas Democratic congressman Phil Gramm, a former economics professor at Texas A&M, for example, cosponsored the Gramm-Latta Budget, which increased military spending, cut domestic spending, and implemented Reagan's tax cuts in the Economic Recovery Tax Act of 1981. Shortly after his reelection in 1982, Gramm was removed from the House Budget Committee for supporting Reagan's tax cuts. In response, Gramm resigned his House seat on January 5, 1983. He then ran as a Republican for his own vacancy in a special election held on February 12, 1983, won, and returned to the House as a Republican—but other Democrats who might have been inclined to support Reagan got the message loud and clear.

Put simply, even though Ronald Reagan and his conservative allies had won the vote in the 1980 election, they hadn't won control of the government—the day-to-day work of the government was being done by Big Government Washington insiders of both political parties.

The Republican leaders on Capitol Hill had opposed Reagan and his policies in the Republican primaries, and the Democrats, such as House Speaker Tip O'Neill, had fought him tooth and nail in the general election.

Things were not much better for conservatives over at the Republican National Committee.

Despite the fact that President Reagan's confidant, Senator Paul Laxalt, and Reagan's daughter Maureen Reagan had big titles at the RNC, the chairmanship of the Republican National Committee and its day-to-day operation remained firmly in the hands of Party insiders, not ideological conservatives.

The RNC chairmen during the Reagan years, Dick Richards and Frank J. Fahrenkopf Jr., were longtime Party men, not movement conservatives. Fahrenkopf was a Nixon supporter who went on to have a distinguished career in several of DC's most powerful law and lobbying firms and to head the gambling industry's national association.

Senator Baker, Congressman Michel, and the rest of the establishment Republicans in Washington weren't necessarily bad people, but their lack of commitment to the conservative principles that Reagan ran on, and that grassroots conservatives expected the GOP to deliver on, meant that the debate that went on in the Republican primaries between Big Government Republicans and the Reaganites who wanted to shrink government never really ended.

Practically from day one of the new administration, Reagan had to fight the Washington insiders of his own party just as hard as he had to fight the liberals and Democrats. In 1982, twenty to twenty-five national conservative leaders (both Old Right and New Right) met with the then RNC chairman, Dick Richards, to let him know we were unhappy with what was going on at the RNC—and at the Reagan White House. In hindsight, while we loved and respected Ronald Reagan the person, during the Reagan years the road to progress on our issues was often rocky.

However, we knew that even if a specific issue on the conservative agenda wasn't getting the attention we thought it deserved, with Ronald Reagan it was never off the table, and our job was to bring it to the president's attention—sometimes whether he wanted to hear it or not.

One night around 1983, after we'd had our Wednesday dinner meeting, everybody had left except Howard Phillips, Newt Gingrich, and me. In my living room Newt began to explain how he was going to run for president. More than ten years before becoming Speaker, he was thinking about how to get himself elected to the White House.

At every meeting we would have an easel with paper or a blackboard, and when we would come up with a problem, Gingrich would go to the board and write:

- Vision

- Goals

- Strategy

- Tactics/Projects

And an hour later, after we had filled in those four concepts, we would have a way forward.

Great leaders like Eisenhower and Churchill talk about how a plan is indispensable in preparing for a battle. However, the number one benefit of writing the plan is not the plan—that's important, but it is secondary. The number one benefit of writing the plan is the exercise of writing the plan, because it clarifies and helps crystallize your thinking.

Congressman David Stockman, whom President Reagan appointed to head the Office of Management and Budget, exemplified one of the problems we faced.

Stockman was criticizing Reagan's proposed spending cuts and tax plan, and leaking uncomplimentary comments to the media before the ink was even dry on his White House commission.

Here was the guy who was supposed to be in charge of developing the economic justification of Ronald Reagan's fiscal plan and selling it on Capitol Hill telling the press (and anyone else who would listen) that Reagan was wrong.

Stockman was one of the first on the Reagan team to clamor for a tax increase, long before the Reagan tax cuts had a chance to work. Reagan later wrote, "Many times when I suggested that we push Congress to cut spending on a certain program, his [Stockman's] response was that it was hopeless—or in his words, 'DOA'—on Capitol Hill."[1]

This pattern repeated itself throughout Reagan's presidency.

Some of the early entries in Reagan's diary for 1982 illustrate the problem:

Jan. 11
Republican House leaders came down to the W.H. Except for Jack Kemp they are h—l bent on new taxes and cutting the defense budget. Looks like a heavy year ahead[2]

Feb. 23
Met this a.m. with our [Republican] Congressional leaders. They are really antsy about the deficit and seem determined that we must retreat on our program—taxes and defense spending. Yet they seem reluctant to go for the budget cutting we've asked for.[3]

Reagan was under constant pressure to raise taxes. In 1982 the establishment Republican leaders in Congress urged Reagan to make a deal with the Democrats "to support a limited loophole-closing tax increase to raise more than $98.3 billion over three years in return for their agreement to cut spending by $280 billion during the same period." Congress later reneged on the deal, and Reagan wrote ruefully in his biography that it was one of the greatest mistakes of his presidency because "we never got those cuts."[4]

Reagan's battles with Congress over aid for the Contras in Nicaragua and rolling back Communist incursions in Central America were met with similar progressive Republican resistance on Capitol Hill.

Even though Republicans had captured control of the Senate and increased their numbers in the House, prohibitions or restrictions on aiding the Contra rebels—generally attached to bills like the Defense bill, which President Reagan could not veto—routinely passed Congress.

In 1986, Reagan's request for aid to the Contras was made part of a pork-filled $1.7 billion supplemental spending bill that Republican stalwart Rep. Henry J. Hyde of Illinois characterized this way: "What you're saying to Mr. Reagan is: 'If you want the $100 million, it's going to cost you $1.7 billion,'" and White House spokesman Larry Speakes termed putting aid for the Contras in the supplemental bill as being "given the shaft" by opponents of Reagan's Contra policy.[5]

On one crucial vote, sixteen establishment Republicans in the House, including Ohio congressman Chalmers Wylie and future Big Government Republican governors Congressman Tom Ridge of Pennsylvania and Congressman John Rowland of Connecticut, abandoned Reagan, while almost forty Democrats supported him.

The defection of the sixteen Republicans was enough to defeat Reagan's plan and give a victory to Speaker O'Neill—and of course to Moscow. Within a few days of the vote, the Communist Sandinistas attacked the main Contra base well inside Honduras, forcing the

Hondurans to ask for emergency US assistance to repel the invasion.

Ultimately, what kept aid to the Contras alive were Reagan's skills as a communicator and conservatives working outside the establishment Republican Party to bring pressure to bear on soft Republicans and persuadable Democrats.

When Congress finally passed a comprehensive aid package designed to end the Communist threat in Central America, it was once again due to conservatives acting as a "third force," as much or more than it was to Capitol Hill Republicans who mostly acted as if restoring freedom in Nicaragua was an inconvenience and they just wanted the problem to go away.

President Reagan's proposal for his Strategic Defense Initiative (SDI) got much the same reaction from the Republican establishment.

Congressman Tom Ridge of Pennsylvania and the same establishment Republicans who undercut Reagan by supporting a nuclear freeze and opposing aid to the Nicaraguan Contras undercut him again by saying Reagan's Strategic Defense Initiative "left us with a serious defense problem."[6]

Ridge and others like him in the House, who wanted to restrict research and stifle funding for SDI, were joined by establishment Republican senators such as his fellow Pennsylvanian, Arlen Specter, and Nancy Landon Kassebaum, daughter of liberal Republican presidential candidate Alf Landon, who, incidentally, later married fellow establishment Republican Howard Baker.

Establishment Republicans, such as Senators Baker and Charles Percy of Illinois, even went so far as to trek down to the White House on the eve of a Reagan summit with the Soviets to harangue the president into abandoning the SDI initiative on the theory that it might lead to an arms race the Soviets would lose—thus upsetting the balance of power and the old Mutual Assured Destruction (MAD) formula propounded by Nixon and Kissinger.

It was an article of faith among Baker, Percy, Kassebaum, Specter, Ridge, and other establishment Republicans that America must accept the existence of the Soviet Union and simply live with the threat of international Communism and nuclear annihilation.

I was always amazed and saddened at those establishment Republicans and Democrats who talked about their compassion for those in need—the poor, the downtrodden, etc., but during the Cold War with the Soviet Union they supported—or at least refused to try to turn back—the enslavement of a billion people under Communism.

The establishment, including Republicans and Democrats, by encouraging détente, and thereby supporting continued Communist rule through trade deals and other economic means, subjected a billion children, men, and women to continued starvation, torture, political prisons, and death. Some compassion.

I remember being on TV around 1985 with a *Time* magazine reporter who expressed concern that American (read: Ronald Reagan's) foreign policy might lead to the fall of the Soviet Union. The reporter's dismay that we might win the Cold War was far from the isolated opinion of one liberal crackpot; it was a common feeling among the liberal elite, the so-called best and brightest, who constituted America's ruling class during much of the Cold War.

Reagan had a different idea; he saw Communism as an existential threat to America and the freedom of all mankind.

Reagan's approach to dealing with the Soviets was simple, as my friend Dick Allen, who served as President Reagan's first White House national security advisor, once explained.

One day at the golf course, Allen related to me how in 1977 he had contacted Reagan to let him know that he was exploring a run for governor of his home state of New Jersey, and if he decided to get in the race, he would have to bow out as Reagan's campaign advisor on national security matters.

Reagan liked and relied on Allen and didn't want to lose him, so he said, "Dick, do you want to know what my approach to dealing with the Soviets will be when we get to the White House?" Allen said he'd like to know, and Reagan replied, "I tell them, 'We win, you lose.'"

Richard Allen passed on running for governor of New Jersey, staying with Reagan as his senior foreign policy advisor during the 1980 campaign, and eventually serving as President Reagan's national security advisor to help see to it that the Soviets did in fact lose the Cold War.

However, establishment Republicans, such as Senator Baker, were too shortsighted and lacked the vision to recognize that SDI was an important part of Reagan's strategy to draw the Soviets into a race they couldn't win, on either the technology or the economic front.

What's more, they just couldn't grasp that Ronald Reagan passionately hated the very idea of a nuclear war that could destroy mankind and he actually believed that MAD was immoral, and that he meant it when he said of SDI: "Isn't it worth every investment necessary to free the world from the threat of nuclear war? We know it is."

The liberal Union of Concerned Scientists (UCS), a leading critic of SDI, put out information that "exposes the inherent technical and strategic flaws" in the program. At the same time, organizers of two other separate opposition efforts by liberal scientists actually sought to limit "star wars" research.[7]

But Reagan was sincere about the SDI program, both as a tool to bankrupt the Soviet Union and as a way to preserve mankind from the sure destruction a nuclear war would bring.

Martin Anderson has vividly described Reagan's 1979 visit to the NORAD's Cheyenne Mountain complex, and how troubled he was by the powerlessness of a system that could detect impending annihilation but could do nothing to stop it. As a presidential candidate in 1980, Reagan was lobbied on missile defenses by Wyoming senator Malcolm Wallop.[8]

Once again, it was conservatives working outside the establishment Republican Party who kept public support for the SDI program alive and the establishment's feet to the fire on one of President Reagan's most important defense initiatives.

One of the two times Ronald Reagan called me while he was

president was to thank me for what I was doing to help generate public support for SDI.

The real heavy lifting was done by General Dan Graham and the organization High Frontier, which he founded and that is still going today under the leadership of former ambassador Hank Cooper.

I first met General Graham at a dinner at Morton and Helen Blackwell's home. Through High Frontier, Graham built public support for the program. As one of Ronald Reagan's military advisers in his 1976 and 1980 campaigns, Graham had helped convince Reagan of the folly and culpable negligence of the establishment politicians who accepted leaving America totally undefended against incoming nuclear missiles.

Graham lobbied other public officials and opinion makers that it was sound political and military strategy; he assembled the scientists and engineers who proved it would work, and through High Frontier he raised the funds to do all of the above.

The Science and Engineering Committee for a Secure World and Dr. Kim Holmes, national-security analyst for the conservative Heritage Foundation, also worked to educate Congress and the public that SDI was feasible.[9]

Establishment Republicans on Capitol Hill once again went soft on the effort, cutting funding and leaving Reagan to plaintively appeal in his final State of the Union address, "Our funding request for our Strategic Defense Initiative is less than 2 percent of the total defense budget. SDI funding is money wisely appropriated and money well spent."

Yes, on Election Night in 1980, it seemed as though all of our efforts to build the conservative movement and our long fight to nominate and elect a conservative presidential candidate had finally been rewarded.

But when push came to shove, the toughest opposition to Ronald Reagan's most revolutionary ideas, such as defeating, not accommodating, Communism, cutting spending and regulation to spur economic growth, and freeing the world from the threat of nuclear war, didn't come from the Democrats and liberals; it came from the establishment Republicans who refought the arguments of the 1980 Republican primaries every time Reagan sent a proposal to Capitol Hill.

In the great hundred-year battle for the soul of the Republican Party, conservatives have faced three challenges: the first was to defeat the GOP establishment and nominate a conservative for president, which we did in 1964 by nominating Senator Barry Goldwater; the second was to nominate, and elect, a conservative president, which we did in 1980 with Ronald Reagan. Our next challenge will be to nominate and elect a conservative as president, and provide him or her with a conservative majority in Congress and the states so that he or she can actually *govern* as a conservative.

5

THE 1988 PRIMARY CAMPAIGN: THE ESTABLISHMENT STRIKES BACK

The passage of twenty-five years has largely obscured the fact that Vice President George H. W. Bush ran for president in 1988 as a conservative; or, like Mitt Romney in 2012, at least as much of a conservative as he could pretend to be.

Although most conservatives did not trust Bush or regard him as Reagan's logical heir, the proof that Ronald Reagan's first decision as the Republican candidate for president was his worst decision—choosing Bush as his running mate—wasn't made manifest until after Bush won the 1988 presidential campaign.

Going into the 1988 campaign, many conservatives allowed themselves to be convinced that Bush would continue to pursue and perhaps bring to fruition many—if not most—of the policies that Ronald Reagan ran on and pursued as president.

Most important, there was no conservative heir apparent to Reagan. The conservative movement and Ronald Reagan's conservative coalition had no strong, obvious, clear alternative to the vice president the Republican establishment had urged upon President Reagan.

Every Republican on Capitol Hill with presidential ambitions claimed to be a supporter and friend of Ronald Reagan's, even those like Senator Bob Dole of Kansas, who had at best a spotty record of supporting Reagan's policies.

The small cadre of principled conservatives in Congress who regularly fought for conservative principles (such as reducing taxes, reining in spending, and cutting welfare) was often frustrated when Reagan would make a deal with the Democrats that undercut what they were trying to do in order to pursue his primary policy goal of rebuilding America's defenses and defeating the Soviets.

Congressman Jack Kemp, a favorite of movement conservatives, drew Reagan's ire on a number of occasions. Reagan privately referred to Kemp as being "unreasonable" when he tried to hold the president's feet to the fire on economic issues and to fan the flames of the revolution Reagan had lit.[1]

And let's face it—Ronald Reagan's outsized political skills, his commanding presence on the world stage, and the reverence in which he was held by grassroots Republicans made every other potential Republican candidate for president appear to be just another politician.

The bottom line was that going into the 1988 primaries, conservatives did not have control of the Republican Party infrastructure, nor did they have a clear leader.

Vice President George H. W. Bush's strategy out on the stump in the primaries was to sell himself to skeptical grassroots conservative voters as Ronald Reagan's loyal helpmate and the candidate to finish Reagan's work.

Bush had the support of the Republican establishment, so he would get no criticism nor have those claims questioned by anyone in the Party organization. Plus, like Mitt Romney in 2012, Bush was willing to at least say the right things to conservatives, even when what he was saying contradicted his past statements and his record.

I had on occasion criticized Jack Kemp because it seemed to me he could only get a sense of outrage at fellow conservatives, not the Left. Like some of our other conservative friends who were strong supply-siders, Kemp was focused on growing the economy, but not necessarily shrinking government and cutting spending, and this frustrated many conservatives who took seriously Reagan's argument that the growth of government was undermining the Constitution and eroding liberty.

In 1985, my wife, Elaine, and I were at the Plaza Hotel in New York for the *National Review*'s thirtieth anniversary gala dinner. During conversation with Jack and Joanne Kemp, Jack looked at me with a smile and said, "Richard, just once would you say something nice about me?"

In 1987, Pat Buchanan gave serious consideration to running for president in 1988, and I was ready to help him, but he decided to defer to Kemp as the conservative standard-bearer. In 1987 Kemp asked me to take charge of his campaign's direct mail, which I did strictly as a volunteer. This proved to be a very difficult job because, like all too many other conservative candidates who may be personally conservative, Jack Kemp had by then surrounded himself with a lot of Big Government Republicans.

Kemp was a favorite on the Republican Lincoln Day Dinner circuit. He drew large crowds wherever he went and was one of the most recognized Republican members of Congress. Despite all that, his campaign never really got off the ground organizationally.

One grassroots Republican operative, and Kemp supporter, described it as "more of a traveling policy seminar than a campaign," with Congressman Kemp delivering great (and long-winded) speeches on economic opportunity, cutting taxes, and spending discipline in cities where he didn't even have a campaign coordinator or a get-out-the-vote effort in place.

Rev. Pat Robertson's campaign was better organized than Congressman Jack Kemp's. Robertson's *700 Club* program on Christian television made him a well-recognized figure on the Religious Right, and he had a prebuilt grassroots organization in charismatic churches across the country. Robertson came in second to Senator Bob Dole in Iowa. Robertson won the disputed Washington Republican caucuses, as well as caucuses in Alaska, Hawaii, and Nevada, but his appeal was largely limited to voters of the Religious Right, and he never seemed to make any inroads with voters outside this core constituency.

Robertson was also attacked by the fearsome Bush smear machine, which went after him for allegedly inflating his Marine Corps record and using his father, Virginia's late US senator Absalom Willis Robertson, to escape combat duty during the Korean War. When Robertson's campaign stumbled in South Carolina in the face of the Bush assault and he failed to win any of the other Bible Belt states, he folded his campaign.

From the perspective of building the conservative movement, all was not lost in Robertson's failed campaign; in fact, far from it. Out of that campaign came the Christian Coalition, which played a major role in the Republican congressional victory of 1994 and gave many Christian conservatives, especially young conservatives such as Ralph Reed and my longtime associate Ben Hart, valuable national leadership experience.

Sen. Bob Dole, who had a deep and abiding dislike of George H. W. Bush, ran against Bush for being a "wimp." Dole's charge was to some degree an indictment of Bush for abandoning his previous moderate principles (if there is such a thing), in favor of Reagan's conservatism.

Dole camped out in Iowa "like he was running for county sheriff," as one wag put it. Dole's long service as Kansas's senator made him an expert on the issues and concerns of voters in the Midwest, and his rise from poor farm boy to seriously wounded World War II hero to law school grad to United States senator, and then to Republican candidate for vice president in 1976, was a compelling story. When presented to voters out in the Farm Belt, it made for an especially appealing contrast with the privileged background of Vice President Bush.

Dole won the Iowa caucuses, despite a strong challenge from Rev. Pat Robertson, and had Bush on the ropes going into New Hampshire.

Dole's challenge was brought to an abrupt end when the

Republican establishment pulled out all the stops for Bush and saved him from defeat in New Hampshire.

New Hampshire governor John Sununu crisscrossed the state with Bush—who would later reward him with the job of White House chief of staff—and busloads of Bush campaign volunteers were shipped to New Hampshire to knock on doors.

Bush's New Hampshire comeback was made easier by Senator Dole's meltdown at a press conference where he angrily accused Bush of "lying about his record" on taxes because Bush had run ads accusing Dole of not supporting what Bush called "the Reagan–Bush plans to cut taxes."

Dole continued his campaign, but the damage was done. Dole ended up winning Iowa, his native Kansas, Minnesota, South Dakota, and a few other Farm Belt states in the upper Midwest, but that was it.

Vice President Bush's nomination was probably assured when the Reverend Jerry Falwell, leader of the Moral Majority, gave his organization's endorsement to Bush instead of endorsing the candidacy of fellow Christian conservative Rev. Pat Robertson or conservative congressman Jack Kemp, both of whom were running in the primaries as the conservative alternative to Bush.

I will leave it to someone else to write a more detailed history of the 1988 campaign. Much more could be said about the personal rivalries, backstage intrigue, and political blunders that led to the strange circumstance of establishment Republican George H. W. Bush being anointed to continue the conservative revolution that he ran against in 1980, and that his acolytes in the Reagan–Bush administration had argued and fought against at every opportunity during the eight years of Ronald Reagan's presidency.

George H. W. Bush's 1988 primary victories provided the model for Mitt Romney's 2012 primary campaign because in many cases the people surrounding Mitt Romney—such as former New Hampshire governor and Bush White House chief of staff John Sununu and establishment Republican super-lobbyist and Massachusetts GOP national committeeman Ron Kaufman—were the same establishment Republicans, or at least the understudies of the establishment Republicans, who had guided Bush to victory in 1988.

Once the 1988 Republican primary season was over, and Bush's nomination was assured, it appeared that for all intents and purposes, conservatives were rudderless and leaderless.

There was a good bit of talk and complaining about Bush, the failures of the conservative candidates in the primaries, and general kvetching—but there was no plan as to what conservatives should do at the Republican National Convention.

Unlike the Ron Paul supporters in 2012, the supporters of Jack Kemp and Pat Robertson—the conservatives who lost out in the 1988 primaries—had no plans to go to the Republican National Convention in New Orleans and make the case for their candidate and his ideas.

Even worse, until just before the convention opened, there was no real push for Bush to select a conservative running mate. Reagan had been pushed to select a moderate, such as former president Ford or Bush himself, to unite the party and ensure that the Republican establishment would support him, but conservatives had no similar effort under way after the 1988 Republican primaries ended.

In the days before the Republican National Convention, conservatives finally began an intense lobbying effort to ensure that a conservative would be nominated for vice president. The media picked up the story of conservative disgruntlement with Bush, and with Bush down in the polls, his advisors knew something had to be done.

Conservatives were persistently and loudly pushing for a conservative to get the nod. But who would Bush choose?

The names of practically every Republican elected official above sanitation commissioner were floated and analyzed by the media. California governor George Deukmejian said he didn't want the job. Republican governors and senators from other key Electoral College states were weighed, with the list eventually being pared down to Senators Bob Dole of Kansas, Pete Domenici of New Mexico,

Dan Quayle of Indiana, and Alan Simpson of Wyoming, Rep. Jack Kemp of New York, and Elizabeth Hanford Dole, wife of Senator Bob Dole and a former transportation secretary.

Domenici and Simpson were both respected members of the Capitol Hill establishment, and Simpson in particular was a familiar face on television, but neither of them were conservatives, and neither came from states that added anything significant to Bush's Electoral College prospects.

The conventional wisdom said Bush should choose Senator Bob Dole or Congressman Jack Kemp, both of whom were perceived to have a national following because they had run in the Republican primaries.

Bush and Dole just plain didn't like each other, so Dole was never really in the running despite public protestations to the contrary from the Bush camp. Mrs. Dole was there solely as window dressing for feminists, so that Republican national politics wouldn't appear to be strictly a male sport.

Clearly, Jack Kemp was the choice of many, if not most conservative leaders, but he certainly wasn't the conservative who was most congenial to George H. W. Bush and his inner circle.

Kemp had been brash enough to try to hold Reagan's feet to the fire on taxes, and as the convention opened, he continued to go on television to talk about his signature issues. This contradicted Bush's idea of a vice president as a loyal helpmate, as he saw his role with Reagan.

Bush had no intention of having Jack Kemp hold *his* feet to the fire on conservative principles from inside the White House, and the more Bush saw Kemp's face on TV, the lower Kemp's prospects fell.

This, by process of elimination, left Senator Dan Quayle of Indiana.

In 1981 Elaine and I hosted an evening party for a hundred or so at our McLean, Virginia, home to celebrate and welcome about twenty newly elected conservative members of Congress. Dan Quayle was one of the stars that night as a young and promising conservative Senator.

Quayle had an impeccable conservative pedigree as the grandson of conservative newspaper magnate Eugene C. Pulliam, who, by the way, received an award for service to the conservative cause at the great Young Americans for Freedom rally at Madison Square Garden in March 1962.

Senator Quayle was also seen as something of a political giant killer, having won a tough GOP primary to take on and defeat one-time Democratic presidential contender Senator Birch Bayh in 1980.

During his time on Capitol Hill, Quayle established himself as a strong anti-Soviet national defense conservative and a reliable vote for Reagan's defense build-up. He also subscribed to Kemp-style "optimistic conservatism" and the signature legislative achievement of his Senate career was probably a job-training bill he sponsored with liberal icon Ted Kennedy.

Quayle had another set of assets not obvious to outsiders at the time; he shared a number of Washington's big-name political consultants with Bush, and they spoke highly of Quayle's abilities as a grassroots campaigner.

Dan Quayle's boyish good looks, handsome young family, and gregarious personality made him appear as if he had been plucked straight out of central casting for the part of the youthful face of the Republican Party to complement Bush's grayed-at-the-temples experience.

What's more, Bush liked Quayle, who had made a point of stopping by his office on the Senate side of the Capitol to talk national security with the former CIA director and US ambassador to China.

Finally, and perhaps most importantly, Bush saw in Quayle a loyal subordinate, and many of Bush's staff and senior advisors saw someone who might be personally more conservative than they were, but who would not be a threat because he would not bring a cadre of movement conservatives with him to upset their plans to roll back the Reagan Revolution in favor of a "kinder, gentler nation."

Without pressure from conservatives to choose one of their national leaders—and indeed without an obvious conservative national leader to get behind—George H. W. Bush and his people had the freedom to make much the same calculation about Dan Quayle that Nixon had made about Agnew: he wouldn't get in the way once the election was won.

And they were right.

After a lackluster performance on the campaign trail, made worse by constant leaking and sniping from inside the Bush campaign, Quayle was largely isolated in the administration and settled into his office in the West Wing to handle the ceremonial duties of the office and to come out to try to calm waters whenever Bush riled conservatives.

6

"READ MY LIPS . . ."

The 1988 presidential campaign may have pitted two of America's least appealing politicians against each other. However, it showed that when Republicans nationalize the election and Americans are presented with a clear alternative between a conservative vision of America and a liberal version of America, voters usually choose the conservative candidate.

While George H. W. Bush was one of the most experienced men ever to run for president, having served as a member of Congress, CIA director, ambassador to China, and chairman of the Republican National Committee, he was not well liked by most of political Washington.

All his political life George Bush had been "selected" on the basis of his old Republican establishment connections (his father had been a Republican senator from Connecticut) and money. The media regarded him as thin-skinned and gaffe-prone, and they also bought, and readily promoted, the idea that, despite his heroism in World War II, Bush was a "wimp."

While he inspired intense loyalty among his close friends and aides, conservatives on and off Capitol Hill didn't trust Bush to actually produce on promises to follow through on Reagan's agenda.

But Bush had one thing going for him: he had trained a lifetime to be president, and after twenty-plus years in public life, he had an unmatched Rolodex of establishment Republican Party leaders, donors, and contacts who owed him favors large and small.

Democratic Massachusetts governor Michael Dukakis was a flinty "process liberal"—a Harvard grad that came across as both holier-than-thou and smarter-than-thou.

Dukakis was an unlikely standard-bearer for Democrats in a year when Congressman Richard Gephardt, Big Labor's best friend in Congress, was on the ballot, as was Rev. Jesse Jackson, favorite of the hard Left and African-American voters.

But Dukakis was a tough campaigner, and his campaign team was master of the negative ad and the behind-the-scenes smear—which eventually took out two of his principal rivals, Gephardt and Senator Joe Biden.

Dukakis was almost matched measure for measure as a negative campaigner by Sen. Al Gore, who first brought the infamous Willie Horton to prominence in an ad against him in the Democratic primaries.

Dukakis also had the distinction of being a governor, which gave him a gravitas that a mere House member could never hope to match, and he could run on the so-called Massachusetts Miracle.

The "Miracle," which was as much, if not more, attributable to the economic and national defense policies of Ronald Reagan than it was to Dukakis, allowed him to present himself to traditional Democratic Rust Belt voters and hard-pressed populist farmers as the guy who was going to make things fair and revitalize their faltering economic bases.

When Dukakis was not trashing his Democratic rivals, he didn't campaign against George H. W. Bush and the Republicans in general; he campaigned against Ronald Reagan.

And it seemed to be working.

Running as a technocrat, on a platform that was little more than a claim of "competence," Dukakis won thirty states and over

40 percent of the Democratic primary vote in a crowded field. Coming out of the Democratic National Convention, some polls had Dukakis ahead of Bush by as much as seventeen points.

If coming out of the Democratic Convention the 1988 race seemed to favor Dukakis, coming out of the Republican National Convention the tide quickly turned in Bush's favor when he gave one of the best speeches of his life, vowing to continue Reagan's policies and embracing the Reagan legacy by saying:

> For seven and a half years I have helped the president conduct the most difficult job on earth. Ronald Reagan asked for, and received, my candor. He never asked for, but he did receive, my loyalty. Those of you who saw the president's speech this week, and listened to the simple truth of his words, will understand my loyalty all these years. . . . I am here tonight—and I am your candidate—because the most important work of my life is to complete the mission that we started in 1980.[1]

Bush went on to list the bill of particulars that would be used against Dukakis for the rest of the campaign in terms every Reagan voter would understand.

> Competence is the creed of the technocrat who makes sure the gears mesh but doesn't for a second understand the magic of the machine . . . The truth is, this election is about the beliefs we share, the values that we honor, and the principles we hold dear.
>
> They call it a Swiss cheese economy. Well, that's the way it may look to the three blind mice. But . . . but . . . when they . . . when they were in charge, it was all holes and no cheese.
>
> Should public school teachers be required to lead our children in the pledge of allegiance? My opponent says no—and I say yes.
>
> Should society be allowed to impose the death penalty on those who commit crimes of extraordinary cruelty and violence? My opponent says no—but I say yes.
>
> And should our children have the right to say a voluntary prayer, or even observe a moment of silence in the schools? My opponent says no—but I say yes.

And should . . . should free men and women have the right to own a gun to protect their home? My opponent says no—but I say yes.

And is it right to believe in the sanctity of life and protect the lives of innocent children? My opponent says no—but I say yes.[2]

From the Second Amendment to American exceptionalism to the right to life that Bush had once opposed by backing *Roe v. Wade* and abortion on demand, George H. W. Bush hit all the notes conservatives were hoping to hear from the Republican presidential candidate and emphasized the social issues establishment Republicans always do their best to avoid.

Absent the acceptance speeches of Barry Goldwater and Ronald Reagan, I doubt there was ever a more conservative acceptance speech delivered at a Republican National Convention. Many of the voters who voted for Bush based on his acceptance speech didn't realize it, but they were voting for speechwriter (now *Wall Street Journal* columnist) Peggy Noonan, not George H. W. Bush.

And the fiscal conservatives and small-government-types were particularly cheered when their newly nominated Republican candidate for president, George H. W. Bush, said:

And I'm the one who will not raise taxes. My opponent . . . my opponent now says . . . my opponent now says he'll raise them as a last resort, or a third resort. But when a politician talks like that, you know that's one resort he'll be checking into. My opponent won't rule out raising taxes. But I will. And the Congress will push me to raise taxes, and I'll say no, and they'll push, and I'll say no, and they'll push again, and I'll say, to them, "Read my lips: no new taxes."[3]

In an address full of big ideas and eloquent lines, delivered by the famously ineloquent Bush, the most forceful and memorable paragraph was Bush's embrace of conservative orthodoxy on not raising taxes—and of making Congress, not just Dukakis and the Democrats, the tax-raising boogeyman.

Legend has it that there was a lot of debate in the Bush inner circle about whether or not this commitment should be included in the acceptance speech.

But the debate wasn't about whether or not Bush intended to keep the commitment not to raise taxes, or what the ramifications of breaking the commitment might be—the debate was about whether the phrase "read my lips" was undignified and inappropriate for inclusion in such a weighty address by the Republican nominee for president.

The lone conservative voice questioning Bush was Barry Goldwater, who, while introducing Senator Quayle at a speech to a Rotary club in Phoenix, admonished Bush's running mate, "I forgot something that I had to say, and I hope you take this kindly. But I want you to go back and tell George Bush to start talking about the issues, okay?"

According to the Associated Press, Goldwater did not elaborate, and afterward he avoided reporters, saying, "I'm not talking. I want to get the hell out of here."

But the dig appeared aimed at Bush's capture-the-flag campaigning, including his pillorying of Governor Dukakis for vetoing a 1987 mandatory Pledge of Allegiance bill for Massachusetts schools. Quayle laughed and said only, "I wish Barry would just say what's on his mind."[4]

Goldwater may have had his doubts about the tone of the Bush campaign, but when George H. W. Bush finished his acceptance speech and the balloons dropped in New Orleans, whatever doubts about the nominee's commitment to conservative principles others had were mostly kept them to themselves. Bush campaigned on conservative themes and relentlessly hammered Dukakis's liberal values from the Right.

Bush may not have *been* a conservative, as events would later prove, but unlike Mitt Romney in 2012, in 1988 Bush *ran* as a conservative. He nationalized the election, and much as Obama countered Romney's technocratic campaign with a values campaign from the far Left, Bush hammered Dukakis's technocratic campaign with a values campaign from the Right.

It was no contest in either election.

Bush and Quayle defeated Dukakis and Bentsen by over seven million votes, garnering 53.37 percent of the popular vote and 426 Electoral College votes. Then Libertarian candidate Ron Paul and his running mate didn't even break half a million popular votes.

But Bush's huge popular and Electoral College victory did not have any coattails—unlike Reagan's 1980 win, Republicans actually lost seats in the House of Representatives and in the Senate, where four incumbent Republican senators were defeated, while Republicans picked up three Democratic seats, giving them a net loss of one.

And there were clues that what Bush had in mind was not the third term of Ronald Reagan, as Nancy Reagan expressed her disappointment with Bush's messaging by asking, "Kinder and gentler than who?"

George H. W. Bush's relationship with conservatives may be best illustrated by his response to a CBS television interview Howard Phillips and I had with Dan Rather at the 1984 Republican National Convention. We pounded Bush for his lack of commitment to conservative principles and what we saw as his "inside the White House" fifth column against Reaganism. The following evening, Rather interviewed Bush and said in so many words, "Mr. Vice President, last night I had Richard Viguerie and Howard Phillips on the show, and they say you're not a conservative. Mr. Vice President, are you a conservative?" Bush replied, "Yes, Dan, I'm a conservative, but I'm not a nut about it."

I'm proud to say that I was then and am now a "nut" about liberty.

It was later shown that what George H. W. Bush was a nut about was growing government, and driving all conservatives out of the White House, the executive branch of the federal government, and the Republican Party.

7

GEORGE H. W. BUSH ABANDONS REAGAN'S PRINCIPLES ᴀɴᴅ TRASHES ᴛʜᴇ REPUBLICAN BRAND

S ome of us who have been around conservative politics for a while remember the smirk on Democratic senator George Mitchell's face when he conned Republican president George H. W. Bush into abandoning his "read my lips" promise to oppose new taxes.

If "Read my lips: no new taxes," was the most memorable line of the 1988 campaign, George H. W. Bush's decision to abandon that commitment was, politically, the most momentous act of his presidency.

The decision to go back on his pledge not to raise taxes didn't take place until well into his term. But Bush's betrayal of the Reagan Revolution started the minute he took the oath of office. Within hours of Bush's inauguration establishment Republicans, such as James Baker III, who had opposed many of Reagan's initiatives from within the administration, were promoted. But throughout the government Reagan's conservative appointees, many of whom were loyal Republicans who had supported Bush, were forced to resign, were stripped of their duties, or were summarily fired by a new administration that wanted no part of the relatively few movement conservatives left in the government on the day Ronald Reagan departed Washington for California.

During Reagan's presidency conservatives frequently said, "Personnel is policy," and Bush's Inauguration Day massacre was a sure sign that he intended to abandon Reagan's policies, and his principles.

While Bush partisans argued that the new president was justified in putting his own people in place, the 1989 "Inauguration Day Massacre" firings were more akin to political executions; lists of those to be "executed" were drawn up, and they were fired before sundown of the first day of the new Bush administration in a well-planned agenda to replace conservatives (be they Bush supporters or not) with establishment Republicans.

While most commentators tend to focus on "Read my lips," Bush quickly walked away from conservative principles on a long list of policies and decisions.

- Bush reversed himself and imposed a temporary ban on semiautomatic rifles—so-called assault weapons—after first opposing the idea.

- He signed and advocated the Americans with Disabilities Act, creating a whole new realm of litigation nightmares for businesses large and small.

- He bailed out the troubled savings and loans banks.

- He signed the Civil Rights Act of 1990, making it easier for employees to sue employers.

- He bought into global warming by signing the Framework Convention on Climate Change.

- He created a "no net loss of wetlands" policy out of whole cloth, with little legislative authority, outraging farmers and landowners across the country.

- And in what was perhaps his most lasting and damaging betrayal of conservatives, he appointed an obscure state judge, David Souter of New Hampshire, to the Supreme Court.

The appointment of Souter, whose only obvious qualification to sit on the Nation's highest court was that he was a crony of former New Hampshire governor and White House chief of staff John Sununu, was a disaster from which the damage haunts us to this day.

We could go on—the point is, establishment media commentators tend to focus on "Read my lips" to sum up Bush's administration, but there were a host of policies where Bush deviated not just from Reagan's principles of government, but from conservative policy goals that had broad grassroots support.

While it was hard for Bush and his advisers to believe that he could go from over 90 percent approval when Operation Desert Storm ended in 1991, to getting just 37.5 percent of the popular vote in the 1992 election, it is easily explained when you look at the litany of me-too policies he backed and the liberal bills he signed.

Support for the Second Amendment and property rights, imposing moral hazard, instead of government bailouts for failed business transactions and investors, and opposing the creation of new "protected classes" of potential litigants were all broad conservative, and Republican, principles that predated Ronald Reagan.

Bush walked away from all of them and in the process not only abandoned the policies of Ronald Reagan, but he destroyed the Reagan coalition, and did serious and long-lasting damage to the Republican brand.

What's more, Reagan's character was such that he was utterly confident in himself—like Lincoln, he was not afraid to build the Party and strengthen his coalition by bringing in one of his primary opponents as vice president.

Bush was just the opposite—he was tentative and thin-skinned—so the very idea of having Jack Kemp, Senator Bill Armstrong, or one of the other leading New Right conservatives as his running mate never seriously entered into his calculations.

One reason Bush had such a strong election in 1988 was that, particularly after his acceptance speech, voters thought they were voting for the third term of Ronald Reagan. Once he got out from under Reagan's shadow and voters saw the real George H. W. Bush, they decided they didn't particularly like Bush and his establishment Republican administration.

Who you walk with says much about who you are. Reagan surrounded himself with conservative leaders and the self-made California entrepreneurs who formed his old kitchen cabinet; Bush filled his administration with people from the Yale Alumni Association and the Social Register—the contrast was obvious and telling.

Much as when Teddy Roosevelt introduced "progressivism" into the Republican Party, and made it the creed of establishment Republicans, President George H. W. Bush's kinder, gentler Big Government Republicanism made it difficult for voters to differentiate between the parties and their policies.

Were Republicans for lower taxes and fiscal discipline, or were they for more spending? Were Republicans the party of less government and more personal freedom, or were they the party of more government regulation and lawsuits from the Americans with Disabilities Act and "no net loss of wetlands"?

No one knew, and if there's not a bright, clear line and a clear contrast drawn between the parties and their candidates, as Democratic president Harry S. Truman so memorably put it, "why vote for a dime store Democrat when you can have the real thing?"

Establishment Republicans led by George H. W. Bush had ignored the profound wisdom of the Bible: "For if the trumpet makes an uncertain sound, who will gird himself for battle?" (1 Cor. 14:8).

Millions of center-right voters decided they wanted no part of Bush's dime-store Democrat policies, so they walked away from Bush and the Republican Party to support Ross Perot's independent run for president. Millions more just stayed home. In 1992, Bush's popular vote fell off from his 1988 total by some eight million votes; he garnered fewer votes than the man he beat four years earlier and earned less than half the votes he won in the Electoral College landslide he booked in 1988.

Republicans on Capitol Hill had not seen any coattail effect from Bush's 1988 victory, but they were not trounced in his defeat. Bill Clinton and Al Gore swept into office with a gain of one seat in the Senate and a net loss of nine Democratic seats in the House and what they thought was a liberal mandate to roll back the Reagan Revolution.

Had the hapless President George H. W. Bush been reelected, it is a near certainty that the Democrats would have made major gains in the 1994 midterm elections. They probably would have gained congressional seats in 1994, and picked up the White House in 1996. It would have been a wipeout down ballot as well. Someone like Al Gore might have been in the White House on 9/11.

8

THE NEW MEDIA AND THE RISE OF THE CONTRACT WITH AMERICA CONGRESS

The damage George H. W. Bush did to the Republican brand was severe, but it was about to be reversed with the help of the same tools that had helped launch the New Right and the Reagan Revolution a decade earlier—the new and alternative media, now augmented with the growing talk radio phenomenon.

During the 1992 campaign, Clinton and Gore had made the economy their priority, as Southern political sage James Carville plastered around their campaign headquarters, "It's the economy, stupid."

But Clinton and Gore did not ignore the larger liberal agenda, and at the top of their list once they were elected was "giving" the American people health care, as Clinton once put it.

President Clinton placed First Lady Hillary Clinton and liberal policy wonk Ira Magaziner in charge of the effort to draft, build support for, and pass a national health care plan, and with Democrats holding decent majorities in both houses of Congress, it looked as though it should be easy.

What Clinton and Gore failed to understand going into what became known as the "Hillarycare" fight was that there was a change brewing in Congress and in how public opinion was being molded.

The change brewing in Congress was that the old go-along, get-along establishment Republicans who accepted that the GOP was destined to be a permanent minority in the House were being replaced by new, aggressively partisan conservative Republicans, led by House minority whip Newt Gingrich.

While the gentlemanly deal-maker Bob Michel of Illinois remained House minority leader, the rest of the House Republican leadership team was made up of conservatives: Minority whip Newt Gingrich, chief deputy whip Robert Smith Walker, House Republican conference chairman Richard Armey, conference vice-chairman Bill McCollum, and conference secretary Tom DeLay.

While Gingrich, Walker, Armey, McCollum, DeLay, and Sen. Bob Dole ultimately joined the battle against "Hillarycare," they weren't really there at the beginning—Dole even had his own Big Government national health care bills.

The real leadership of the effort to defeat Hillarycare came from outside Congress—conservative grassroots organizations, commentators, and journalists who pressured Republicans to fight the Clinton health care bill on conservative principles—and who demanded that there be no deal and no compromises.

While talk radio has become one of the main media of choice for conservatives, back in 1992 it wasn't obvious that talk radio would be almost strictly a conservative domain.

In the 1992 presidential election, Bill Clinton had "played talk radio like a piano," said *Talkers Magazine* editor and publisher Michael Harrison.

The talk-savvy new president had plans to continue exploiting talk radio once he became president. He did eighty-two radio interviews during his first two years as president, while Hillary did eighty.

One of the Clinton's major radio initiatives centered on Hillarycare, and it was the first really big thrust of the Clinton agenda. To help sell the proposal, the president invited more than two hundred talk radio hosts from all over the country to Washington.

They received a briefing on September 21, 1993, followed by a lawn party two days later where they could broadcast their shows "direct from the White House."

Top administration officials, including Hillary Clinton, HHS secretary Donna Shalala, presidential advisor David Gergen, Tipper Gore, and health care czar Ira Magaziner, were made available to the talk radio hosts to help sell Hillarycare.

The problem was that America was not responding well to the sell. As *Talkers Magazine*'s Harrison put it, "the initial infatuation with the health care plan is fading as a majority of those who choose to express themselves don't trust Clinton, don't trust government and don't trust anything that smacks of socialism."

Rush Limbaugh's program had only been on the air nationally for about five years, but Limbaugh jumped into the fray against Hillarycare with both feet.

While Rush was leading the on-air charge against Hillarycare, in Washington Bill Kristol (formerly Vice President Dan Quayle's chief of staff and now editor of the *Weekly Standard*) channeled the brewing popular revolt into legislative opposition. Part of that campaign was very public—but the most important part may have been behind the scenes.

Three or four times a week, Kristol sent a barrage of faxes to thousands of conservative leaders, providing talking points against Hillarycare as well as practical advice on defeating the measure in Congress and the court of public opinion. Each new fax would be on opinion-molders' desks the very first thing in the morning.

Talk radio first showed its potential as a political force when a few talk radio hosts began to push the idea of voters mailing tea bags to Congress to protest a proposed congressional pay raise. The idea quickly gained currency and was promoted vigorously on air. Thousands of tea bags were mailed to Washington, and the fax machine, first used between a mere dozen talk hosts in the "tea bag" campaign, became a full-fledged member of the alternative media.

The establishment media was not absent from the battle, and the *Wall Street Journal*, one of the last conservative-leaning daily newspapers in America, waged a relentless campaign against Hillarycare, backed up by its stable of accomplished economic conservative opinion writers and commentators.

Direct mail also played a key role in the fight against Hillarycare. Dozens of conservative organizations—such as the American Conservative Union (ACU), under the leadership of David Keene and Don Devine, and the United Seniors Association, led by Sandra Butler and Kathleen Patten—mailed between twenty and twenty-five million letters.

As just one example of the breadth and depth of the campaign against Hillarycare, the Viguerie Company had the American Conservative Union as a client—in a period of one hundred days we mailed thirteen million letters, others were mailing as well, but we led the direct-mail charge in rallying grassroots conservatives to oppose Hillarycare and turn it into a nightmare for the Clinton administration.

The Democratic leadership on Capitol Hill was frozen by the outpouring of public opposition, and it stalled Clinton's legislative agenda just as the scandals began multiplying to further bog him down. More importantly, through talk radio, millions of outside-the-Beltway Americans were empowered to express their opinions, understand that they were not alone, and rally like-minded people to their cause.

The Democrats didn't really understand what they were up against.

At the height of the Hillarycare battle, I attended a policy forum, and one of the largest events was a panel presentation on Hillarycare, with ten panelists from the Clinton administration and an eleventh panelist from the insurance industry—a guy about 60 percent in favor of Hillarycare.

Mrs. Clinton was there watching, and they all talked as though (and apparently assumed that) Hillarycare was a fait accompli. I remember thinking, *Do you have any idea what we're doing?*

Apparently they didn't, because the new and alternative media of direct mail, faxes, talk radio, etc., were all under the establishment's radar.

They sure understood afterward.

Hillary Clinton sat down to a series of interviews with sympathetic liberal reporter Adam Clymer of the *New York Times*. Clymer's October 3, 1994, article, titled "Hillary Clinton Says Administration Was Misunderstood on Health Care," put the blame—or credit—right where it belonged: "This battle was lost on paid media and paid direct mail," the First Lady complained.

The new Republican majority that was elected to the House in 1994 believed that talk radio played such an important part in their victory that the Class of 1994 made Rush Limbaugh an honorary member of their caucus.

While Limbaugh, Kristol, and other conservative activists made opposition to Hillarycare the rallying point for opposition to Clinton and the Democrats, that effort by itself wasn't enough to rebuild the Republican brand after the damage George H. W. Bush had done to it.

What was needed was a new platform and new faces for the GOP, and going into the 1994 midterm election, Newt Gingrich, Dick Armey, and the new conservative leaders of the Republicans in the House had a plan to rebrand the Republican Party, and in the process repair much of the damage Bush had done.

It was called "The Contract with America." You can find the Contract with America in appendix 4 of this book.

While many members of the Gingrich leadership team have claimed a hand in the Contract with America, it was pure Ronald Reagan, and according to Reagan biographer Lou Cannon, it took much of its substance from Reagan's Second Inaugural Address.

While Newt Gingrich later wrote (with typical hyperbole) that "there is no comparable congressional document in our two-hundred-year history," he was right in the sense that never before had the technique of nationalizing an election been applied with such discipline to congressional campaigns.

And, I might add, never before had an effort been made to so completely expunge the legacy of a president only two years after his defeat, since practically everything in the Contract with America was intended to scream at voters, "We're not George Bush!" and at least one of the provisions of the Contract, that on compensation of property owners, was intended to mitigate the harm caused by Bush's wetlands policy.

As Jeffrey B. Gayner, writing for the Heritage Foundation, noted in 1995:

> The revolutionary character of the change represented by the Contract went beyond the US House of Representatives. Not only did the 367 Republican candidates for the House of Representatives who signed the document run election campaigns based on its provisions, but many of the campaigns for the US Senate, as well as state and local government races, also pivoted around the fundamental questions concerning the role of government in society as reflected in the Contract. In short, the Contract may come to symbolize the most profound change in the American political landscape in the last half century and, in many respects, determine the character of American government well into the 21st century.[1]

Gingrich, Armey, and the rest of the new House Republican leadership were helped in this effort by the retirement of long time minority leader Bob Michel—the old establishment Republicans who had accepted minority status as their lot in life (and learned to like it) and who had opposed the policies of Ronald Reagan were now mostly gone.

In their place were young, principled conservatives who were prepared to not just talk a good game, but (unlike George H. W. Bush) actually act on those promises.

The Contract with America was introduced at a big Capitol Hill rally, September 13, 1994, about six weeks out from Election Day 1994. The Contract with America allowed House Republicans to shift the debate in the last six weeks of the campaign to the size, scope, and intrusiveness of government, and almost as important, to the elitist character of Washington and its permanent liberal majority.

Democrats and the establishment media jeered, but the voters embraced the Contract with America, and the result was a fifty-four-seat swing from Democrats to Republicans.

Democratic House Speaker Tom Foley was defeated for re-election in his district, becoming the first Speaker of the House to fail to win reelection since the Civil War. Scandal-tainted Ways and Means chairman Dan Rostenkowski of Illinois was defeated, as was House Judiciary Committee chairman Jack Brooks of Texas. In all, thirty-four incumbent Democrats were defeated.

Republicans gained a majority of seats in the United States House of Representatives for the first time since 1954, and Newt Gingrich was set to be elected Speaker.

The Contract with America showed once again that conservative principles, clearly articulated, win elections.

And as Speaker, Gingrich made good on the Contract—within the first 102 days of the new Congress, all of the provisions of the Contract with America got a vote . . . at least in the House.

In the Senate, it was a different story, with the Republican establishment's 1994 senate candidates, such as Mitt Romney, opposing the Contract with America before the election, and establishment Republican senators, such as Oregon's Mark Hatfield, opposing it on the floor of the Senate; as House Republicans sent bills over to implement it, many of the most popular provisions of the Contract (such as the Balanced Budget Amendment) failed by narrow margins in the Senate.

Next to congressional term limits, the Balanced Budget Amendment was probably the most popular element of the Contract with America, and all but one of the Senate's fifty-three Republicans voted for the amendment, along with fourteen of forty-seven Democrats. But that was still one vote shy of the two-thirds majority required for passage of any proposed constitutional amendment. The House had passed the measure by a vote of 300 to 132, well over the margin.

Thanks in large measure to opposition from establishment Republican senators, most of the Contract got the promised House vote, but never became law, causing CATO Institute chairman Ed Crane to observe in 2000 that the budget for those programs the Contract had proposed to abolish had growth of about 13 percent since the Contract with America was announced and Republicans took control of the House.[2]

Clearly, something was amiss in the re-branded Republican Party.

9

BIG GOVERNMENT REPUBLICANS BACK in CONTROL

When Democratic president Bill Clinton said in his January 23, 1996, State of the Union Address that "the era of Big Government is over," and "We know Big Government does not have all the answers. We know there's not a program for every problem. We have worked to give the American people a smaller, less bureaucratic government in Washington. And we have to give the American people one that lives within its means," it sounded as though conservatives had won; we could fold our tents and go home.

Of course, 1996 was an election year, and politicians, particularly Democrats like Bill Clinton, are prone to say anything they think will get them elected or reelected, and in this case Clinton was simply facing reality. With Newt Gingrich holding the Speaker's gavel and the House leadership by and large in the hands of conservatives, the era of Big Government seemed to be on the ropes.

The question was, would Big Government go down for the count, or come back to go another round?

The Republican presidential primary elections and the budget impasse between Clinton and Gingrich, which resulted in two government shut downs lasting a total of twenty-eight days, dominated the political environment when Clinton gave his 1996 State of the Union Address.

Establishment Republican Bob Dole, the Senate majority leader, was running for president in 1996, and the Iowa caucuses and New Hampshire primaries were looming. Dole wanted to put the budget crisis behind him and get out on the road to campaign, despite the willingness of other Republicans to continue the fight unless their demands were met.

Gingrich for once failed to effectively make the case for conservative policy on the budget and came away looking as though the budget fight with Clinton was personal.

Democrats and their allies in the media attacked Gingrich's motives for the budget standoff. The polls began to suggest that the standoff and Gingrich's comments were damaging the Speaker politically, and he later referred to his comments as his "single most avoidable mistake" as Speaker.

Clinton's approval rating fell significantly during the shutdown, indicating that the public also blamed the president for the government shutdown, but once the fight was over, Clinton's approval ratings shot back up to the highest level seen since his election.

Gingrich later argued that the government shutdown led to the balanced-budget deal of 1997 and the first four consecutive balanced budgets since the 1920s. He also argued that the 1996 election brought about the first reelection of a Republican majority since 1928, and that was due in some measure to the Republicans' willingness to go to the mat on the budget.

Gingrich was right; while the 1996 Republican candidate for president, Bob Dole, went down in defeat and Republicans suffered a net loss of eight seats in the House, they managed to retain a 228–207 seat majority in the House, and in the Senate Republicans actually gained two seats.

The problem for Republicans was that the budget standoff with Clinton revealed the continuing fault line in the Republican Party and reenergized the Republican establishment to undercut conservatives on the budget and fiscal policy.

Once again, the toughest battle for conservatives was not with Democrats and liberals; it was with the establishment Republicans, like Bob Dole, who were only too happy to spend more and let government grow if it would just keep the budget battle off the front page.

After a rough start, Dole vanquished his conservative rivals, Senator Phil Gramm, magazine publisher Steve Forbes, and political commentator Pat Buchanan, to become the face of the Republican Party in 1996.

Dole's 1996 campaign was a classic example of a content-free establishment Republican presidential campaign—the same kind of résumé-heavy campaign that Mitt Romney ran and lost in 2012.

Republicans never, ever win the presidency unless they nationalize the election by campaigning on a conservative agenda—drawing a sharp contrast between the Democrat worldview and the conservative worldview.

One of the best examples of nationalizing a presidential election is, of course, Reagan's 1980 campaign, but the 1994 "Contract with America" congressional campaign also drew a sharp contrast with Democrats on balancing the budget, term limits, and other issues. Likewise, in 2010, Tea Party candidates, without any real direction from the national GOP, drew a sharp contrast with Big Government Republicans and with the Democrats on taxes, spending, the growth of government, and especially on Obamacare, to power the GOP to pick up six Senate seats and win historic sixty-three seats in the US House of Representatives, recapturing the majority, and making it the largest seat change since 1948 and the largest for any midterm election since the 1938 midterm elections.

Sometimes Democrats assist in this effort by being Democrats—as Walter Mondale famously did in 1984 when he admitted, "Reagan won't raise taxes; I will."

If the campaign becomes, as Democratic Speaker of the House Tip O'Neill said, "all politics is local," Democrats will win—they are the party of the delivery of ever-increasing services, and Republicans will never outbid them for the votes of special-interest groups or payments to the aggrieved, nor should they try.

In 1996, Bob Dole ran on his biography as a war hero, attacked Bill Clinton's character, and tried to make himself out to be a conservative, but you couldn't find the social issues or any part of the conservative agenda in a Dole campaign ad. The low point in Dole's campaign came when, in a ham-handed effort to appeal to conservatives, Dole said, "If that's what you want, I'll be another Ronald Reagan."[1]

The "stand for nothing" strategy didn't work for President Ford's 1976 campaign, it didn't work for President George H. W. Bush's reelection, and it certainly didn't work for Bob Dole—or John McCain's losing 2008 campaign, or Mitt Romney's losing 2012 campaign.

My old friend, conservative author, and Reagan administration official Jeffrey Bell's insightfully wrote:

> Social issues were nonexistent in the period 1932 to 1964. The Republican Party won two presidential elections out of nine, and they had the Congress for all of four years in that entire period. . . . When social issues came into the mix—I would date it from the 1968 election . . . the Republican Party won seven out of eleven presidential elections.[2]

The American electorate was already polarized on fiscal and social issues; it was waiting for a candidate to step forward and seize the opportunity to make the case for the conservative policies that Gingrich and the conservative leadership of the House had fought for—but Senator Bob Dole was not that candidate.

Social issues have come to the fore on the GOP side in two of the past six presidential elections. As I have noted there were only two elections since Reagan where the Republican Party won by a majority of the popular vote. It isn't coincidental that when the Republicans run on conservative issues, they win.

Like any good establishment Republican, President George H. W. Bush avoided the social issues in 1992, and Bill Clinton, who ran for president and defeated Bush in 1992, was a death-penalty advocate who promised to "end welfare as we know it" and make abortion "safe, legal, and rare."

Dole missed that lesson entirely, and by running a content-free campaign, Clinton's reelection was never really in doubt. He led the public opinion polls throughout the campaign. On Election Day, Clinton won a decisive victory over Dole, becoming the first Democrat president to win reelection since Franklin Roosevelt.

Clinton garnered 379 Electoral College votes to Dole's 159; although Clinton outpolled Dole by over 8.2 million votes, he did not win an absolute majority of the popular vote.

The media and establishment Republican postmortem of the 1996 campaign was brutal—but it was mostly aimed at conservatives, not Dole's content-free campaign.

In much the same way that the establishment tried to blame conservatives for Mitt Romney's loss in 2012 by claiming that he was "forced" to embrace unpopular conservative positions, the establishment blamed Dole's loss on the government shutdown and the conservative agenda pursued by House Republicans and largely ignored by the Senate that Dole led.

There was, however, one voice that got it right.

On the eve of Election Day 1996, conservative columnist and opinion leader George F. Will gave this "pre-mortem" to the Dole campaign:

> Bob Dole's unintelligible campaign—the "Finnegan's Wake" of presidential politics—was premodern in its indifference to the rhetorical dimension of the modern presidency, and postmodern in its randomness. His contention that the liberal media made matters worse called to mind the sign on the ruins of an ancient British church: "Anyone damaging these ruins will be prosecuted.[3]

"Reagan," said Will, "faced media much more hostile than the often affectionate media Dole faced, but Reagan won because his candidacy, unlike Dole's, was about something larger than the candidate's lust for the last rung up the ladder. Which is to say, the secret to getting out a message is to have one."

Will saw in Dole "an incoherence and superficiality born of his intellectual laziness and the incompetence of his staff of rented strangers [that] trivialized every issue he touched, from the coarsening of the culture as exemplified by partial-birth abortions to the Balkanization of the country by racial preferences." He predicted, "On Tuesday the country will make the mistake of extending a squalid presidency, but the country cannot be said to have missed the chance for a luminous presidency."

George F. Will's devastating indictment of the 1996 Dole–Kemp campaign included a number of criticisms that bore an eerie resemblance to what conservatives would say about the failures of the 2012 Romney–Ryan campaign, and with good reason. In both campaigns, the Republican establishment forced their candidate, and their policy of running a content-free campaign, down the throats of the conservative grassroots of the GOP, and lost the election to a Democratic candidate that in any rational universe would have been soundly defeated by a competent candidate and campaign.

Dole lost not because conservatives on the House side of Capitol Hill pursued a conservative agenda—he lost because he was at heart a supporter of Big Government who failed to embrace the reconstituted coalition of social and economic conservatives that, joined by national defense conservatives, supported the Contract with America.

But at least Bob Dole remained true to his Big Government principles. Long after he was out of office and had ceased to be relevant in Republican politics, he joined with another "great compromiser," Howard Baker, the former Republican senator from Tennessee, and his predecessor as Senate Republican leader, to support the passage of Obamacare.

"This is one of the most important measures Members of Congress will vote on in their lifetimes," the former Republican Senate majority leader and presidential candidate told an audience in Kansas City. "If we don't do it this year I don't know when we're gonna do it."[4]

With a "commitment" to conservative principles like that, it is no mystery why Bob Dole was soundly defeated in 1996—the question facing Republicans in the aftermath of Dole's defeat was, what was going to happen next?

10

CONSERVATIVES OPEN the DOOR to ANOTHER BUSH

n the aftermath of the GOP's 1996 defeat, it was clear that Bill Clinton hadn't won the election so much as Republicans had given it away.

Newsweek magazine noted that even "the most loyal Democrats [ascribed] Bill Clinton's victory to anybody or anything but Bill Clinton." In *Newsweek*'s analysis, Clinton "was neither beloved as a leader nor trusted as a man; his first term had generated scandals enough to shadow his second before it had begun; his fellow Democrats avoided using his likeness in their advertising; his average grade as president in a nonpartisan Pew Research Center poll was a merely passable C."[1]

And Clinton still outpolled Bob Dole by over eight million votes.

As Republicans and conservatives surveyed the political environment in the wake of the 1996 election disaster, there was a tremendous leadership vacuum in the GOP at the national level. Leading fiscal conservative Senator Phil Gramm of Texas, and economic conservative magazine publisher Steve Forbes, had run against Dole in the presidential primaries and been soundly rejected by GOP primary voters. Principled conservative political commentator and former White House advisor Pat Buchanan had run against both

George H. W. Bush and Bob Dole and had defeated Dole in the New Hampshire primary in 1996.

However, it was clear the Republican establishment was never going to forgive or forget that Buchanan had run against incumbent Republican President George H. W. Bush in 1992. What's more, Buchanan's unfiltered political commentary, which was loved by grassroots conservatives, came back to haunt him by providing his establishment Republican detractors and the liberal establishment media with unlimited fodder with which to attack him. Buchanan's campaign soon wilted under the harsh flame of their attacks, and Buchanan returned to the role of conservative commentator. Republican voters may have liked what Pat Buchanan said, but it was clear they weren't going to make him president.

Going into the 1996 election, former congressman Jack Kemp had been viewed by many conservatives as the leading voice of conservatism. Even though Kemp had declined to run for the presidency in 1996, he remained a popular and influential figure in conservative circles, and the fact that Kemp was put on the ticket as Dole's running mate was taken as some evidence that even the tone-deaf Dole campaign team recognized that the campaign was DOA unless it found the means to energize grassroots conservatives.

Unfortunately, Kemp did not distinguish himself during the 1996 campaign. To the great disappointment of his many friends and supporters in the conservative movement, far from being the voice of principled conservatism that would fire up grassroots Republican voters, Kemp often came across as a zombielike figure who went through the motions of advocating a cause he knew was lost.

When Kemp did wake up, it was usually to criticize the inside workings of the Dole campaign or to declare his intention not to be "divisive" or otherwise take up the cudgel and play the role of aggressive conservative warrior against the liberal policies of Clinton and Gore.

The low point in the Dole–Kemp campaign for conservatives probably came during the Kemp–Gore debate in which Kemp, a gifted speaker and favorite on the Lincoln Day circuit, was expected to demolish Gore. But Kemp was flat, weak, and disappointing in the debate with Gore; he did not demolish Gore as expected, and even Kemp's close advisors admitted he did not take the debate seriously. As one Kemp staffer put it, "There was no quarterback's pre-game drill before a big game like the Rose Bowl or the Super Bowl" before the Kemp-Gore debate.

As soon as the campaign was over, Kemp went back to running Empower America and promoting his brand of optimistic economic conservatism. Jack Kemp still had many friends in the conservative movement and grassroots Republican politics, but he was no longer seen as a potential president by most observers of the national political scene.

In the headlines of the national media, the most recognized Republican was Speaker of the House Newt Gingrich. Gingrich, largely by dint of his fierce and tireless partisanship, was the leading conservative opponent of President Clinton and his agenda. And in the two years since the "Contract with America" Congress had been elected, Gingrich's fight with Clinton and the business-as-usual Washington establishment over spending and balancing the budget had largely erased the me-too Republicanism of President George H. W. Bush, and effectively re-branded the Republican Party as the Party of fiscal conservatism.

However, Gingrich's larger-than-life personality and his tendency toward bombast and hyperbole—especially when describing his own contributions to the American historical record—were beginning to wear thin on many of his colleagues in the House, and especially on other members of the House Republican leadership.

Less than six months into the first Republican-controlled House to be re-elected in half a century, Gingrich would be the target of a rebellion by some of his closest colleagues in the House leadership.

Gingrich survived the rebellion; it turned out the rebels were fractured and riven by the same conflicting personal ambitions that brought them together to plot Newt's demise.

Still, the rebellion generated a great deal of negative publicity about Gingrich's leadership style, and it weakened him as a national leader. Coupled with his personal foibles, and the constant negative media to which he was subjected, Gingrich was a declining force in national politics; he just hadn't yet expended quite all of the energy stored in his meteoric rise to the Speakership.

Bill Kristol, editor of the *Weekly Standard*, described this period as "the winter of the Republican discontent" in an article urging the party to rally behind both Gingrich and an aggressive conservative agenda. In an interview, Kristol called the nervousness within party ranks over Gingrich "a sign of the disarray of the party" and not the cause of it.[2]

"To be defeated by Clinton again was a blow," Kristol said. "To have gotten 38 percent (1992) and 42 percent (1996) in successive presidential elections is a blow. And to have proclaimed a revolution, foolishly, and not to have had a revolution happen has caused them [Capitol Hill Republicans] to overreact to a kind of timidity and even dispiritedness."[3]

Kristol criticized Republicans for slamming on the brakes in reaction to past missteps, saying he feared that "the party has decided they shouldn't go anywhere. No speed is the favorite speed." In some respects, the agenda favored by many Republicans in 2012 remains similar to the one that shaped the Contract with America in 2014. But there are important differences now in how vigorously the party may pursue those policies.[4]

If the losing 1996 Republican candidates for president had failed to establish themselves as conservative leaders and potential candidates for the presidency in 2000, and Newt Gingrich and the conservative leaders of the House were diminishing themselves by the minute in internal squabbles, who was left to provide leadership to conservatives and Republicans at the national level?

The consensus gradually emerged that, if new leadership was going to be found, it would be found among the GOP's governors, who had not been tainted by the infighting endemic to the nation's capital and who were implementing a host of conservative ideas about how to encourage economic development, and deliver needed public services while balancing their budgets and holding down taxes.

The 1996 election produced mixed results for the Republican governors. Their numbers remained at thirty-two. They lost New Hampshire but gained West Virginia. However, in eight states, the Republicans weren't able to deliver their states to Dole, and in four of them—Pennsylvania, Michigan, California, Illinois—the Democrats won the state legislature, too.[5]

The thirty-two Republican governors were by no means thirty-two movement conservatives, and they were by no means happy with the conservative agenda adopted by Newt Gingrich and the House conservatives.

At the postelection 1996 meeting of the Republican Governor's Association, Wisconsin's establishment Republican governor Tommy Thompson came right out and said, "What happened is we went too far. . . . The Democrats picked up on the severity of our rhetoric and threw it back on us."[6]

Even if establishment Republican governors, like Tommy Thompson, weren't happy with the conservative agenda, voters in other parts of America outside the Beltway were.

After the 1996 election, Democrats held a 20 to 18 edge in the Kentucky Senate.

That margin disappeared overnight when five Democrats refused to follow the customary procedure of meeting in party caucus to elect leaders of the new Senate, condemning the procedure as undemocratic. "Secret caucuses," said state senator Larry Saunders (D), are "why people in Kentucky have such low esteem for elected officials." So he and four Democratic colleagues teamed up with Republicans to select the new Senate leaders.[7]

The Kentucky state senate revolt was sparked in large measure by Democratic governor Paul Patton's liberal higher education agenda and the liberal Democratic leadership's plans to stymie conservative legislation on abortion and other social issues.

In New Jersey's off-year gubernatorial election, liberal Republican governor Christine Todd Whitman had a big lead in the polls, but was worried about Rep. Robert Andrews, her probable Democratic opponent. Andrews was seen as a good candidate who would not be the easy target for Whitman that tax-increasing governor Jim Florio was in 1993, because Andrews had inoculated himself by signing Grover Norquist's no-tax-increase pledge.[8]

Conservative ideas were not defeated in the 1996 election, because, just like in 2012, the Republican presidential candidate did not run on a conservative agenda. The conservative Republican Congress had been re-elected, in spite of the controversy and media antagonism Speaker Newt Gingrich generated.

What conservatives were lacking after the 1996 election defeat was not a change in the agenda, as suggested by establishment Republicans such as Wisconsin governor Tommy Thompson; it was a leader who would run on and advocate the conservative agenda without the personal controversy and bombast that had become the hallmark of Gingrich and the leading House Republicans.

The next term of Congress would see more dilution of the message that brought Republicans to power in 1994, and just as important, the utter abandonment of the grassroots conservative campaigns that had powered insurgent conservative Republican candidates to victory.

As Paul Weyrich of the Free Congress Foundation said in a 1998 election postmortem meeting, Republicans, generally speaking, won the "air war" (commercials and similar activities) in 1998 while the Democrats won the "ground war" (voter identification and turnout). "You can be 7 percent ahead and if the other side knows where their voters are and turns them out, you lose," said Weyrich.

Morton Blackwell of the Leadership Institute added in the same meeting that campaigns must be about more than raising money and spending it on advertising, activities that, he said, not coincidentally permit campaign consultants to keep 15 percent of expenditures. Campaigns must include training, voter ID, precinct organization, turnout activities, etc.

The Republican House majority's aggressive solicitation of special-interest campaign funding and embrace of the Big Government that Washington insiders feed off had disconnected them from the conservative grassroots voters who elected the "Contract with America" majority.

The way I saw it, Republicans lost because they had become the establishment.

Into that leadership vacuum swaggered a young Republican governor who had a reputation for getting conservative policies past a Democratic legislature, a bankable national name, a base in one of the nation's most powerful Republican states, and a man who wowed his fellow Republicans when he said:

> I base my decisions on principle and on a conservative philosophy that most Texans share. And I want you to know I'm proud to be a Republican, just like I know you're proud to be a Republican as well.
>
> Ours is a party that stands for something—a conservative philosophy that is fair and decent and compassionate and full of hope for the future of our great country. We must proclaim our principles with pride and conviction, because I know and you know that when acted upon, our philosophy will make our country a better place for every American.
>
> Republicans must outline our hopes for America's future. We must make our case with reason and respect. We must inspire others to follow. In short, we must lead. And our leadership must be based upon principles and core convictions from which we will not waver.[9]

That Republican governor, with what he claimed was a set of conservative "principles and core convictions from which we will not waver," was Texas governor George W. Bush.

11

THE SELLING of GOVERNOR GEORGE W. BUSH as a "CONSERVATIVE"

George H. W. Bush was never a conservative, but he was able to use his role as Reagan's vice president to secure the GOP nomination and be elected president in 1988. His one term in office was an affront to Reagan conservatives, as he began his term in office with an "Inauguration Day Massacre" that swept most Reaganites—even ones who had worked tirelessly for his election—out of the federal government, and he broke his promises to us and the American public, most infamously by breaking his "read my lips" pledge never to raise taxes.

Many conservatives responded in 1992 by staying home or supporting third-party candidate Ross Perot, and as a result, Arkansas governor Bill Clinton, with only 43 percent of the vote, brought the White House back under Democratic control.

This was a setback to the progressive establishment of the Republican Party who had backed Bush, and benefited politically from his presidency, but it was a boon to conservatives, who channeled a rebellion against Bill and Hillary Clinton's Big Government initiatives to win conservative GOP control of the House of Representatives in 1994, ending forty years of Democratic rule.

The 1994 rise of the "Contract with America" Congress coincided with and was fueled by an expansion of the conservative media. No longer confined to a few publications of limited circulation, and with the use of direct mail to bypass the establishment media filter, conservatives expanded the new and alternative media of talk radio, cable TV, and the Internet to spread the conservative message and generate public opposition to Big Government Clinton-style.

In 1996 Republicans (much as they did again in 2012 by nominating Mitt Romney) largely squandered the enthusiasm and power of the 1994 "Contract with America" grassroots rebellion by nominating Senator Bob Dole, another "it's his turn" establishment presidential candidate, and Clinton was handily reelected, despite his scandal-plagued first term in office.

As the 2000 primaries approached, Washington's inside elite of both parties was exhausted. What's more, the GOP was tarnished by the Clinton impeachment and the attendant PR disaster for congressional Republicans, who found themselves labeled as hypocrites when it was revealed that a number of their leaders who had attacked Bill Clinton for his adultery and lies were guilty of the same sins.

The stage was set for Republicans to look outside of Washington for their presidential nominee, and against that backdrop Texas governor George W. Bush announced his candidacy for president.

Lined up against Bush were Arizona senator John McCain, social conservative activist Gary Bauer, businessman Steve Forbes, Utah senator Orrin Hatch, former ambassador Alan Keyes, former Tennessee governor Lamar Alexander, former Red Cross director and cabinet member Elizabeth Dole, Ohio congressman John Kasich, and former vice president Dan Quayle.

Forbes campaigned on the flat tax and worked hard to attract support from social conservatives. Although Forbes was a close second to Bush in the Iowa caucuses and tied with him in the Alaska caucuses, the only other candidate to move the needle against Bush and win any of the GOP primaries was Arizona's John McCain.

McCain didn't fit neatly into any political box, and he liked it that way. Even though he had a solid conservative voting record on many issues, he seemed to relish antagonizing and picking fights with leaders of the conservative movement—especially social conservatives.

Senator McCain's "base," to the extent he had one, like Bob Dole, was the establishment media. The media loved McCain's frequent sallies against conservatives and those he labeled "special interests." Even though McCain himself was a darling of those who wanted to reform Washington's corrupt lobbying and campaign finance system, the defense industry largely escaped his jibes and calls for reform because he was one of the defense industry's most reliable votes in the Senate and a major beneficiary of their special-interest political contributions and support.

If McCain was the alternative to the Republican establishment, many of the other candidates qualified as more conservative, but none of them attracted the money or support as did Governor George W. Bush.

Hailing from Texas, Bush started out with an extensive fund-raising advantage, and an "in" with the state's large group of conservative activists and donors.

But Bush had a number of negatives, not the least of which was his name and his lack of personal political skills. It hardly seemed possible, but going into the 2000 Republican primaries, George W. Bush was a weaker public speaker and more uncomfortable in front of a TV camera than his father had been, leading one longtime conservative political operative who saw Bush and McCain side by side in New Hampshire to conclude (wrongly, it turned out) that there was no way anyone could be elected president who was as bad onstage as Bush was.

However, Bush's lack of stage presence was compensated for by his money, organization, and vast army of consultants, family political contacts, retainers, and acolytes. Only the Kennedys could match Bush in having a ready-built national political franchise—no one on the Republican side was even close.

Bush's 2000 campaign was, according to the London *Independent's* writer Andrew Marshall:

[O]ne of the most highly organized in the long history of American politics. Every base is covered. The candidate is just the tip of the spear, almost an incidental: there are the advance men, the press handlers, chartered aircraft, the coaches [buses] lined up outside, speech writers, conference calls, banks of telephones primed to ring every voter in the state, television studios churning out attack slots and crash ads, computers running Microsoft Access databases, Palm Pilots crammed with telephone numbers and dates and names, senators, congressmen and mayors just waiting to make endorsements, websites, virtual press conferences, and bank accounts as deep and wide as the Atlantic ocean."[1]

Fourteen years later, historians and pundits are still arguing over whether Bush won South Carolina by deploying the infamous Bush smear machine that has worked over every candidate who ever ran against a Bush, or whether it was McCain's lack of organization and campaign by personal caprice that led to his defeat in South Carolina.

Certainly the hammering McCain took from the smear machine hurt him, and South Carolina has been the home of a well-organized group of Bush-family operatives since at least 1988, as Andrew Marshall noted in his article for the *Independent*.[2]

And the value of the personal Bush-family relationships in South Carolina could not be overestimated, as the *Boston Globe* observed in March of 1999, "Some of the same forces that crushed Pat Buchanan's insurgency in the 1996 South Carolina primary and helped Lee Atwater throw up a 'firewall' in the state to protect George Bush in 1988 are at work to give an advantage to the former president's son in next year's primary."[3]

However, South Carolina was also the first state where social conservatives had a major say in the outcome of an election, and in 2000 Governor Bush learned from his father's mistake in alienating conservatives.

The younger Bush worked hard to convince conservatives, especially social conservatives, that he was "one of us," by campaigning on the social issues in South Carolina while McCain campaigned mostly on being McCain.

Bush's compassionate conservatism graced every speech, woven through promises to improve education, keep the peace, and cut taxes.[4]

Bush opened many rallies and appearances with a local dignitary reading a letter from the most loved politician in the state, Senator Strom Thurmond, who endorsed Bush, saying, "After eight years of Clinton–Gore, the stakes are too high to stay at home. My friends in South Carolina have been with me through many campaigns and we've done right by South Carolina. I ask everyone here tonight to join in one more crusade and support George W. Bush as he leads our country forward in the 21st century."[5]

While some conservatives remained skeptical, after being clobbered in New Hampshire, despite outspending McCain by a substantial amount of money there, Bush convinced enough conservatives to vanquish McCain in the crucial South Carolina primary, largely on the strength of his conservative support.

George W. Bush gathered that conservative support by presenting himself as a man of principles, more than on the strength of any of his policy prescriptions, which were mostly mainstream Republican proposals that had been around Capitol Hill for years.

Governor Bush said in his victory speech the night he won the South Carolina primary, "I'm often asked about my tax cut plan. They say it's not popular in the polls. 'Why won't you back down, Governor?' And I say, you've got the wrong man. I make my decisions on what's best for America. I make my decisions based upon principle, not based upon polls and focus groups." It was that commitment to principles, presumably conservative principles, not the tax plan, that won Bush the South Carolina primary and ultimately the White House.[6]

McCain went on to win other primaries, including Michigan, just days after his defeat in South Carolina, but conservatives had made up their minds to support Texas governor George W. Bush, and the 2000 Republican presidential nomination was never really in doubt after South Carolina.

In hindsight, it was clear George W. Bush had no intention of pursuing a conservative agenda as president. However, he was well advised enough to understand that, if his chief opponent was John McCain, he could only get to the White House with conservative support, and as a South Carolina voter interviewed by the *Independent*'s Andrew Marshall said with a hint of guilt for being inclined to support the Texas governor early in the South Carolina primary, "He's a politician, sneaky, in a subtle sort of way."[7]

12

CONSERVATIVES BETRAYED:
THE PRESIDENCY OF GEORGE W. BUSH

As the 2000 presidential campaign unfolded, some conservatives were disturbed by George W. Bush's use of the term "compassionate conservatism," which seemed to imply that "regular" conservatism was not compassionate.

We remembered how our movement's first political leader, Barry Goldwater, scorned the progressive establishment Republicans' use in his day of the term "progressive conservatism." "This is a strange label indeed," he wrote in *The Conscience of a Conservative*. "It implies that 'ordinary' conservatism is opposed to progress. Have we forgotten that America made its greatest progress when conservative principles were honored and preserved?"

"Compassionate conservatism," also had a strong scent of the "kinder, gentler" conservatism that Bush's father had described in his acceptance speech at the 1988 Republican National Convention and that we soon learned was not conservatism at all, but a return to the progressive Republicanism of Teddy Roosevelt, Tom Dewey, Dwight Eisenhower, Nelson Rockefeller, and Richard Nixon.

Despite the misgivings of some conservatives, when George W. Bush was inaugurated as our forty-third president, with a Republican majority in the House and Senate to back him up, the average grassroots conservative voter thought that Bill Clinton's statement that "the era of Big Government is over" was about to become reality. Boy, were they ever mistaken.

Clinton, of course, knew full well that Big Government was growing and would continue to grow. What he probably didn't anticipate was that, as fast as government grew under his administration and a Democratic Congress in 1993–94, it would grow much faster under a Republican president with a Republican Congress.

Once George W. Bush was sworn in as president and Republicans had control of both elected branches of the federal government, the era of Big Government really was over, and the era of Obese Government had begun!

When Bill Clinton made his (possibly tongue-in-cheek) claim about the era of Big Government being over, the federal government was spending $1,635.9 billion. Just seven years later, in 2003, the federal government was spending $2.3 trillion, and by the end of President George W. Bush's second term in 2008, the federal government was spending $3.2 trillion, almost double what it was spending when the era of Big Government supposedly ended. For that we can thank both Republicans and Democrats, but most Democrats don't claim to be, or campaign as, fiscal conservatives, as George W. Bush did.[1]

With the solid backing of conservatives, Republican George W. Bush won the presidency in 2000 and the succeeding election as well. We gave a Republican president, who ran as a conservative, a Republican House in 2000, 2002, and 2004, and a Republican Senate in 2000 (until the defection of Vermont senator Jim Jeffords), 2002, and 2004. We conservatives had every right to expect that *finally* we'd see government spending brought under control, and the size of the federal government cut back.

Instead, the size of the federal government increased at a faster rate under the Bush administration and a Republican Congress than at any time since President Lyndon Baines Johnson and the Great Society. The Bush years were responsible for a near doubling of the federal budget and set the stage for the unprecedented spending of President Barack Obama and the Pelosi–Reid Congress that followed.

How could this happen? It happened because there was what was for all intents and purposes a corrupt bargain struck between President Bush and the leaders of the Capitol Hill Republican establishment, particularly establishment Republicans Speaker of the House Dennis Hastert and majority whip Tom DeLay.

Hastert and DeLay sought to shore up their Republican majority in the House and at the same time impose an ironclad discipline upon it through "earmarks" and pork-barrel spending of the taxpayers' hard-earned money.

Far from being fiscal conservatives, these two cynical politicians saw the federal budget as their personal political slush fund to be used to advance their personal power and to permanently entrench themselves, and their cronies, in positions of power.

Here's how it worked.

Typically, an individual member of Congress, with the approval of the majority leadership, inserted an "earmark" into a spending bill. The president didn't request such spending, and it evaded the usual procedures for competitive bidding, expert review, and cost-benefit analysis.

"Each one of these," said the *Washington Post*, "as Mr. Reagan understood, but Mr. Bush apparently doesn't, amounts to a conscious decision to waste taxpayers' dollars."

There really is no better illustration of the corrupting influence of power on the principle-free Republican establishment than the explosion of "earmarks" and pork-barrel spending projects during the presidency of George W. Bush.

When Reagan said, "I haven't seen so much lard since I handed out blue ribbons at the Iowa State Fair," in March 1987, he then vetoed the Transportation bill because it contained 152 congressional earmarks. When his veto was overridden with the help of thirteen Republican senators, he had his OMB director, Jim Miller, look into the Constitution to see if there was any way to stop earmarks from being implemented in the Omnibus Appropriation Bill Congress later passed.[2] According to Phil Kerpen's "Earmarks and the Executive" in *National Review*,

> Miller checked with attorneys and legal scholars and discovered that committee report language, which is where earmarks appear, should not be treated as law since it fails to meet the requirements of the Presentment Clause of the Constitution.
>
> Acting in accord with the Constitution, Miller told executive agencies to comply with the law and spend money on accounts for which it was appropriated. Meanwhile, he instructed agencies to treat report language properly—in other words, as not binding—and to disregard earmarks in committee reports. Spending decisions would thus be merit-based and not subject to political manipulation. Appropriators and other Members of Congress predictably were outraged, and they used every lever of power available to retaliate. (They even threatened to de-fund Miller's Office of Management and Budget.) Reagan, who had his hands full with Iran-Contra, ultimately backed down.[3]

Since then there has been a conspiracy of silence; members of Congress have struck an agreement: "I won't object to your earmark if you don't object to mine." And the leaders of key committees get the lion's share of earmarks. You don't complain about that, either, if you ever hope to get legislation through their committees.

Although the establishment news media loved to portray them as skinflints, when it came to spending, the Republicans who controlled Congress during the Clinton years weren't exactly bashful about popping in some pork spending for their districts. But when the Republicans took over the White House and the Congress, the flood of earmarks became downright obscene.

Despite the fact that these "earmarks" were not part of his budget request and distorted the policies of his administration, especially in the areas of defense and transportation spending, President George W. Bush never vetoed a budget.

President Bush kept his part of the bargain with Hastert and

DeLay. In return for no trouble on his military adventures overseas, he let the Republicans on Capitol Hill have their way on spending.

Omnibus spending bills are a favorite place in which to hide these earmarks. The bills are so huge (often thousands of pages in length) and members have so little time in which to consider them (usually a couple of days or less), that no one is likely to discover a piece of pork, no matter how ludicrous, until a congressman brags about it to the folks back home, and then it's too late.

But transportation bills, like the one Reagan vetoed because it had 152 earmarks, are even worse. The transportation bill enacted in 2005, for example, was the most expensive public works legislation in our nation's history, and printed out at 1,752 pages. It was also laden with no fewer than 6,373 pork-barrel earmarks. Unlike President Reagan, when a pork-laden transportation bill passed in 2005, President George W. Bush didn't blink at signing into law a pigsty piece of legislation containing 6,373 earmarks.

Back in the bad old days, when Republicans derided Democrats as tax-and-spend liberals, the late senator Robert Byrd (D-WV) was castigated as the king of pork. His state typically received two dollars in federal largesse for each one dollar it produced in tax revenue.

During the Bush years, the king of pork indisputably was Don Young, the Republican congressman from Alaska and chairman of the House Transportation Committee. His state got five dollars back for each one dollar paid in taxes, thanks to taxpayers in the other forty-nine states.

Young, it seems, has no shame. He bragged that the 2005 transportation bill was stuffed "like a turkey" with pork dressing, including a $231 million bridge in Anchorage to be named "Don Young's Way." But the real poster boy in Don Young's pork bill is the now infamous "Bridge to Nowhere."

Congress authorized $223 million to build a mile-long bridge connecting Gravina Island, Alaska (population fifty), with Ketchikan, Alaska (population 8,044, with a median household income 9 percent higher than the national median). It was designed to rise two hundred feet above the water, almost twice as high as the 119-foot-high Brooklyn Bridge.

It's not as if the fifty residents of Gravina Island are cut off from civilization. A ferry transports them to Ketchikan in five minutes. And yes, there's a small airport on the island, but anyone in Ketchikan who wants to catch a plane can also use that five-minute ferry ride. Because of the mountainous topography, and thus the circuitous route of the highway connecting with the bridge, it would actually take longer to get to the airport via the highway and bridge.

Parade magazine sent a reporter to Ketchikan and Gravina Island to see if there was some urgent need for the bridge that hadn't come to anyone's attention. What he found was this sort of attitude, coming from a local politician: "The general feeling here is that if someone else is paying for it, sure, why not?"

Why not, indeed? Especially when a one-fourth interest in thirty-three acres on Gravina Island, within a mile of the proposed construction, is owned by a woman named Nancy Murkowski, who happened to be the wife of the governor of Alaska and the mother of US Senator Lisa Murkowski (R-AK). Senator Murkowski, you may recall, took to the Senate floor to defend the Bridge to Nowhere project when an attempt was made to use some of the money for New Orleans disaster relief instead.

"Someone else," not the residents of Gravina Island, is paying for the Bridge to Nowhere. You, dear reader, are that "someone else." Or, more precisely, your children and grandchildren, since establishment Republicans believe in using deficits to finance bloated government.

During the Bush–Hastert–DeLay years, if you were a member of Congress and played ball, you got a "bridge to nowhere."

If you crossed them or opposed their schemes, you could get kicked- off your committee, and as punishment, legitimate federal responsibilities in your state might not get funded.

Jeff Flake spent much of his House career in purgatory for opposing earmarks and pork-barrel spending, but his 2012 election to succeed dyed-in-the-wool pork-barrel spender Jon Kyl as Arizona's junior senator is proof you can stick to your principles and succeed in Washington politics.

But it was even worse if you were a lobbyist or interest group—you allegedly had to make sure that you hired one of DeLay's friends or someone who would play ball with him; otherwise your issues were likely to be declared DOA by the majority whip.

DeLay was able to pull this off by co-opting what had been a private initiative to get the business community behind the conservative agenda of lower taxes and less government—the so-called K Street Project, which later became infamous for its association with Jack Abramoff.

Conservatives had long criticized the national business community's established organizations and various industry and trade associations for the craven influence peddling in which they engaged by hiring former liberal Democratic members of Congress and Hill staffers as lobbyists.

These individuals would cash million-dollar paychecks and then often work harder lobbying their new employers to support the Big Government policies of Democrats on Capitol Hill than they did trying to get their former congressional colleagues to reduce taxes and regulations to free the job creation engine of our free enterprise system.

However, in the hands of the Capitol Hill's establishment Republican leaders, the idea quickly morphed from what Tom DeLay said was "just following the old adage of punish your enemies and reward your friends," into what many observers said was "a pay-to-play system."[4]

And the cash at stake was and is colossal: Back in 2004 federal lobbyists spent $2.1 billion, and that rose to $2.8 billion for lobbying by 2007, according to political watchdog opensecrets.org. In 2010, during the height of the battle over President Obama's health care overhaul, more than $3.55 billion was spent on lobbying. Now that Obamacare has passed and the establishment seems to have accepted it as just another cost of doing business that's trended down somewhat, "only" $3.28 billion was spent on lobbying in 2012.

This pay-to-play mentality permeated the entire fabric of the GOP Capitol Hill establishment, so decisions weren't made on the basis of conservative principles; rather, they were made on the basis of whose friend was asking or if the right lobbyist was advocating the project.

The result was a complete breakdown of the system of checks and balances that should have restrained the growth of spending and the size of the federal government with Republicans controlling both ends of Pennsylvania Avenue.

What this means for future generations of American taxpayers is best illustrated by the passage of the Medicare Part D prescription drug benefit.

About an hour before sunrise on November 22, 2003—5:53 a.m., to be exact—the Republican members of the House of Representatives showed what they were made of.

After Republican leaders kept the House in session through the night, members of Congress finally caved in to pressure from the White House and the GOP leadership and approved President Bush's Medicare prescription drug program. The legislation passed the entire House by a vote of 220 to 215 (204 Republicans approving, 25 opposed) and sailed into law.

By that narrow margin, they increased the future indebtedness of the already-bankrupt Medicare program by $8 trillion.

This was, in effect, a new entitlement at a time when existing entitlements were already threatening the economic health of the nation, and it represented the largest increase in the welfare state since the Great Society of Lyndon Baines Johnson. This was an abuse of our children and grandchildren, who will be paying for this monstrosity the rest of their lives.

In the Senate, on the key vote that decided whether the program would pass, two Republican senators voted no. Not fifty-two. Not forty-two, or thirty-two, or twenty-two, or twelve.

Two. John McCain and Chuck Hagel.

President Bush and Karl Rove wanted a Medicare drug prescription bill for one simple reason: to bribe the nation's senior citizens to vote for Bush in the 2004 election. To their way of thinking, a prescription drug bill, no matter how reckless it was economically, was the way to win over a voting bloc that traditionally has been up for sale to the highest bidder in presidential elections.

The bribery strategy may have worked for 2004, but long-term it boomeranged.

Discontent with the results of the drug prescription "entitlement," structured as it was to appease the big pharmaceutical companies, was so intense, it ranked as one of the top reasons Democrats took over Congress in 2006 and the White House in 2008. (I am reminded of the Democratic strategists who thought the Clintons' health care plan in 1993 would seal a Democratic majority for a generation, then watched as the GOP took both the Senate and House of Representatives in 1994.)

Back in 2003, Bush's Big Government Republicans were bragging how they had made great strides with the senior community, and as evidence, they pointed to the support given by the American Association of Retired Persons, now known simply as AARP.

AARP is a corporation that sells insurance and provides discounts and other benefits. It is influential because of its mailing list, its publications, and the fact that some politicians and the media treat it as "the senior citizens' lobby."

It is no such thing.

AARP doesn't determine its positions based on the opinions of its members; its high-paid, left-wing Washington staff represents no one but itself.

The AARP *Policy Book* touts the group's liberal views on a plethora of issues, including capital gains taxes, the marriage penalty, gun control, a balanced budget constitutional amendment, and—get this—estate taxes.

The group denies that there is a crisis in Social Security, now or in the near future, and states, "For years, each political party has accused the other of raiding the Social Security trust funds. In fact, no one has raided the funds." In the past AARP provided a letter to Senate Minority Leader Harry Reid, which was read on the floor of the Senate, opposing an amendment to the budget bill to require that Social Security surpluses be used only for retirement purposes.

AARP is the epitome of Washington corruption, taking its members' hard-earned money and using it for causes they oppose and that are against their best interests. Not surprisingly, AARP stood with Rove in supporting the prescription drug scheme. Not surprisingly, AARP, to which the Bush White House had given great credibility, turned around and played a leading role in quashing Republican efforts to reform Social Security.

What makes Republicans' behavior on the prescription drug issue even harder to accept is the tactics they used to get the measure passed; these tactics included outright lies and even bribery. Members of Congress were told that the cost of this new welfare scheme would be no more than $400 billion over ten years. Richard Foster, the chief Medicare actuary, calculated a higher estimate, $534 billion for the first ten years, but he was told he would be fired if he blew the whistle.

Most House votes last about fifteen minutes. House leaders kept this one open for three hours overnight, resulting in that final vote at 5:53 in the morning. Egged on by greed for power and by lots of coffee, the GOP leadership kept hammering away at conservative resistance until it got the votes it needed.

Conservatives voting no were restrained from leaving the floor of the House until they could be pressured into changing their votes. "Doormen" were stationed at exits to make sure they couldn't escape. Congressmen Jerry Moran (KS) and Charles Norwood (GA) managed to outmaneuver them and got away, but Jo Ann Emerson (MO) had to hide on the Democratic side, crouching down to avoid being seen by the Republican search team—Emerson was eventually found and switched her vote to "aye" under pressure from the party leadership.

The weekend the Medicare Part D bill was about to be voted on, I attended a conservative event at the Breakers hotel in Florida, where Tom DeLay was present. When I discussed it with DeLay and urged him to hang tough against this vast expansion of government, he deceptively avoided getting his fingerprints on the bill—and certainly never gave any indication that it would be he who was breaking arms and legs to get the last few Republican votes to pass the bill only hours later.

I'm not kidding. This was your Republican-controlled House of Representatives I'm talking about—Speaker Dennis Hastert, Majority Leader Tom DeLay, Majority Whip Roy Blunt—not Boss Tweed and some nineteenth-century Tammany Hall ward heelers.

The lowest point involved strong-arm tactics against Michigan Congressman Nick Smith. Smith was retiring after that session of Congress, and his son Brad was one of five candidates running to succeed him. Majority Leader Tom DeLay offered to endorse Smith's son and raise money for him in exchange for a "yes" vote.

According to testimony by a Republican staffer, Rules Committee chairman David Drier of California offered to find Smith's daughter a job as an actress in Hollywood. (Drier denied this.) Congresswoman Candice Miller, a fellow Michigan Republican, cursed Smith for voting no. To his credit, Smith stood firm.

The late conservative columnist Robert Novak reported that, "after Nick Smith voted no and the bill passed, Duke Cunningham of California and other Republicans taunted him that his son was dead meat." Other Republicans voting against the bill were told that they were endangering their political futures.

Major contributors warned then representative Jim DeMint they would cut off funding for his Senate race in South Carolina. A Missouri state legislator called then representative Todd Akin to threaten a primary challenge against him. Duke Cunningham, as you may recall, later went to prison for taking bribes.

DeMint, by the way, stood firm against the bill, and became Senator DeMint, now president of the Heritage Foundation, the nation's largest conservative think tank. Akin stood firm against the bill, and was reelected in 2004 with 65 percent of the vote and earned the gratitude of many conservatives who continued to support him even after his verbal stumbles brought down his 2012 Senate campaign. They are proof that you don't have to cave in to spending pressure, or "go along to get along."

Had a Republican president been facing a Democratic Congress intent on doubling the budget over the course of just a few years and enacting a vast, new, unfunded, or at least underfunded, entitlement program, there's no doubt that the president would have pulled out all the stops to defeat such a raid on the taxpayers—including vetoing the bill or at least rescinding some of the spending.

But President Bush, faced with a runaway Republican Congress, did no such thing.

During his eight years in office, President Bush spent almost twice as much as his predecessor, President Clinton. Adjusted for inflation, in eight years, President Clinton increased the federal budget by 12.5 percent. In eight years, President Bush increased it by a whopping 53 percent.[5]

During President Bush's first five years in office, the federal budget increased by $616 billion. That's a mammoth 33 percent jump in the size of the federal government in just his first five years! To put this in perspective, this increase of $616 billion is more than the entire federal budget in Jimmy Carter's last year in office. And conservatives were complaining about Big Government back then! How could Bush, Hastert, DeLay, Boehner, Frist, McConnell, and company look us in the eye and tell us they are fiscal conservatives when in five short years they increased the already-bloated government by more than the budget for the entire federal government when Ronald Reagan was assuming office?

Now, the excuse we hear most often goes something like this: "Federal spending has increased because of the War on Terror. In time of war, spending has to increase, just as it did during World War II and the Cold War."

In the eyes of the military-industrial complex and their neo-con allies on Capitol Hill, the implication is that you're unpatriotic if you complain about spending a few more dollars, or several hundred billion dollars. This is a total cover-up of the real situation, as I'll now show you.

First, there is an assumption that the Pentagon and Homeland Security budgets should be sacrosanct. But the Pentagon is spending much of its budget on expensive weapons systems that are unsuited for fighting Al-Qaeda, or for the kinds of wars we are likely to fight in the foreseeable future. And there are tens of billions in appropriations the Department of Defense cannot account for. As for the Department of Homeland Security, it has quickly become the largest bureaucratic mess outside of the Pentagon, and we saw what we got for our money when Hurricane Katrina struck. It is past time for conservatives to realize, acknowledge, and act as if the Pentagon, military, Department of Homeland Security, and Justice Department are part of the government and subject to the same waste, fraud, and abuse issues that plague all government programs.

Second, whatever one thinks about the wars in Iraq and Afghanistan, demanding that the Pentagon and the military be run efficiently and with an eye for the same kind of waste, fraud, and abuse that has been found at GSA, the IRS, and other agencies of the federal government isn't unpatriotic, so it is time to admit that the argument that the increase in federal spending can be blamed on the War on Terror is a smokescreen.

Don't believe me?

Let's look only at discretionary domestic spending. This covers all the other departments of the government, from agriculture and education to human services and the environment and all the rest. These are the areas that take up most of the time on Capitol Hill. Because they are discretionary (not entitlements that are automatically paid out by a preset formula) and domestic (nothing to do with national defense), they should be the easiest to cut or freeze.

Not a chance.

Discretionary domestic spending, adjusted for inflation:

LBJ	+4.1 percent
Nixon/Ford	+5.0 percent
Carter	+1.6 percent
Reagan	-1.4 percent
Bush 41	+3.8 percent
Clinton	+2.1 percent
Bush 43	
2005 =	+3.0 percent
2006 =	+0.9 percent
2007 =	+0.2 percent
2008 =	+36.8 percent
2009 =	+14.2 percent

When we strip away defense, homeland security, and entitlements, and adjust for inflation, leaving only discretionary domestic spending, George W. Bush grew the federal government at a faster pace than Lyndon Baines Johnson. Only another Big Government Republican, Richard Nixon, outmatched his record for profligate spending. And when Bush's second term was over, Bush held the record as the president who had grown the federal government at its fastest pace in modern times.[6]

Unlike Bush, father or son, Ronald Reagan actually cut discretionary domestic spending in inflation-adjusted dollars. He was the only president to do so since the end of World War II.

That's because he didn't follow Lyndon Johnson's so-called guns-and-butter formulation of high spending on both military and domestic programs. Reagan knew he had to increase defense spending in order to win the Cold War—a mission that really was accomplished—so he insisted on controlling domestic programs to keep the budget on an even keel. Defense spending went up by 19.2 percent, but Reagan cut discretionary nondefense spending.

In cutting back on domestic spending during the Cold War, Reagan was following the path blazed by FDR and Truman during World War II and the Korean War. Roosevelt cut domestic spending by 20 percent between 1942 and 1944, during World War II, even agreeing with Congress to abolish some of his favorite programs, including the Civilian Conservation Corps, the National Youth Administration, and the Works Projects Administration. And after the start of the Korean War, Truman and his Democratic Congress cut domestic spending by 28 percent in the first year.

Not so George W. Bush. He followed in LBJ's guns-and-butter footsteps.

Reagan's accomplishment is all the more remarkable given the fact that the House of Representatives—where spending bills originate—was under Democratic control during both of his terms, at one point by more than one hundred seats. And Bush's cave-in is all the more inexcusable given the GOP's control of Congress during most of his two terms.

While spending is the most easily quantified aspect of the corrupt—if tacit—bargain between President George W. Bush and Capitol Hill's big-spending, Big Government establishment Republicans, this shameful insider deal had many other policy effects—and none of them good for the conservative cause, the Republican Party, or America.

In politics there are two types of theft. One is illegal theft, which we all too often read about in the media. Usually it is small potatoes—Congressmen Duke Cunningham, Bill Jefferson, Jesse Jackson Jr.; their thefts were unfortunate, but they were caught and punished, and the magnitude of their thefts did not affect the quality of life for ourselves, our children, and our grandchildren.

In 1849, French philosopher Claude Frédéric Bastiat identified another kind of theft—legal plunder. Legal plunder, or legal theft, is when politicians use taxpayer money to bribe voters with benefits, bailouts, roads, and bridges for the corrupt and immoral purpose of getting reelected.

Legal theft has cost trillions of dollars; it affects our quality of life for generations, and indeed threatens the very future of our country.

Both parties engage in this legal theft. I sometimes fanaticize about a fictitious meeting early in 2001 at the Bush White House to strategize how Republicans could hold power for generations to come. Instead of standing for conservative principles, someone says, "I've got an idea! How about bribery? Let's bribe the voters to vote for us." And so they used legal theft to bribe seniors with a new prescription drug benefit. Florida, which Bush won by only 537 votes, was soon awash in federal largesse, paid for by future generations of Americans, and it flowed wherever it was needed to shore up the political prospects of George W. Bush and his allies in Congress.

Due to the 9/11 attacks, and the reflected glow of the outstanding performance of the United States military and intelligence personnel in overthrowing the Taliban regime in Afghanistan, George W. Bush had received a pass from many grassroots conservatives for his betrayals of conservative principles during his first term.

However, by the time Inauguration Day 2005 rolled around, and the urgency of defending Bush against a Democratic opponent had evaporated, conservatives began a hard-nosed assessment of the Bush presidency—and their conclusions weren't pretty.

The wars in Iraq and Afghanistan had turned into exactly the kind of "nation-building" exercises many grassroots conservatives and libertarians opposed, and that Bush had campaigned against in 1999 and 2000.

"Maybe I'm missing something here," candidate George W. Bush said in a debate with Democratic rival Al Gore. "I mean, are we going to have some kind of nation-building corps from America? Absolutely not."[7]

Almost eight years later, US interagency "provincial reconstruction teams" were trying to rebuild the economy and government in Afghanistan and Iraq. The US Army's just-revised field manual put military post-conflict "stability operations" on a par with fighting wars, and conservatives and libertarians had concluded that George W. Bush was just another politician who would say anything to get elected.

What's more, these great sacrifices of blood and treasure were being ineptly and arrogantly managed according to what were obviously political calculations, not sound military principles.

On the domestic policy front, spending was out of control, and while the Bush administration hewed to some conservative principles, in opposition to expanding federal funding for embryonic stem cell research, for example, most of the conservative agenda had long ago been put by the wayside in a rush to expand the federal government's role in housing, through Bush's "ownership society" initiative and in education, through the "No Child Left Behind" legislation, and along with a host of other programs that appeared to be straight out of the liberal Democrat's playbook.

To the extent that there were conservative initiatives, such as Social Security reform, they were quickly abandoned in the face of liberal opposition.

Still, Bush had won reelection—if only narrowly—and conservative leaders were prepared to see George W. Bush's second term as an opportunity to move the ball down the field, if only by a few yards.

That is, until Bush decided to nominate Harriet Miers, his chief

White House counsel, and longtime Bush family friend, to the United States Supreme Court.

Harriet Miers was a political unknown outside of Texas, where she was seen as a capable and successful business community lawyer.

Her views on the key social issues that concerned conservatives, such as religion in the public square, abortion, and same-sex marriage, were unknown.

Conservatives recalled with growing alarm President George H. W. Bush's nomination of an unknown New Hampshire judge named David Souter, who, once confirmed, became one of the Supreme Court's most reliably liberal votes.

Conservative columnists George Will and Charles Krauthammer knocked Miers as an intellectual lightweight, and they were right—there were plenty of other potential nominees who would add conservative intellectual horsepower to the court's conservative bloc, such as Fourth Circuit Appeals Court judge Michael Luttig, Judge Michael McConnell of the Tenth Circuit, Judge Janice Rogers Brown, and Georgetown University law professor Viet Dinh.

From the conservative perspective, Harriet Miers had absolutely nothing to recommend her as a Supreme Court justice, except a close friendship with the president of the United States and his family.

Just before the announcement, key conservative leaders, such as Dr. James Dobson, "got a personal phone call from Karl Rove," President Bush's top political adviser, who assured them that Miers would prove to be a justice "the Religious Right would be mighty pleased with."

According to published reports, Rove told these conservative leaders, "Harriet Miers is an Evangelical Christian, that she is from a very conservative church, which is almost universally pro-life, that she had taken on the American Bar Association on the issue of abortion and fought for a policy that would not be supportive of abortion, and she had been a member of the Texas Right to Life."

Some conservative leaders were inclined to accept Rove's word on the matter, others, such as Gary Bauer, were not.

"If an individual goes his or her whole life," Bauer wrote, "without writing or speaking about the horrid court decisions—abortion-on-demand, same-sex 'marriage,' removal of public displays of the Ten Commandments—why would they suddenly find their voice when they get on the Supreme Court?"

Bill Kristol, editor of the *Weekly Standard*, waded in to say, Miers "has no constitutional credentials that I know of." George F. Will said, "There is no evidence that she is among the leading lights of American jurisprudence, or that she possesses the talents commensurate with the Supreme Court's tasks."

Washington Post columnist Charles Krauthammer wrote, "If Miers were not a crony of the president of the United States, her nomination to the Supreme Court would be a joke, as it would have occurred to no one else to nominate her."

A nominee with such a thin public record invited intense scrutiny, and the media soon discovered that in the late 1980s Miers had donated $1,000 to Al Gore's failed presidential bid and another $1,000 to the Democratic National Committee.

When further research revealed that Miers told a homosexual rights group that she supported civil rights for homosexuals and said the city of Dallas has a duty to fund AIDS education and "patient support services," conservatives were outraged.

But when a 1993 speech that Miers delivered to a group called the Executive Women of Dallas surfaced, conservative opposition to Miers solidified. As the *Washington Post* reported, "Miers appeared to offer a libertarian view of several topics in which the law and religious beliefs were colliding in court." She endorsed "self-determination" on issues such as abortion and school prayer.

Remarked Miers during the speech, "The ongoing debate continues surrounding the attempt to once again criminalize abortions or to once and for all guarantee the freedom of the individual to decide for herself whether she will have an abortion."

Miers went on to assert, "We gave up . . . legislating religion or morality." She added, "When science cannot determine the facts and decisions vary based upon religious belief, then government should not act."

To conservatives well versed in constitutional law and the language of the Supreme Court, that sounded suspiciously like the language of the Court's infamous *Roe v. Wade* decision creating a "right" to an abortion.

Miers soon after withdrew her nomination, but the damage was done to President Bush's reputation with conservatives.

"Republicans first" type conservative leaders who had endorsed Harriet Miers realized that they had been deceived by President Bush and Karl Rove. Those who had opposed Miers, or at least not endorsed her, realized just how close one of the grossest acts of cronyism of the modern American political age had come to putting another David Souter on the Supreme Court.

For most conservatives, the fiasco of the Harriet Miers nomination was the last straw. Bush broke too many promises on reducing the size of the federal government, harnessing federal spending, putting into place permanent tax cuts—not to mention gaining control of runaway immigration policies that had failed.

Like his father before him, Bush seemed content with avoiding ideological battles and surrounding himself with longtime family friends. And, like "Bush 41," "Bush 43" seemed more willing to avoid bickering with liberals in Congress than to fight for the campaign agenda that got him elected.

While the sound and fury over the Miers nomination played out on the op-ed pages and among the leaders of the conservative movement, who felt their personal credibility had been betrayed by Bush and Rove, the average conservative voter on Main Street wasn't necessarily invested in the fight the same way.

Unless the Supreme Court issued a big ruling that brought its power home to their neighborhood, it seemed pretty far away.

Sure, they wanted a conservative Supreme Court, but what mattered more to them on a day-to-day basis was what was happening in their own neighborhoods, in their own schools and hospitals, and to their own local taxes.

And one of the most important things that was happening to

those everyday family concerns was (and still is) that illegal immigration is overwhelming America.

Estimates varied as to how many illegal aliens were actually in the United States back during the Bush years. Depending on the source, the numbers range widely—from about seven million up to twenty million or more. During the first decade of the twenty-first century, United States immigration officials have said the number was growing by as much as five hundred thousand a year.[8]

The Republican National Committee and Republicans in Congress had been alternatively hiding from the illegal immigration issue or promising to increase border security and immigration enforcement for years.

Conservatives, such as Colorado congressman Tom Tancredo, had been warning against the economic and cultural cost of this vast influx of people whose presence in the country was based on the commission of a crime, and who had little or no investment in the social order.

On April 19, 2002, Tancredo gave an interview to the *Washington Times* in which he said Bush's immigration policies were political calculations designed to snare Hispanic votes in Texas and California and prop up Mexican president Vicente Fox. He said open-border policies left the nation open to terrorist attack.

Tancredo's remarks invited an angry call from Bush's White House consigliore Karl Rove on the morning the article was published and a sustained campaign to undermine and marginalize Tancredo afterwards—screaming at him that he would never get inside the White House again.[9]

However, with something like one out of eleven Mexicans emigrating to the United States (about half of whom crossed the border illegally), Bush and Rove couldn't deny that local governments were paying billions in increased hospital emergency room costs because illegal immigrants had no health insurance or incentive to pay their medical bills.[10]

Nor could they deny that school budgets and local taxpayers

were being overwhelmed by the cost of educating millions of children whose first language was not English, and whose illegal alien parents chose to live outside the law and could contribute little or nothing to their education.

Conservative icon Phyllis Schlafly later wrote in *Human Events*:

> The Republican National Committee's mail-order fundraisers often contain a comprehensive multiple-choice survey so that prospective donors can give their opinions on topics of national importance. One issue, however, is conspicuously missing from the list: border security/immigration.
>
> The omission isn't an oversight; it's a deliberate policy. The National Republican Congressional Committee has been advising its candidates not to mention this issue in their speeches or campaign literature.
>
> House Minority Leader Dick Gephardt (D Mo.) gave Republicans the opportunity to seize this issue when he addressed the radical left-wing Hispanic group, the National Council of La Raza, in Miami on July 22. He announced a Democratic Party plan to introduce legislation to grant amnesty to millions of illegal aliens.
>
> Nothing is more unpopular with the voters than amnesty (which Senator Robert Byrd (D-W.Va.) called "sheer lunacy"). If the powers that be in the Republican Party don't realize this, they are out of touch with the grass roots.[11]

President Bush deflected the issue by promoting various "guest worker" schemes, saying in a 2005 speech in Arizona that "people in this debate must recognize that we will not be able to effectively enforce our immigration laws until we create a temporary worker program." Said Bush:

> The program that I propose would not create an automatic path to citizenship. It wouldn't provide for amnesty. I oppose amnesty. Rewarding those who have broken the law would encourage others to break the law and keep pressure on our border.

The temporary worker program, by contrast, would decrease pressure on the border. I support increasing the number of annual green cards that can lead to citizenship.

But for the sake of justice and for the sake of border security, I'm not going to sign an immigration bill that includes amnesty.[12]

In the wake of the revelation that many of the 9/11 terrorist attackers were in the country illegally, it seemed like finally Republican promises to stem the tide of illegal immigrants would be kept.

But instead of the immigration enforcement plan that President Bush and Republicans in Congress had been promising Americans who wanted the rule of law upheld, what Bush and his establishment Republican allies on Capitol Hill, such as then senator Jon Kyl of Arizona, eventually came forth with was "comprehensive immigration reform."

No matter how you sugarcoated it, once the details of the legislation were understood, "comprehensive immigration reform" was nothing more than amnesty for illegal aliens—just like Democratic leader Dick Gephardt had promised his radical Left allies at La Raza.

The outraged reaction at the conservative grass roots was immediate; the Capitol Switchboard, talk radio, letters to the editor, and public forums of every sort were overwhelmed by the opposition. Bush was not persuaded or dissuaded by conservative opposition to his plan to grant amnesty to illegal aliens and began an all-out effort to build support for the amnesty bill, including the unprecedented step of putting Vice President Dick Cheney on Rush Limbaugh's syndicated radio program to try to mollify conservatives.[13]

In what may have been one of the few understatements of his long political career, Rep. Tom Tancredo, Republican of Colorado, one of the leaders of the effort to stop the flow of illegal immigrants from Mexico and Central America said, "The emphasis that he [Bush] placed on the amnesty provision will not fly."

Tancredo said Republicans, already facing difficult midterm elections, would suffer if the president was successful in advancing his proposal, which he believed diverged with public opinion and carried the risk of alienating much of the Republican base.[14]

Bush's offer of amnesty sparked mass demonstrations and rallies of illegal aliens which further angered grassroots conservatives and many nonpolitical Americans who simply believed in the rule of law.

Their feelings toward Bush and his establishment Republican allies on Capitol Hill was best summed up by Rush Limbaugh when he said to the millions of listeners who tuned in his syndicated radio program, "My first thought is anger, folks. . . . How can they [the illegal alien demonstrators] just show up and brazenly demand to be . . . allowed to be against the law, and nobody does anything about it? Some of you might say, 'Surround them with INS agents.'"[15]

Bush was increasingly desperate to salvage his proposal and reverse the grassroots landslide moving against it. He lashed out at conservative opponents saying: "If you want to kill the bill, if you don't want do what's right for America, you can pick one little aspect out of it. You can use it to frighten people."[16]

Laura Ingraham, a potent voice in conservative talk radio, said the president's decision to lash out at the critics of the immigration bill had left them feeling jilted, betrayed, and incensed.[17]

Limbaugh said later that the immigration reform debate had broken the back of the president's loyalist base. There are people who are saying, "I've had it. I am through defending him. This is the last straw, because he [Bush] is attacking me here."[18]

If the nomination of Harriet Miers to the Supreme Court had cost Bush his remaining support among conservative leaders, "comprehensive immigration reform" cost him whatever support he had left with the conservative grass roots.

13

THE 2006 ELECTION: AMERICA REJECTS BIG GOVERNMENT REPUBLICANISM

I n 2001, when Karl Rove and Bush came to town, they seemed to adopt a one-word strategy for governing, and that one-word strategy was *bribery*—it was all completely legal, but it was still bribery. As I, and many other conservatives, saw it, the spending and legal theft that the Republicans engaged in under Bush was immoral, but Bush's betrayal of conservative principles didn't stop there.

Republicans as the party of fiscal conservatism? Gone in the hundreds of billions of deficits for a new prescription drug benefit, earmarks, and pork-barrel spending by Republicans in Congress and a Republican president.

Republicans as the party of competent governance? Gone in the vast loss of lives and treasure sunk in the Bush Cheney Rumsfeld–inspired and managed quagmire in Iraq, and the incompetent pursuit of Usama bin Laden.

Republicans as the party of clean government? Gone in the "K Street Project" and the Duke Cunningham, Jack Abramoff, and Bob Ney bribery cases, and the Mark Foley sex scandal.

Republicans as the party of the rule of law? Gone in the blundering attempt to appease the Left and gain Hispanic votes with a bill to grant amnesty to illegal aliens.

Republicans as the political home of conservatives and traditional values? Gone in the cronyism that would have put Harriet Miers—likely another closet liberal like David Souter—on the Supreme Court.

By Election Day 2006 President George W. Bush and his establishment Republican allies on Capitol Hill had effectively destroyed the Republican brand.

As my good friend L. Brent Bozell III put it so well in March 2008, when he looked back and summed up the George W. Bush administration:

> Any hopes that Bush would deliver on a conservative agenda in his second term evaporated almost immediately. We [conservatives] watched with growing fury as he and the GOP leadership promoted one liberal initiative after another. Finally, we openly rebelled, turning on the GOP over the Supreme Court nomination of Harriet Miers, amnesty for illegal immigrants and the Republicans' shameless abandonment of fiscal discipline. What was once a powerful alliance between the Republican Party and grass-roots conservatives had become a political bridge to nowhere. With the GOP facing the loss of Congress in 2006, we shrugged in indifference. The movement that had "nowhere else to go" had gone.[1]

But in 2006 not everyone in the conservative movement was ready to walk away from Bush and the Capitol Hill Republican establishment just yet.

In late September of 2006, my old friend James Dobson, the founder of Focus on the Family, and now with Dr. James Dobson's *Family Talk*, told the estimated three thousand people attending the "Stand for the Family" rally at the Mellon Arena in Pittsburgh, Pennsylvania, that despite his misgivings, they should stick with the Republicans.

"I have flat-out been ticked at Republicans for the past two years," he said. "This country is at a crisis point. Whether or not the Republicans deserve the power they were given, the alternatives are downright frightening."[2]

Jim Dobson was right; it was true that the country was (and is) at a crisis point, but many conservative leaders had already mentally checked out of exerting any effort on behalf of the Republican establishment, even if they hadn't publicly said so.

There was a growing (albeit largely unspoken) conservative consensus that the Big Government Republicans in Washington did not merit the support of conservatives.

President George W. Bush and his establishment Republican allies on Capitol Hill expanded government regulation into every aspect of our lives and refused to deal seriously with mounting domestic problems, such as illegal immigration.

They had busted the federal budget for generations to fund the prescription drug benefit and the creation and expansion of other programs. They had brought forth a limitless flow of pork for the sole, immoral purpose of holding on to office.

As we saw it, they spent more time seeking the favors of Washington's K Street lobbyists than listening to the conservatives who brought them to power. Establishment Republicans wanted, of course, to hold on to power even if it meant the wholesale abandonment of conservative principles. Some conservative leaders, like Jim Dobson, were concerned that the damage Democrats would do would be too great to be undone. However, as I and many other conservative leaders saw things, if we ever wanted to get conservative governance, Big Government Republicans and Big Government Republicanism were going to have to go. We weren't necessarily campaigning against Republicans, but we'd been around long enough and understood history well enough not to fear defeat. We recognized that the defeat of Republican senator Barry Goldwater in 1964, the resignation, in light of the Watergate scandal, of President Richard Nixon in 1974, and the defeat of President Gerald Ford in 1976, and in 1992 the defeat of George H. W. Bush, each swept away many of the older Republican leaders of the time.

As I saw things from the perspective of my then forty-plus years (now fifty-plus years) in conservative politics at the national level, when Republicans were defeated, it has invariably led to the growth of the conservative movement. The resounding defeat suffered by Goldwater at the hands of President Lyndon Johnson in 1964 cleared a lot of dead wood out of the Republican Party, which made it easier for us to increase our influence on the GOP, utilizing new technology, more effective techniques, and fresh ideas. Likewise, the Watergate scandal in 1974 eliminated more Republican officeholders who stood in the way of creating a more broad-based party. It dramatically weakened the Party establishment, making it much easier for Ronald Reagan to mount a nearly successful challenge, just two years later, to an incumbent Republican president. And the 1992 election of Bill Clinton led directly to the conservative "Contract with America" and the Republican takeover of Congress two years later.

Those defeats allowed younger leaders, like former Speaker of the House Newt Gingrich, Dick Armey, Bob Walker, and other young conservatives, to rise to positions of leadership that normally would have taken them another twenty years.

Conservatives turned out for McCain and Romney, but independent voters didn't. Conservative unhappiness reflects what others see; specifically, that there was no clear choice between Big Government Republicans and Big Government Democrats.

Of course the Republican establishment wasn't about to admit that the GOP was very poorly led and weren't going to make any progress until the existing leadership passed from the scene.

Sound familiar?

What I told my friends in 2006 was that we conservatives should not respond to the Big Government Republicans' message of "*Yes, we're bad, but the other guys are worse, so if you don't vote Republican, the boogeyman's going to get you.*"

Conservatives had been threatened with that as long as any of us can remember, and it was my experience that conservatives don't usually have growth until establishment Republicans have losses.

If, in 2006, the Republican leaders of Congress and at the White House didn't recognize that they had a serious problem with the base of the Republican Party, then I expected that Republicans would lose the House and possibly even the Senate.[3]

As I put it in an op-ed I penned for *Washington Monthly*:

> With their record over the past few years, the Big Government Republicans in Washington do not merit the support of conservatives. They have busted the federal budget for generations to come with the prescription-drug benefit and the creation and expansion of other programs. They have brought forth a limitless flow of pork for the sole, immoral purpose of holding onto office. They have expanded government regulation into every aspect of our lives and refused to deal seriously with mounting domestic problems such as illegal immigration. They have spent more time seeking the favors of K Street lobbyists than listening to the conservatives who brought them to power. And they have sunk us into the very sort of nation-building war that candidate George W. Bush promised to avoid, while ignoring rising threats such as communist China and the oil-rich "new Castro," Hugo Chavez.[4]

As the 2006 election approached, conservatives were as angry as I had seen them in my five decades in politics. At that time, I guessed that 40 percent of conservatives were ambivalent about the November election or wanted the Republicans to lose. But a Republican loss of one or both Houses of Congress would turn power over to the likes of Nancy Pelosi and Harry Reid. Did we dare risk such an outcome?

The answer was, we had to take the chance.

As I saw it, the conservative movement, and the cause of conservative governance, can and often did end up in a better position after Republicans lost a given election than it did by backing the Republican establishment—and 2006 was going to be one of those elections.

What's more, the American people were clearly fed up with

George W. Bush and the establishment Republican congressional leadership.

Public-opinion polls in mid-2005 gave Bush his lowest approval rating in office. After averaging a 62 percent approval rating during his first term, just 44 percent of respondents approved of his performance, a national Gallup poll found.

According to Gallup, Bush ranked behind Presidents Eisenhower, Reagan, Clinton, and Truman and was on par with Richard Nixon (44 percent amid the Watergate crisis) and Lyndon Johnson (42 percent during the Vietnam War) at comparable times in their presidencies.[5]

One of Washington's top political analysts, Charlie Cook, publisher of the *Cook Political Report*, surveyed the situation just six months after George W. Bush's 2005 inauguration and reported that "Democratic [congressional] candidates from coast to coast have already taken up the mantra 'arrogant, abusive, and out of touch'—stolen straight from the Republicans' own 1994 playbook. That chant is starting to get under the skin of Republicans, particularly those who were around in 1994."

Charlie Cook also noted that history wasn't on the Republicans' side either.

"In four of the five midterm elections since World War II that were held during a president's second term, the party in the White House got shellacked," said Cook in June 2005. "Today's House Republicans are watching many, if not all, of the factors that led to those losses being replicated before their very eyes."

While it is hard to identify exactly when during the 109th Congress Republicans sealed their fate and the loss of their majority, a good case could be made that it was with the House passage of the 2005 Transportation bill that included the infamous "bridge to nowhere."

At $286 billion it was at that point, the most expensive public works bill ever—passed by the "fiscal conservatives" of the Republican Party and touted as such in news conferences across the country.

As the *Chicago Tribune* observed at the time, "If that's responsible, what would irresponsibility look like?"[6]

The *Trib* took a look back and noted that since Bill Clinton left office, federal outlays under President Bush and a GOP-controlled Congress had risen from 18.5 percent of gross domestic output to 20.3 percent.

In January 2006, as the crucial midterm election year opened, the Cato Institute looked at the George W. Bush fiscal record and labeled Bush "the biggest-spending president since Lyndon Johnson."[7] Nor could that spending all be blamed on the Iraq war and homeland security. When Cato's study excluded defense and homeland security spending from the calculations for both presidents, it found that, even then, "Bush was worse than LBJ."

A few Republicans in Congress had the courage to buck the establishment leadership and admit that their party had gone wrong. "If you look at fiscal conservatism today, it's in a sorry state," principled fiscal conservative representative (now senator) Jeff Flake of Arizona told the *Washington Post*. "Republicans don't even pretend anymore."

While the same could be said of Jeff Flake now that he has moved to the Senate, he had nailed the problem—Republicans didn't even pretend to follow conservative principles anymore.

If Big Government Republicans behaved so irresponsibly and betrayed the people who elected them, and conservatives blindly, slavishly continue backing them, we establish that there is no price to pay for violating conservative principles.

If we gave in, we were forgetting the lesson that mothers teach their daughters: *Why buy a cow when milk is free?*

As I saw it, it would take a Republican defeat to bring about a complete change in the GOP leadership in Washington. Without such a change, real conservatives will never come to power. We were (and still are) like the Jews who wandered the desert for forty years until their flawed leaders passed away; we will never reach the Political Promised Land with these guys in charge.

Many conservatives and right-of-center independents apparently agreed with my analysis, because one by one conservatives decided it was time to stop slavishly giving free milk to Big Government establishment Republicans who did no better than pay lip service to our issues.

The Republican House leaders never seem to learn that going along with Big Government policies is exactly what gets Republicans thrown out of office and relegated to the status of the powerless minority they were from the beginning of the New Deal until the election of Ronald Reagan in 1980.

And without committed conservative support, Republicans were not just beaten; they were wiped out in the 2006 midterm election.

Why did Republicans get wiped out in 2006?

There is no doubt that religious conservatives, an important part of the Republican coalition, were turned off by Congressman Mark Foley's homosexual sex scandal.

But there were other issues at hand.

The media, and more importantly, the candidates, seem curiously unconcerned with another discontented part of the Reagan coalition: economic, small-government conservatives.

It was the Republicans' big-spending, Big Government ways that helped ensure their defeat in the 2006 midterm elections. It wasn't Evangelical Christians or so-called values voters who deserted Republicans. Roughly 70 percent of white evangelicals and born-again Christians voted Republican in 2006, just a fraction less than in 2004.

It was suburbanites, independents, and others who were fed up not just with the war and corruption, but also with the Republican drift toward Big Government who stayed home, or even voted Democratic, on Election Day 2006. That night, more than 65 percent of voters told a pollster they believed that "the Republicans used to be the party of economic growth, fiscal discipline, and limited government, but in recent years, too many Republicans in Washington have become just like the big spenders they used to oppose."[8]

There was a swing of six seats in the US Senate and thirty-one seats in the House of Representatives. Democrats gained control of

Republican-held governorships in Arkansas, Colorado, Maryland, Massachusetts, New York, and Ohio to give the party a twenty-eight to twenty-two advantage in governorships.

More to the point, many moderate and Big Government Republican House members, such as Nancy Johnson, Jim Leach, Anne Northup, Jeb Bradley, Charles Bass, and Sue Kelly, were defeated, demonstrating that being "Democrats-lite" was no protection from the wrath of voters fed up with George W. Bush and his principle-free party on Capitol Hill.

14

2007 AND 2008: GEORGE W. BUSH'S CRAVEN RETREAT AND SURRENDER

After the 2006 wipeout of Republicans, especially the party's congressional candidates, establishment Republicans tried to explain the debacle, and their first instinct was to blame conservatives—but not for staying home. They tried to blame the few examples of Republican adherence to conservative principles they could find—for example, supporting the right to life—rather than Republican betrayal of those principles.

Sound familiar?

After the election, top Republican strategist Karl Rove specifically named the Foley scandal as the cause of the Republicans' loss of Congress.

The big-spending Congress, the Bush failures in Iraq and Afghanistan, the culture of cronyism and corruption that set the checks and balances the Founders built into the Constitution on their heads were not important factors in Rove's eyes.

Even some establishment Republicans were honest enough to argue that the party lost its majority by straying from conservative principles, especially limited government spending.

John Boehner, who became minority leader after the 2006

debacle, accepted that argument when his leadership was challenged by conservatives, but later changed his tune to blame the Iraq war.

Boehner changed his tune because he probably recognized that by such an analysis he was implicitly holding responsible for the defeat those old bulls of the Republican establishment who had put him in power.

Most of the Republican establishment was similarly in denial. Oklahoma congressman Tom Cole, who had just been elected to lead the Republican National Congressional Committee, demonstrated such denial when he claimed, "Oh, I don't think the problem was spending. . . . People who argue that we lost because we weren't true to our base, that's just wrong."[1]

Of course, as a member of the Appropriations Committee, and a prolific pork-barreler, Cole would be indicting himself if he had placed the blame differently, and, as events would prove, continuing the old ways was not a successful strategy for the Republican National Congressional Committee under Cole's leadership.

The way I saw it was that, yes, defeat stings, but in this case it was necessary and could lead to some good results in the future.

The election of Bill Clinton in 1992 led directly to the successful "Contract with America" two years later.

As I've said before, and it bears being repeated regularly, sometimes a loss for the Republican Party is a gain for conservatives.

A little taste of liberal Democrats in power is often enough to remind the voters what they don't like about them, and more important, to focus the minds of Republicans on the principles that really matter. The conservative movement has grown fastest during those periods when things seemed darkest, such as during the Carter administration and the first two years of the Clinton White House; and the first two years of the Obama presidency led to the Tea Party wave election and the biggest GOP victory in seventy-five years.

Conservatives are, by nature, insurgents, and as the eight years George W. Bush was in the White House proved, it's hard to maintain an insurgency when your friends, or people you perceived to

Howard Phillips, Jonas Savimbi, and Richard (pictured left to right) exchange greetings at a dinner honoring Savimbi at the Madison Hotel in Washington, DC, on February 3, 1986.

Richard relaxes at his home in the Northern Virginia countryside.

ABOVE: Richard talks with *Washington Post* journalist David Broder.

BELOW: Ronald Reagan and Richard peruse copies of *Conservative Digest* in the spring of 1975.

Paul and Joyce Weyrich, Elaine and Richard Viguerie, and Senator Paul and Mrs. Carol Laxalt (pictured left to right). Conservative friends gather at a victory dinner honoring Senator Laxalt and Richard for their leadership that led to the defeat of President Jimmy Carter's 1977 attempt to change election laws in favor of the Democrats.

Richard, Congressman Barry Goldwater, Jr., and Congressman Ed Koch (pictured left to right) converse after Richard's testimony at a December 11, 1975, congressional hearing on privacy protection.

Fifty members of Richard's extended family gather on the steps of the Lincoln Memorial as part of his eightieth birthday celebration in September 2013.

"002," "001," and "003" is how Richard jokingly refers to himself and his friends, who are the conservatives who have been active at the national level longer than all other living conservatives. Lee Edwards, Phyllis Schlafly, and Richard (pictured left to right) smile for the camera at a conservative gathering in 2013.

Richard, Joanne Kemp, and Congressman Jack Kemp (pictured left to right) celebrate the thirtieth anniversary of *National Review* at the Plaza Hotel in 1985.

Howard Phillips, Congressman Bob Dornan, Pat Buchanan, and Richard (pictured left to right) meet at a book party for Pat at Gonzaga High School in Washington, DC, in the summer of 1988.

Joseph Farah, Founder, CEO and Editor of WND, Mrs. Jenny Beth Martin, President and Cofounder of Tea Party Patriots, and Author Richard A. Viguerie, Founder and Chairman of American Target Advertising (pictured left to right)

be your friends, are in power.

A Republican loss in 2006 did eventually lead to a rebirth of the conservative movement as a third force independent of any political party. Almost all of the gains made by Democrats in 2006 came from large gains among independents, not Republicans.

Democrats, Republicans, and independents all accounted for proportions of the electorate similar to what they did in 2004. Democrats and Republicans voted nearly as loyally for their parties in 2006 as they did in 2004, but independents exhibited a large swing toward Democrats.

In 2004, independents split forty-nine to forty-six, slightly in favor of Democrats, but in 2006 they voted fifty-seven to thirty-nine for Democrats, a fifteen-point swing and the largest margin among independents for Democrats since the US 1986 midterm elections.[2]

Bringing those independents back to the Republican column by offering a clear contrast with the Big Government liberalism of the Democrats should have been the top priority of President Bush and the Capitol Hill GOP leadership.

Far from standing like Horatius at the bridge, holding off the Democrats until reinforcements could arrive or the bridge could be destroyed and Rome saved, Bush did little to check the spending of the new Democratic majority as long as he got the go-ahead to continue the war in Iraq on his terms. This was, in essence, another corrupt bargain with Congress.

In the short time that George W. Bush was president and the Democrats held the majority in Congress (2007–2008), spending jumped by $700 billion—$4.7 trillion in FY 2006 to $5.4 trillion in FY 2008.[3]

Despite the fact President Bush finally vetoed a few spending bills—four of his vetoes were overridden with establishment Republican votes for such things as a massive water project bill, a massive farm bill, and more Medicare spending.

It bears repeating that Republicans never ever win big elections unless the election is nationalized and a bold contrast is drawn between a conservative Republican agenda and the liberal Democratic agenda.

In Reagan's 1980 and 1984 campaigns, he ran against the Big Government embraced by the Washington establishment of both parties, and he made it clear that his opponent and the Democrats were soft on communism by running against the détente with the Soviets embraced by the establishment of both parties.

In 1994 we achieved a historic turnover in the House by running against Hillarycare, and for term limits and a balanced budget.

In 2000 Republicans won the presidency, the House, and the Senate running against "Clinton fatigue," and for fiscal responsibility and the conservative social agenda.

In 2010 Republicans won another historic turnover in the House by running against Obamacare and for an end to earmarks, out-of-control spending, and cronyism on Capitol Hill.

Establishment Republicans have still not learned the lesson that no one was going to work to get out the vote, raise money, and support a party that was merely "Democrats-lite" on spending, and stood for nothing more than keeping insiders in power.

There is no doubt the Republican Party developed a near-fatal case of split personality disease during the George W. Bush presidency, and in 2006 and 2008 it came close to death by irrelevance.

As the Bush presidency came to a close, there was a real question in the minds of many about whether or not the Republican Party could be revived—and if it was even worth reviving.

15

McCAIN WASTES CONSERVATIVE ENTHUSIASM for PALIN, OBAMA WINS

Many conservatives began the 2008 primary season with a strong sense that the "Bush fatigue" that the establishment media had turned into a constant theme on the nightly news wasn't necessarily bad for our cause—if the right conservative candidate stepped forward to run for president.

The early front-runner in the race was New York mayor Rudy Giuliani. Giuliani was the favorite of Republican moderates and neocons for his liberal positions on the social issues and unabashed support for President Bush's "war on terror," despite the threats to civil liberties that conservatives saw in it and regularly protested.

Giuliani pursued a rather bizarre strategy of passing on many of the states early on the Republican primary calendar to put most of his energy and money into Florida. While Florida has many retired New Yorkers that might have provided Giuliani with a natural base of support, it is not Iowa, where you can campaign across the whole state as if you are running for county commissioner.

Florida spans two time zones and a dozen media markets, some bilingual, and Giuliani was off the front page and out of the national

TV news cycle while he drained his bank account campaigning almost alone in Florida.

Many social conservatives tended to pin their hopes on Arkansas governor Mike Huckabee. Huckabee, an ordained Baptist minister, had a good record of winning in an Old South state that had begun to trend Republican, but he was certainly not an economic conservative or small-government conservative. I think of Mike Huckabee as a Christian socialist; a nice man, caring and compassionate, but not someone who is going to reduce the size of government.

Huckabee's policy of granting ill-conceived pardons to violent criminals, who returned to society to commit further crimes (including murder and rape), also left him open to Willie Horton–style attacks from other candidates and negative commentary from Rush Limbaugh and Michelle Malkin.

Huckabee won the Iowa caucuses, did not do well in New Hampshire, and pinned the hopes of keeping his campaign alive by winning South Carolina to set up a strong showing in other Southern "Super Tuesday" states.

Social conservatives seemed divided on the Huckabee candidacy. Huckabee went on to win the Super Tuesday states of Georgia, Alabama, Tennessee, and West Virginia, and later a lightly contested Kansas race. Although Governor Huckabee said in late February, "I may get beat, but I'm not going to quit," and vowed to stay in the race until the convention, when Huckabee came in second to Senator John McCain in South Carolina, the likelihood of a Huckabee victory became remote at best.

Congressman Ron Paul ran on his platform of libertarian-oriented policies and made significant inroads for his cause, particularly among younger voters. But the Paul movement was not yet mature enough to field the organization necessary to threaten the front-runners. Even though he came in second to Mitt Romney in Nevada, Dr. Paul came in fifth in South Carolina, and won only one county in Iowa, and one in New Hampshire.

Senator Fred Thompson was also briefly a contender in the race, mostly on the basis of the fact that he wasn't one of the other candidates. Thompson's "good old boy" Southern demeanor and fairly conservative voting record made him attractive to those who were turned off by John McCain and his long-running antagonism toward the conservative movement and its leaders and by Mitt Romney's record.

But Thompson never made a compelling case for his own candidacy. A Thompson speech, rather than being an eloquent statement of conservative principles, was more often the rhetorical equivalent of watching a possum wander along on his rounds of the neighborhood garbage cans, knocking them over and making a lot of noise, but not turning up much to sink his teeth into.

Thompson never won a primary and was out the day after he came in third to McCain and Huckabee in South Carolina.

That left Senator John McCain and former Massachusetts governor Mitt Romney as the two leading contenders for the 2008 Republican nomination.

Believe it or not, Romney ran as the conservative alternative to John McCain and garnered a lot of conservative support along the way. Conservative commentators like Laura Ingraham, Mark Levin, Sean Hannity, and Rush Limbaugh—even if they didn't give him their official endorsements—talked him up. Pro–traditional values Senator Rick Santorum gave Romney an official endorsement that, we might add, came back to haunt Santorum during his 2012 campaign against Romney.

Rush justified his supportive commentaries about Romney by saying that McCain represented the GOP's national security wing, Huckabee represented its social conservative wing, and Ron Paul represented the economic conservative wing, but that Romney (version 2008) was the one candidate who represented all three.

Many other conservative leaders and commentators, including me, weren't buying it.

In the fall of 2007, I attended a meeting with Gov. Mitt

Romney and twenty or so conservative leaders in Salt Lake City, Utah. Romney went around the room and invited each attendee to talk about their issues, and what they thought were going to be the important concerns of conservatives in the 2008 campaign.

Each attendee spoke passionately about their particular organization's area of expertise or concern. When it became my turn, I said that with all due respect to my friends, they are wrong. "The most important issue, Governor, is personnel—who is going to populate your White House and administration?"

Who you walk with tells me a lot about who you are. When Ronald Reagan was running for president, every time I saw him, and I saw him quite a bit, he was surrounded by people I knew from conservative politics: Senator Paul Laxalt, Jeff Bell, Lyn Nofziger, Marty Anderson, Dick Allen, Judge Clark, Ed Meese, etc. If you haven't walked with conservatives for the past ten or fifteen years, how can we expect you to have a conservative administration if there are no conservatives around you now?

Romney's reply, somewhat like the government bureaucrats in *Raiders of the Lost Ark*, was that we should not worry; he would hire "the best people" for jobs in his administration. In other words, he planned to staff his administration with his friends from Big Business and Wall Street, not the conservative movement, which meant our conservative issues would never see the light of day.

We looked at Romney's record as governor of Massachusetts and his personal choices—such as to give money to Planned Parenthood—and didn't see a principled conservative. What we saw was a typical Big-Business, nominal Republican.

And then there was Senator John McCain.

McCain had gone from being the frontrunner to having his political obituary written and back to being the front-runner in the space of less than a year.

During the 2008 campaign Senator John McCain's lifetime rating of 82.3 percent from the American Conservative Union was often cited as proof of his conservative credentials. As Randall

Hoven pointed out in an article for the *American Thinker*, an ACU rating of 82.3 percent is not really particularly high.

A rating of 82.3 percent put Senator McCain in thirty-ninth place among senators serving back then. For the years leading up to the 2008 primary season, McCain's record was spotty at best: in 2006 he scored only 65 percent, in 2007 he scored 80 percent, and in 2008 he scored only 63 percent. Other Senate "mavericks," such as Chuck Hagel (R-NE), who went on to serve as President Obama's secretary of defense, scored 75 percent in 2006, 79 percent in 2007, and 73 percent in 2008.

The Arizona senator was also one of the darlings of the influential neo conservative writers and intellectuals who constantly urged a strong national defense and an aggressive US national security posture and could legitimately lay claim to being a "foot soldier in the Reagan Revolution," as he put it.

This, coupled with McCain's record as a prisoner of war in Vietnam, gave McCain a certain amount of credibility with patriotic grassroots conservatives who were critical of or disillusioned with George W. Bush's conduct of the wars in Iraq and Afghanistan.

They somewhat uncritically assumed McCain saw things their way when he criticized Bush, even if their real ally in the debate over the future of American national security policy was more likely to be libertarian-minded congressman Ron Paul.

McCain was also the darling of the establishment media, who ate up his regular criticism of President George W. Bush, his rival in the 2000 Republican presidential primaries. McCain's base, to the extent that he had one, remained the national press corps and its hunger for any story of Republicans criticizing other Republicans.

It wasn't always McCain's positions that caused friction with movement conservatives; he maintained a 100 percent rating with National Right to Life. Further, McCain, like New York governor Nelson Rockefeller before him, seemed to relish picking fights with the leaders of the conservative movement. This alone might have doomed his candidacy, but McCain had one other thing going for him—it was "his turn."

The Republican vote has a strange royalist streak in it, and even though grassroots Republicans had rejected McCain eight years earlier, they began to slowly acquiesce to his candidacy as the 2008 primary cycle built to its climax in February and March 2008.

McCain also made another move that had short-term benefits in helping him sell himself to the GOP establishment, but, in the longer term, doomed his candidacy—he began to hire George W. Bush's staff and consultants to run his campaign.

Nevertheless, conservatives remained fiercely opposed to McCain. After Super Tuesday, "exit polls showed that only in Connecticut did Mr. McCain actually win a plurality of self-identified conservative voters, barely topping Mr. Romney in the Northeastern state. In every other state, he trailed one or both of the other candidates.

"Even in his own home state of Arizona, Mr. McCain trailed badly among conservative voters, with just 36 percent to Mr. Romney's 47 percent. And in California, Mr. Romney won nearly half of conservative voters, with 48 percent, according to the MSNBC exit polls," reported the *Washington Times*' Stephen Dinan.[1]

McCain seemed to recognize that he needed to find some kind of peace with conservatives to have any chance of winning in November, but his only effort in that direction during the primaries came at CPAC, where he held out the olive branch to conservatives, saying:

> I know I have a responsibility if I am, as I hope to be, the Republican nominee for President, to unite the Party and prepare for the great contest in November . . . I am acutely aware that I cannot succeed in that endeavor, nor can our party prevail over the challenge we will face from either Senator Clinton or Senator Obama, without the support of dedicated conservatives whose convictions, creativity and energy have been indispensable to the success of our party that it has had over the last quarter century.[2]

That was all well and good, but McCain seemed to be trying to get our support on the cheap. After the bruising primaries, where he savaged Mike Huckabee, we felt the next step was up to McCain. We conservatives wanted to see if he would reach out—and we were waiting to see who he picked as his running mate.

Dr. James Dobson, founder of Focus on the Family, went so far as to publicly state that he would not vote for McCain. Jim Dobson later softened his rhetoric somewhat, but he remained critical of the Arizona senator throughout the campaign.

"I have seen no evidence that Sen. McCain is successfully unifying the Republican Party or drawing conservatives into his fold," Dobson said in a written statement released in May 2008. "To the contrary, he seems intent on driving them away."

Despite conservatives making clear where they were coming from, McCain failed to reach out and sell himself one-on-one to conservative leaders or actually make a commitment to run as a conservative and pursue a conservative agenda if elected. Instead, he promised conservatives a "kinder, gentler" version of John McCain if they would abandon their principles and support him.

As I've said before, personnel is policy. You couldn't find a leader of the conservative movement anywhere near the top leadership of the McCain campaign.

Who you walk with says a lot about who you are, and if Senator McCain wouldn't surround himself with conservatives during this campaign, when he desperately needed them, why should we think that he would have conservatives making critical decisions in his White House?

By the time Freedom Fest rolled around in July 2008 (this is an annual gathering of libertarians and free-market lovers), I surveyed the state of the campaign in a speech and concluded that conservatives were so depressed over the state of the McCain campaign—particularly its failure to include conservatives and enthuse the grassroots conservative Republican base—that the attendees should began preparing themselves for a monumental GOP defeat in November.

John McCain had the Republican nomination sewn up for five

months and had done little to convince conservatives they should come off the sidelines and fight for him.

Things were so bad that some conservatives were considering voting for Barack Obama, because they feared McCain as president would destroy what was left of the Republican brand and would finish off the conservative movement. Their mood was that of the fatally ill patient who says, "Let's get this over with."

All that changed—at least temporarily—when McCain announced Alaska's boat-rocking conservative governor, Sarah Palin, as his running mate.

Conservatives had refused to fall in line behind the Republican Party's grudging choice of McCain as the nominee—those of us who maintained our independence, at the price of being ridiculed as "cranky" or "impossible to please," had made it clear that, without a strong, principled conservative on the ticket, we would vote for it—but do little else.

We were subjected to some pretty harsh criticism, but as I saw it, we were the ones responsible for John McCain's brilliant, game-changing selection of Sarah Palin.

Those who backed John McCain as the "lesser of two evils" did no favors for themselves, their movement, or for Senator McCain. To unite the conservative grassroots of the party, Senator McCain needed to know what conservatives really thought, and he needed to know what had to be done to get conservatives enthusiastically on board his campaign.

What he had to do was pick Sarah Palin—or some other limited-government constitutional conservative—as his vice presidential nominee.

The conservative base of the party had been listless. But with the selection of Sarah Palin as the Republican vice presidential nominee, nearly all would work enthusiastically for the McCain–Palin ticket.

In fact, when I spoke to conservatives at the grass roots of the party, it seemed they were the most enthusiastic they had been since the era of Ronald Reagan.[3]

To me the choice of Sarah Palin was a grand-slam home run. During the days leading up to the convention and Palin's national debut, it seemed as if conservatives' feet didn't touch the ground.

Some pundits saw the choice of Palin as another in a list of establishment presidential candidates, such as Richard Nixon and George H. W. Bush, choosing a vice presidential candidate who could be isolated and would bring little experience or horsepower to the table to challenge the candidate or his inside circle.

I figured that there was much more to Sarah Palin and was pleased that McCain had chosen to balance his ticket with a principled conservative like her. Governor Palin's life story was one of sticking to principle. She was living proof that a person can take on the corrupt political establishment—including corrupt leaders in her own party—and achieve great things.

There's an old expression in politics: *Go along to get along.* Not this time. The selection of Sarah Palin was one big kick in the pants to the corrupt establishment in both parties.

The problem for Republicans was that John McCain had gone from being a "maverick" at war with the Republican establishment, particularly those associated with the Bush family, to actually surrounding himself with Bush's staff and consultants.

Although he'd made a brilliant move in choosing Sarah Palin as his VP, in most other respects he'd pretty much done the opposite of what Jim Dobson, other influential conservatives, and I had urged—he made peace and unified the Republican establishment. But he then went on to freeze conservatives out of the campaign.

And that was where the McCain campaign would founder; it failed to use Sarah Palin to her full potential to connect with America's conservative grass roots and in the process missed the opportunity to defeat Barack Obama and avoid the disaster for America that the Obama presidency has produced.

In the haze of history and the establishment media's deification of Barack Obama, it is difficult for most Americans to remember that in Gallup's August 13, 2008, daily tracking poll, Barack Obama led John McCain 48 percent to 42 percent. Yet at the close of the Republican National Convention, McCain actually led Barack Obama 49 percent to 44 percent in the September 8 tracking poll—a swing of eleven points. The week that McCain announced Sarah Palin as his running mate—and she gave her electrifying speech at the Republican National Convention—was the only time after Labor Day when McCain led Obama in Gallup's daily poll.[4]

When Sarah Palin left the Convention and hit the road on her own, she was drawing larger crowds than either McCain or Obama, and that immediately began to make McCain's Washington-based staff unhappy.

The sniping from inside the McCain campaign began almost immediately, and Governor Palin, her family, staff, and supporters from Alaska were treated like a bunch of rubes by the snobby alumni of the Bush White House that McCain had hired to run his campaign.

The shabby treatment of Governor Palin was shameful, but what really destroyed McCain's chances of defeating Obama was the campaign's refusal to use Governor Palin to connect with the conservatives who were her natural constituency and whose votes and enthusiastic support McCain needed to have any hope of becoming president.

The McCain campaign had put the conservative "pit bull with lipstick" on a leash. The campaign had surrounded her with people from the Bush administration. And as we could see from the wreckage of the Bush presidencies, these folks didn't have the slightest clue how to make a case to the American people.

By early October it was clear the election was slipping away from McCain, and I began to say what a lot of conservatives were thinking privately: McCain needed to free Sarah Palin to go after Barack Obama and the liberal Democrats, or he would almost certainly lose.

I also said point-blank that McCain needed to get rid of the Bush people around Palin, along with the lobbyists and the folks from the Washington consulting firms, and replace them with principled conservatives who know how to relate to and speak to grassroots America.

As I've said many times throughout this book, Republicans never win big elections unless they nationalize the election and draw a clear distinction between the liberal vision for America and the conservative vision for America. America is a center-right country. So, for four decades, when national elections break along the liberal-conservative fault line, the more conservative candidate wins. Nationalizing the election along liberal-conservative lines was McCain's only path to victory.

Of course, elections don't happen in a vacuum, and Obama and his liberal allies were ahead because they were making the 2008 election about the record of the Bush administration and the GOP leadership in Congress—ironically, a record of cronyism and Big Government that McCain could credibly argue he had opposed.

Personnel is policy!

And having surrounded himself with lobbyists and Bush White House alumni who were part of the problem, McCain suddenly found it impossible to campaign against the cronyism, corruption, and follies of Fannie Mae, Freddie Mac, and Wall Street that he had railed against during the entire eight years of the Bush presidency.

Contrast that with Reagan. Almost all of his top advisors were from outside the Beltway; Ed Meese, Mike Deaver, Judge William Clark, Lyn Nofziger, Dick Allen, and his California kitchen cabinet were all from outside of Washington, and were not beholden to the entrenched special interests of the DC establishment.

John McCain had forfeited his outsider status and was not willing and able to cast the 2008 election as a choice between one side that is center-right and the other that is extremely liberal. Only Governor Palin could do that.

Palin brought together all the types of conservatives—economic conservatives and religious conservatives, libertarians and "values voters," and people who are simply fed up with Washington's culture of corruption—and she appealed to millions of Americans in the center.

This is why the Left hates Sarah Palin to this day. And this is why she represented McCain's last, best chance. To have any hope of winning, McCain needed to remember why he picked Governor Palin, and unleash her to do what she did best: rally grassroots conservative and independent voters to support the McCain–Palin ticket.

Predictably, the response from the McCain inner circle was to do pretty much the opposite of what conservatives suggested.

I won't go into a state-by-state analysis of why McCain lost. One example will suffice: New Hampshire, where McCain twice won the Republican primary, but lost in the 2008 general election.

The McCain campaign's New Hampshire staff had prohibited any communication between Palin's advance team and the local right-to-life leadership due to the fact that the state GOP leadership was feuding with the right-to-life community.

A small group of right-to-lifers gathered outside Palin's hotel in the hopes of catching a glimpse of the governor, and when told that, yes, the entire family was along, including Bristol and Trig, they burst into spontaneous applause. Startled advance people later concluded it was their way of affirming their support for the Palin family's commitment to the right to life, despite the fact that they had been given the back of the hand by the McCain campaign.[5]

Rather than bring conservatives, such as the New Hampshire right-to-life community, into the campaign, McCain ceded his New Hampshire operation to the state's Republican establishment and operatives working for establishment Republican senator John Sununu and Rep. Jeb Bradley, who of course found it impossible to run against the cronyism and Big Government of the Bush years because they were part of the problem.

The result was predictable. Tied to the discredited Big Government Republican policies of the Bush presidency and bereft of conservative support, Bradley was defeated in his bid for re-election, Sununu was defeated in his bid for reelection, and McCain lost a state that had twice resuscitated his presidential ambitions.

Instead of running as outsiders and turning Governor Palin

loose to appeal to America's center-right voters, the McCain campaign represented many things Americans do not like about politics. Senator McCain spent more than a quarter century in Washington as a "moderate" and "insider," and his campaign was run by longtime Washington insiders and lobbyists for Big Government.

In the 2008 elections, voters did not reject conservatism; they rejected Big Government Republicanism in all its forms, including the Bush administration and the Republican leadership in Congress, who undoubtedly sealed their fate when they passed TARP and protected Wall Street and K Street and forgot about Main Street.

The disastrous defeat of 2008 must be laid at the feet of the Big Government corporate Republicans, because they abandoned the Reagan Coalition, massively expanded government, and ignored the needs and values of America's center-right grassroots voters.

As the conservative vice presidential candidate yoked to the blundering establishment campaign of GOP presidential candidate John McCain, Sarah Palin often drew larger and more energetic crowds than her running mate. In large measure this was because she gave voice to the frustrations of middle-class Americans in what Washington's inside elite derisively call "flyover country."

It is not a stretch to say that the outpouring of populist support for Sarah Palin's vice presidential run was a precursor to the Tea Party movement, and that the thousands of conservative voters whom she energized with the message that the establishment could be beaten were going to be heard from again, and soon.

In postelection comments I remarked that Republicans would make a comeback only after they returned to their conservative roots. The battle for the heart and soul of the Republican Party had stepped up in intensity and although Republicans had lost the presidency in 2008, the good news for conservatives was that new troops were coming onto the battlefield on our side.

16

THE TEA PARTY BECOMES
THE OPPOSITION TO OBAMA

People looking for the roots of the Tea Party movement should start with the grassroots response to the Sarah Palin candidacy for vice president—both at the grassroots and in the inner circle of the Republican establishment. The people who showed up at Sarah Palin's events were different. They were not the usual back-slapping corporate types and ladies with rhinestone elephant pins that made up the crowd at many Republican events for the past two decades.

Instead there were people in well-worn work clothes, the clean Carhart jackets and jeans or logo-embroidered shirts that guys wear when they come to give you an estimate for a new furnace or wait on you at the local computer shop. And they brought their children, especially their daughters and their children with disabilities, to see "their" candidate—Sarah Palin.[1]

The trashing of Sarah Palin by the Republican Party's inside elite, particularly those associated with the George W. Bush White House, demonstrated the level of contempt in which grassroots conservative Republicans were held by the professional political class in Washington.

Palin was, and is, a genuine populist phenomenon, and her

appeal showed a way forward to rebuilding the Republican majority, one more attuned to the views and values of the limited-government constitutional conservatives of the Party's grassroots. It was also a clarion call for new leadership in the GOP, and the Republican establishment wasn't about to hand over power without a fight.

One can't understand the Tea Party movement unless one understands that it is as much a rebellion against the Big Government Republican establishment and the entrenched leadership of the Republican Party as it is driven by opposition to specific liberal policies of President Obama, such as Obamacare or the growth of spending, the deficit, and the federal debt.

Why? Because the Republican establishment, while often talking a good game, has been complicit in the spending, deficit, and debt and in the creation of all of those Big Government programs that drive it.

The Republican Party's Capitol Hill leaders never seem to learn that going along with Big Government policies is exactly what gets Republicans thrown out of office and relegated to the status of the powerless minority they were for the better part of the fifty years from the beginning of the New Deal until the election of Ronald Reagan in 1980.

When Big Government establishment Republicans are the face of the Party, Republicans lose, most recently in 2006, 2008, and 2012.

What's more, in addition to being seen as "Democrats-lite," establishment Republicans just plain aren't very well liked by the grass roots of the GOP. They are viewed as out of touch, elitist, and arrogant—and that's by the grass roots of their own party. Imagine what the conservative independents, Reagan Democrats, and liberty-minded voters that Republicans need to attract to win national elections think?

Enter CNBC correspondent Rick Santelli and his February 19, 2009, "Rant Heard 'Round the World."

Santelli went on air from the Chicago Mercantile Exchange and called for a "Chicago Tea Party" and urged a revolt against the Obama administration's mortgage bailout plan.

The video immediately "went viral" and was seen by millions of people who shared Santelli's view that those who had paid their mortgages on time, and scrimped, and saved, and did without to meet their obligations should not be forced to bail out those who had overextended themselves, or in many cases engaged in outright fraud, to purchase an extravagant lifestyle.

Rick Santelli was right, and unlike the establishment Republicans, who spent the first months after their 2008 defeat mealy-mouthing about how they wanted President Obama to succeed, principled conservatives outside of the Capitol Hill Republican establishment understood that millions of grassroots conservatives did not want Obama's socialist agenda to succeed. The attitude of these millions of grassroots conservatives was perhaps best summed up by Rush Limbaugh in remarks he made at CPAC in February 2009.

Limbaugh spoke for millions when he asked the audience at CPAC, "What is so strange about being honest about saying I want Barack Obama to fail if his mission is to restructure and reform this country so that capitalism and individual liberty are not its foundation? Why would I want that to succeed?"

Less than a month after Barack Obama took the oath of office and began the "transformation" of America, the "TEA Party," or Taxed Enough Already, movement was born.

The viral response to Rick Santelli's "we need a Chicago Tea Party" monologue was not lost on grassroots, limited government and constitutional conservative activists around the country.

Within twenty-four hours of Santelli's broadcast there was a conference call of about fifty or so grassroots, limited-government constitutional conservative activist leaders to discuss how to organize the opposition to Obama's liberal agenda. Through the efforts of Michael Patrick Leahy, Jenny Beth Martin, Mark Meckler, Amy Kremer, Eric Odom, Stacy Mott, Christina Botteri, Lorie Medina, and dozens of others, the first "Nationwide Chicago Tea Party" was organized and the Tea Party movement was born.

At that time I saw things a little differently from some of my friends. Yes, it was important to motivate these newly energized conservative voters to oppose President Obama's destructive policies, but even more important, all the people who were going online to watch Rick Santelli's comments and forwarding them to their friends were the new troops we needed to win our fight for the soul of the Republican Party.

It's the primaries, stupid!

It wouldn't do the cause of conservative governance much good if all of these newly energized voters showed up and elected establishment Republicans in the mold of Mitch McConnell, John Boehner, Denny Hastert, Bill Frist, George W. Bush, and John McCain.

The Republican establishment still hadn't figured out that the Tea Party activists were the new GOP, and they were no longer interested in the go along, get along politics of the Big Government Republican establishment.

While I won't go into all the legends and myths surrounding the growth of the Tea Party movement, I will cite one example of how the Republican establishment did its best to smother this new conservative movement at birth.

President Obama nominated progressive Republican John McHugh of New York to be secretary of the Army and a special election to fill the seat was called.

The Democrats nominated liberal activist Bill Owens, and the Republican establishment pulled out all the stops to hand the nomination to Republican New York assemblywoman Dede Scozzafava—who was even more liberal than the incumbent Republican John McHugh.

Sarah Palin, many leading conservatives, Tea Party activists, and other conservative movement organizations, such as the Club for Growth and Freedom Works, threw their support behind Doug Hoffman, a conservative activist who had challenged Scozzafava for the GOP nomination and won the nomination of the New York Conservative Party in New York's unique multiparty system.

The Republican establishment did everything they could to force

Dede Scozzafava down the throats of the conservative voters of New York's Twenty-Third District, but she just wasn't selling—even after a host of the Republican Party's more conservative insiders, such as Newt Gingrich and Republican Study Committee chairman Jeb Hensarling of Texas, endorsed her.

With Scozzafava fading and conservative Doug Hoffman surging and having the potential to win the three-way race, the Republican establishment was in a panic. Then, with just a few days left in the campaign, Scozzafava withdrew from the race and endorsed the Democrat, Bill Owens.

The GOP leadership's backing of Ms. Scozzafava was a slap in the face to Tea Party activists, town hall protesters, and conservatives across the country who wanted change. The American people were beginning to realize that the GOP leadership and establishment were (and are) as much a part of the problem as are the Democrats.

Doug Hoffman and NY-23 were an earthquake in American politics in 2009, and were the first of many challenges to establishment Republicans that would be seen in the 2010 elections and beyond. Ramming the Scozzafava nomination down the throats of conservatives was one more example of the "closed tent" mentality of Big Government, establishment Republicans who have worked long and hard to keep conservatives out of power at the national, state, and local levels. The outrageous decision by Republican leaders to pour nine hundred thousand dollars into the NY-23 race against a conservative unleashed a fury against the National Republican Congressional Committee that caused many conservatives to withhold their donations. I hoped that fury would lead to new GOP leadership.

Hoffman lost, but the race was still quite close, and it proved once again that rather than give an opening for the principled conservative to take the seat, many establishment Republicans would back a Democrat.

The Republican establishment was humiliated by Dede Scozzafava and her withdrawal and endorsement of the Democrat, and consequently, going into the 2010 Republican primaries they were much more reluctant to play favorites and try to muscle the grass roots into backing a Big Government "Democrat-lite" candidate, which ultimately worked in the favor of the GOP during the 2010 campaign.

As I saw it, the actions of the GOP establishment demonstrated who the immediate opponent was to the grassroots activists of the new New Right—the Tea Party movement activists, Obamacare town hall meeting protesters, and grassroots conservatives across the country—and it was the Big Government Republican establishment, not President Obama, House Speaker Nancy Pelosi, Senate majority leader Harry Reid, and the Democrats.

We may have lost the Doug Hoffman congressional campaign, but conservatives, and especially the newly energized activists of the Tea Party movement, were beginning to understand: "It's the primaries, stupid!"

But before limited-government constitutional conservatives of the Tea Party movement could get down to the business of nominating and electing candidates, they had to relearn the lessons that Barry Goldwater and Ronald Reagan taught us in the 1960s and 1970s about the folly of forming a third political party.

Due to New York's unique system of allowing candidates to run on more than one "line" on the ballot, and combine the votes, Hoffman could present himself as a candidate for both the Republican and the Conservative parties. This was a feat that could not be replicated in any other state.

Many grassroots conservatives began the year 2010 with the idea that the only way to defeat the Republican establishment was to bolt the party and form a new party.

My counsel to Tea Party movement leaders, then and now, is that they should work to be a third force operating in the Republican Party, but should not try to organize themselves into a third party.

A third party would be a disaster for the cause of limited government. It would split the center-right vote and put liberals in charge with unstoppable majorities that would soon act to make sure conservatives were frozen out of the legislative process permanently and completely.

Instead, Tea Party members and other grassroots conservatives should focus exclusively on the Republican and Democratic primaries, I told those assembled for a January 29–31, 2010, meeting of 125 Tea Party leaders for a grassroots training event at the Dallas–Fort Worth Airport Westin hotel.

Essentially, I told them not to think about 2012 at all, not even about November 2010. The focus, I emphasized, should be to challenge every establishment Republican and Democrat in all federal, state, and local primary races.

What I told the Tea Party movement leaders back in January 2010 still holds. Our country didn't get into the mess we're in because of the policies and skills of Barack Obama, Nancy Pelosi, or Harry Reid.

The people who are responsible for handing power to the liberals in 2006, 2008, and in 2012, are the Republican establishment: George W. Bush, Karl Rove, Tom DeLay, Dennis Hastert, Bill Frist, John McCain, Mitt Romney, John Boehner, Eric Cantor, Mitch McConnell, and other establishment GOP leaders.

The disastrous policies of the Big Government Republicans and their content-free campaigns caused the voters to want to fire Republicans in 2006 and 2008—and certainly gave voters little or no reason to hire them in 2012.

Too many conservative leaders have been complicit in this because most conservative leaders just kept quiet while Bush, Rove, DeLay, Hastert, Frist, McConnell, and Boehner ran full speed ahead with all their spending, deficits, and principle-free legislative agenda.

But Tea Party activists are different. The power of the Tea Party movement is that it is unfettered to the old ways of doing things and the old leaders of the Republican establishment. Limited-government constitutional conservatives believe in principles, not just political power. What a tremendous improvement.

On the one-year anniversary of Rick Santelli's "We need a Chicago Tea Party" broadcast, I saw a grassroots movement that had already contributed much to the cause of conservative governance.

In the year or less that the Tea Party movement had been in existence, their grassroots activism was already paying dividends. If there had been no Tea Party opposition to President Obama's legislative program, Obamacare, cap and trade, union card check, and much more federal spending would probably have been enacted into law in 2009.

That year, the Tea Party had become the fastest-growing political movement perhaps in American history. It was getting bigger by the day, and efforts by the political and media establishment to denigrate it merely fueled it. I expected more establishment Republican defeats in primaries that year than ever before.

With only a little hyperbole, I suggested in an op-ed for *Investor's Business Daily* that "most Big Government incumbents would be well advised to follow Senators Bayh, Dodd and Dorgan and voluntarily retire, or the revitalized conservative movement led by Tea Partiers will enforce retirement this November."

At the time much was being written about the phenomenon called the Tea Party movement, some accurate, and some fantastical.

Few commentators in the establishment media grasped that at its core, the Tea Party movement is a revolution of fed-up middle-class Americans of the "Country Class" Angelo Codevilla has written about, and a response to political arrogance—and that it was as much a rebellion against the Republican establishment leadership as it was a revolt against the specific policies of President Barack Obama and the Democratic majority in Congress.

The Tea Party movement developed independently from the conservative movement, but at the local and state level is a natural ally to the cause of small, limited, constitutional government. However, at the national level most conservatives are fettered to the Big Government establishment Republican leadership. The Tea Party started precisely where the conservative movement once had, as outsiders to the political establishment.

As I often do, I began my speech to the Tea Party leadership in Dallas by looking at my watch and saying, "Hi. Where have you been? [pause] I've been waiting for you. [pause] I've been waiting for fifty years for you people."

I had been working and waiting fifty years for this populist, principled, and constitutional groundswell against Big Government and the quasi-socialistic, crony capitalist establishment institutions that have abused power and trust at the expense of hard-working Americans, their children, and their grandchildren.

Due to the enthusiasm, tireless work and commitment to principle of the Tea Party movement and the candidates they fielded and supported, the 2010 election turned out to be almost everything I had hoped.

One of the first big wins for the Tea Party movement was in South Carolina, where Nikki Haley, Tim Scott, and Trey Gowdy won great victories against establishment Republican candidates in the state's primary election.

South Carolina congressmen Gresham Barrett and Bob Inglis both supported the $700 billion Wall Street bailout. In the governor's race (Barrett) and the two congressional races, the candidates associated with the Washington Republican establishment, like Bob Inglis, lost, and the small-government constitutional conservative Tea Party candidates, Nikki Haley, Trey Gowdy, and Tim Scott, won landslide victories.

This was alarming news for GOP establishment politicians such as John Boehner, Mitch McConnell, and all closely associated with them. The Tea Party steamroller was rolling Big Government Republicans right out of town, and it was too late for the Republican establishment to stop it.

If they couldn't stop it, they could try to co-opt it, which they did with their so-called Pledge to America, billed as a follow-up to the Contract with America that had helped lead Republicans to the House majority in 1994.

The Pledge to America was, as Erick Erickson of *RedState* put it so well, "mom-tested, kid-approved pablum" designed only to help Republicans in the 2010 congressional elections. And to that end it might have had some small benefit, but it wasn't a real legislative agenda, and unlike the Contract with America which actually got a vote, at least in the House, the Pledge quickly faded from view after the election.

As a practical matter the Pledge to America was mostly about Republicans promising not to do things they had relished doing in the previous decade.

In many respects the Republican Party is like a business that has an exceptionally good product that is not selling because the sales people are not trusted.

All too often the GOP is represented by guys who come across as scam artists with loud suits and bad toupees, who need a breath mint and whose sales pitch is not believed because they are obviously more interested in their commission than in serving the customer.

When the face of the GOP is not the scam artists of the Big Government Republican establishment the party tends to do well.

The establishment GOP could make all the pledges it wanted, but if it did not push hard in the new Congress to return America to limited constitutional government, establishment Republicans could expect most Republican incumbents to be seriously challenged by Tea Party movement candidates.

The 2010 election, as everyone now knows, proved to be a historic "wave election," and Republicans had their best election in six or seven decades.

Several things happened to make the Tea Party wave possible.

One was the Tea Party movement: a citizen uprising that provided Republican candidates across the country with hundreds of thousands of grass roots volunteers, small donors, and advocates.

We have the radical policies of the first two years of the Obama presidency to thank for creating the middle-class rebellion that became the Tea Party movement. "We the people" were rising up, but it would never have happened without Barack Obama, Nancy Pelosi, Harry Reid, and their radical Left agenda.

Ever since I've been in national politics, people have periodically asked me, "Richard, how can we stop America's slide toward socialism?" I reply that our slide toward socialism could stop only when things get real bad, real fast—just like the old frog-in-boiling-water story.

Put a frog in a pot of boiling water and he will immediately jump out. Put him in a pot and then slowly turn up the heat and the frog will stay there until he is cooked. When Big Government progressive Republicans and Democrats were in charge, we were being slowly cooked, but with the radical liberal Obama in charge, things got really bad really fast and the frogs started jumping out of the pot to create the Tea Party movement.

Equally important was that the face of the opposition to the Democrats was not the usual Big Government, Karl Rove–type Republicans. In 2010, when voters saw the opposition to Obama and the Democrats, they saw Rand Paul, Marco Rubio, Mike Lee, the Tea Party volunteers, Rush Limbaugh, Sean Hannity, and Mark Levin. Clearly they liked that better than the Republican establishment.

And here were the results:

- The Republican Party gained sixty-three seats in the US House of Representatives, recapturing the majority, and making it the largest seat change since 1948 and the largest for any midterm election since the 1938 midterm elections.

- The Republicans gained six seats in the US Senate, expanding its minority.

- The GOP gained 680 seats in state legislative races, to break the previous majority record of 628 set by Democrats in the post-Watergate elections of 1974.

- This meant Republicans controlled twenty-five state legislatures, compared to the fifteen still controlled by Democrats going into the crucial post census reapportionment.

- And finally, after the election, Republicans took control of twenty-nine of the fifty state governorships.

There were, along with this remarkable victory, some notable failures. For example, Nevada Republican Senate candidate Sharron Angle, who emerged from a crowded field to take on the Senate's Democratic majority leader, Harry Reid, and Delaware's Tea Party–backed Republican Senate candidate Christine O'Donnell, who knocked off liberal establishment Republican congressman Mike Castle to claim the nomination. Both O'Donnell and Angle lost in spectacular fashion.

In postelection armchair quarterbacking, the defeats of Angle and O'Donnell in two potentially winnable elections were taken by the Republican establishment as evidence that the Tea Party was somehow a drag on the GOP.

This rewriting of history conveniently overlooks the fact that the Republican establishment immediately abandoned Angle and O'Donnell as soon as they won their primaries. If the Republican establishment considered them to be "not ready for prime time," they did nothing to help them get ready, and plenty to damage their campaigns by criticizing them and filling the media with GOP insider predictions of inevitable losses now that their favored candidates were rejected by the voters.

In reality, there was no evidence to suggest that a candidate, such as liberal Delaware Republican Mike Castle, who was defeated in the primary, was going to automatically prevail in the general election. The claim that the Tea Party cost the GOP control of the Senate was solely based on the idea—thoroughly discredited in 2006 and 2008—that conservatives and right-of-center voters had "no place to go" and would always vote Republican.

What's more, it ignored the tough Senate races that were won, such as Illinois, Pennsylvania, and Wisconsin, in all likelihood only because of the new energy and new voters brought to the campaign by the Tea Party.

The newly elected Tea Party–backed public officials hadn't even been sworn in yet when we began to hear from the likes of Sen. Lindsey Graham (R-SC), and lobbyist Trent Lott, that Republicans would have done much better without the Tea Party. The blame for the GOP's failure to capture the Senate lay, in their view, with Sen. Jim DeMint (R-SC), former Alaska governor Sarah Palin, the Tea Party Express, and their grassroots, limited-government constitutional conservative voters.

Because political parties always do better without actual supporters, right?

The RINOs, reaction to the 2010 election results was a reaction that can only be described as deluded, or insane or (dare we say it?) DeMinted. It was also further evidence that, while the Republican Party is alive and well at the grass roots; its Big Government establishment wing is flailing in its death throes.

Sen. Lindsey Graham's grousing showed that the Big Government Republicans no longer contribute to the party's success either intellectually or in putting boots on the ground. They contributed only money and kvetching, plus an occasional last-minute endorsement of a Democrat running against a Tea Party–backed Republican.

The 2010 election made it clear: the era of Big Government Republicanism was ending.

I wrote in an op-ed in the *Washington Times* that "Big Government Republicans [should] take their place in the dustbin of history beside the slavery-accommodationist wing of the Whig Party, it is time for Tea Partiers to take the next logical step in the development of their movement."

Limited-government constitutional conservatives need to begin the hard work that will ensure that future Republican nominees, at all levels from constable to president, are supporters of Tea Party principles. It is time to flood GOP meetings, to seek party offices ranging from precinct committee member to national convention delegate, and to gently (or not) push aside the party's moribund, incompetent leadership.

How incompetent? Polls show that conservatives outnumber liberals by more than two to one nationally, and that conservatives outnumber liberals in forty-nine of fifty states, yet the Left dominates our country's politics, media, academia, and, increasingly, big business.

Such is possible only because members of the Republican establishment are more concerned with the needs of Washington, DC, lobbyists and Wall Street than the needs of Main Street. They worry more about their popularity down at the country club than about the concerns of working-class and small-business-class Americans.

And they know so little about how politics really works that, offered the opportunity to tap into the energy and activism of tens of millions of Tea Partiers, they greet these new recruits with derision and disdain.

I am regularly asked how conservatives and the Tea Party movement hope to pressure Republican leaders or influence the Republican Party.

Wrong question!

With regard to the GOP, the proper goal of the Tea Party movement should not be to pressure Republican leaders, but to become the Republican leaders. The goal should not be to influence the Republican Party, but to become the Republican Party.

It is hard for conservatives to understand that establishment Republicans are the enemy. They are not people who can simply be talked out of their commitment to Big Government; they must be defeated because they are blocking the path to saving America.

The Democrats under President Obama and House Speaker Nancy Pelosi drove millions of voters right back into the arms of the Republicans. But if Republicans return to their bad habits—if they start working for K Street lobbyists instead of Main Street—they will, in my estimation, pay a terrible price.

People will say, "Fool me once, shame on me. Fool me twice, and the Republican Party is dead."

Voters had given Republicans one more chance to get it right. They were on probation.

Senator-elect Marco Rubio of Florida, one of the great Tea Party successes of the 2010 election, and because of his embrace of amnesty for illegal aliens, one of its greatest subsequent disappointments, said much the same thing in his victory speech.

"We make a great mistake if we believe that tonight, these results are somehow an embrace of the Republican Party," Senator-elect Rubio said after handily defeating his two opponents. "What they are is a second chance—a second chance for Republicans to be what they said they were going to be, not so long ago."[2]

17

ESTABLISHMENT REPUBLICANS THROW AWAY THE 2010 REALIGNMENT

S ince the formation of the Reagan coalition, and the wise decision of Reagan's team to welcome social conservatives into the Republican Party, the conservative movement consisted of three legs: (1) fiscal conservatives, (2) national defense conservatives, and (3) social or traditional-values conservatives.

In 2010 the Tea Party movement became the fourth leg of the conservatives' new big table. It not only brought millions of new people to the political process; it also brought more energy, enthusiasm, and excitement to politics than we've seen in the last one hundred years.

However, it was an open question after the election whether Republican leaders would have the wisdom to welcome the Tea Party movement into the GOP in the way that Ronald Reagan and his team showed in welcoming social conservatives into their coalition and the Republican Party.

It didn't take long to figure out that the short answer was no. The Republican leaders of today don't have the wisdom of Reagan and his team, and it appeared to me that today's Republican leaders would rather be in charge of a permanent minority than share power in a winning coalition.

Senator Jim DeMint spelled out the challenge for the newly elected Tea Party–backed members of Congress in an op-ed in the *Wall Street Journal* welcoming freshmen senators to Washington: *"You must now overcome determined party insiders if this nation is going to be spared from fiscal disaster."*

Or as I put it in an interview with the *New York Times* as the 2010 campaign drew to a close, "We're all on the same page until the polls close Nov. 2." After that, "a massive, almost historic battle for the heart and soul of the Republican Party begins."

Jim DeMint understood how the Capitol Hill establishment worked better than just about anybody.

He was warning Tea Party leaders, and the millions of grassroots, limited-government constitutional conservatives who voted for Tea Party–backed candidates, that the minute the polls closed on Election Day 2010, all promises in the establishment Republicans' Pledge to America were null and void, and that a promise from Republican insiders not to go back to the old ways of earmarks, pork, and deficits was only as good as the Tea Party's willingness to hold the GOP's feet to the fire.

One of the first indications of just how hard this was going to be was to be found in the deliberations of the House Republican Steering Committee and its decisions about who would chair committees in the new Congress.

Two of the most important committees that could make a real difference if chaired by a limited-government constitutional conservative were the House Appropriations Committee and the House Committee on Energy and Commerce.

The choices Republicans offered to head the House Committee on Energy and Commerce were Texas congressman Joe Barton and Michigan congressman Fred Upton.

Electing Barton would require waiving the term-limit rule because he had previously chaired the committee and then served as ranking member. Barton's close ties to the oil industry made critics of corporate welfare nervous, but he had an otherwise conservative voting record. The alternative, Fred Upton, was rated as the tenth most liberal Republican in the House, based on lifetime American Conservative Union ratings.[1]

Upton had also drawn conservative ire by serving as the Republican sponsor of the "light bulb law of 2007," a measure that effectively outlaws the traditional incandescent bulb, and earlier he had supported oil- and gas-drilling bans in the Gulf of Mexico and the Great Lakes.[2]

Upton "has never fought for anything on our side in his life," one conservative activist told the *Washington Examiner*'s Tim Carney. "Since he doesn't believe what we believe, how is he going to get out the message?" "Anybody but Upton!" became the conservative battle cry.

While the conservative grass roots focused on Upton's ideology, those of us who have been around Washington for a while recognized that, regrettably, a lawmaker's voting record isn't how party loyalty is measured on the Hill.

Leadership staffers and K Street lobbyists and others with an inside track on the Republican Steering Committee's deliberations recognized that Upton had raised a lot of money for other Republican candidates through his TRUST PAC by hosting fund-raisers, and by transferring funds from his campaign.[3]

Joe Barton and Speaker-in-waiting John Boehner were rumored not to get along, which made a waiver of the Republican term limits rule unlikely. Three other conservatives who might have made a claim on the chairmanship were Florida's Cliff Stearns, Illinois congressman John Shimkus, and Pennsylvania's right-to-life hero Joe Pitts. Sterns, an outspoken advocate of repealing Obamacare and expanding domestic energy production, seemed to have the most support from conservatives; Shimkus was a dogged supporter of ethanol mandates and subsidies, which were precisely the sort of Big Government corporate welfare programs that Republicans should be using their new power to dismantle. But none of the three ever mounted a serious challenge to Upton.

Despite a strong campaign to influence members of the Republican Steering Committee and John Boehner, including editorials from conservative publications detailing why Fred Upton was "wholly unsuited for the job," Upton was elevated to one of the most visible and powerful chairmanships in the House.[4]

The election of the chairman of the House Appropriations Committee was even more disheartening for conservatives and Tea Partiers.

The candidates for chairman of the House Appropriations Committee, arguably the most powerful committee in the House, were California representative Jerry Lewis, the current ranking member, who was supposedly term limited but chose to ask for an exception to the term limits rule; Georgia congressman Jack Kingston, who, despite his otherwise conservative voting record, had been blasted by Citizens Against Government Waste for earmarks that doubled the Pentagon's request for passenger jets in the 2010 Defense Appropriations Act; and "the Prince of Pork," Kentucky's Congressman Hal Rogers.[5]

Rogers, in the previous year alone, had sponsored or cosponsored fifty earmarks totaling $93.4 million, ranking him tenth out of the 435 representatives, according to the Center for Responsive Politics.[6]

Not one genuine fiscal conservative was even in the running for chairman of the committee that is the first line of defense against the continuation of the massive growth of spending, deficit, and debt that are driving America toward national bankruptcy.

Rogers eventually prevailed and became chairman of the House Appropriations Committee, and while he talked a good game by publicly repudiating earmarks, he has since been a regular and strident advocate of more, not less spending.

Roger's tenure as chairman of the House Appropriations Committee has been a far cry from the fiscal conservative spending discipline Tea Partiers thought they would get when they restored Republicans to the House majority in the 2010 midterm election.

The last time the Republicans were in charge, they became the party of Big Spending, Big Government, and Big Business. They abandoned the philosophy of Ronald Reagan and cozied up to lobbyists and special interests.

If the selection of Fred Upton and Hal Rogers as chairmen of two of the most powerful committees in the House was any indication, the Republican establishment hadn't gotten the message that they were on probation and the voters that handed them back the majority expected a change—or else.

The good news was, so far, the Tea Party showed no appetite for the diet of corporate welfare, Keynesian economic policies, and big business rent-seeking that characterized the Republican Party under the suzerainty of George W. Bush.

Indeed, the Tea Party began to be criticized because it stood for conservative principles, especially on taxes and spending. The Washington establishment soon began to lament that Congress "can't get anything done." What that really means is that they can't grow government if Tea Party–backed members of Congress stand in the way.

Thomas E. Mann and Norman J. Ornstein perhaps best captured this attitude in an article they penned for the *Washington Post*. They claimed that the Tea Party–inspired Republican Party had "become an insurgent outlier in American politics. It is ideologically extreme; scornful of compromise; unmoved by conventional understanding of facts, evidence, and science; and dismissive of the legitimacy of its political opposition."

Let me translate what Mann and Ornstein are saying. Conservative Republicans are making it more difficult for Democrats to reduce your liberty, freedom, and rights and grow the power of the federal government.

It is completely dishonest for the Left and progressive Republicans to use words like *obstructionist* and *gridlock* as opposed to recognizing that there is a real ideological difference between conservatives and progressives. The real problem is not that conservatives are "obstructionist" but that for the first time in one hundred years, the Left and progressive Republicans have some serious opposition, and they don't like it.

Conservatives are standing and fighting because there is a clash of two diametrically opposed worldviews colliding—progressives and the Left believing in the dominance of government, and a powerful government controlling people's lives; conservatives stand for freedom, and the rule of law limiting government. This isn't "obstructionism," but exactly the kind of checks and balance the Framers of the Constitution envisioned. When Tea Partiers began to organize opposition to Big Government, regardless of which Party was behind it, that was exactly what Madison had in mind when he wrote in Federalist no. 44, "In a last resort a remedy must be obtained from the people, who can by the elections of more faithful representatives, annul the acts of the usurpers."

The bad news is that Republican headquarters is still inside the Beltway and, as Senator Jim DeMint observed after the 2010 election, "The establishment is much more likely to try to buy off your votes than to buy into your limited-government philosophy."

The point at which the Republican establishment leadership gave the Tea Party the back of the hand and made it clear they really weren't welcome at the Mitch McConnell–John Boehner–Reince Preibus table was the 2011 battle to raise the federal debt ceiling.

In 2010, most, if not all, Tea Party–backed candidates campaigned against the out-of-control spending, deficits, and debt of the Bush and Obama years.

Many made a solemn promise to their constituents not to vote for a debt ceiling increase, or at least not to increase it without real spending reform.

As the vote to raise the debt ceiling loomed, the newly elected Tea Party–aligned congressmen and women began to see that the challenge lay not with Nancy Pelosi's plaintive demands for a seat at the budget negotiation table. It was in their own leadership ranks, where the willingness to sell out the taxpayer to corporate welfare seeking was unabated among establishment Republicans.

The vote to eliminate funding for a second engine for the F-35

Joint Strike Fighter was an instructive example of this fault line in the Republican Party. This wasteful pork for the military-industrial complex was eliminated only through the support of a strong core of Tea Party–backed freshmen, despite the opposition of top House Republicans who supported General Electric and Rolls Royce over hard-pressed American taxpayers.

In the view of many grassroots Tea Partiers and limited-government constitutional conservatives, this willingness to subsidize favored interests with the taxpayers' money and pick winners and losers by legislative fiat rendered establishment Republicans indistinguishable from Democrats.

The newly elected Tea Party–backed members of Congress were also being educated on just how Washington's insiders worked, and just how divergent the interests of Main Street America and inside the Beltway Washington had become.

As the House was debating under what conditions Congress should raise the debt ceiling, US Chamber of Commerce chief Tom Donohue peremptorily warned Tea Party–aligned members of Congress that if they voted against raising the debt ceiling, "We'll get rid of you."[7]

Missing from that threat was any acknowledgment that congressional spending always chases the funds available to be spent. Nor was Donohue prepared to acknowledge that corporate welfare, bailouts, and subsidies that benefited chamber members, such as General Electric, had anything to do with the fiscal crisis that is destroying this nation.

Tea Party and conservative activists understood that Congress must act to cut spending to solve our nation's spending, debt, and deficit crisis—that's where the Taxed Enough Already acronym came from!

Establishment Republicans were facing a choice that would determine whether or not the party remained a relevant force in American politics. If Republicans caved in and followed the establishment line to raise the debt ceiling, while claiming they would address the spending crisis sometime in the future, they would render the GOP irrelevant to solving the greatest political problem of our times.

As the vote to raise the debt ceiling loomed, and with the newly elected Tea Party–aligned members of Congress making up a substantial part of the Republican majority, holding the line on the debt ceiling and making real cuts in the size of government should have been a no-brainer.

One might think that corporate interests would oppose raising the debt ceiling because they would never run their businesses the way the federal government is run. But Donohue's comments were a stark reminder of the major fault line in the Republican Party.

Donohue and establishment Republicans understood all too well that solving the federal budget and debt crisis means derailing the federal gravy train and ending the Wall Street bailouts, corporate welfare, and pork-barrel spending that got us into the spending, deficit, and debt cycle in the first place. Clearly, that would be bad for a lot of US Chamber members who had become addicted to profiting from the axis between Wall Street, Washington, and Silicon Valley.

"Raise the debt ceiling or we will get rid of you"?

What Donohue and the Republican establishment didn't seem to understand was that every time Republicans in Congress voted for the corporate interests over the national interest, they widened the fault line in the party and made more Tea Party candidates in Republican primaries.

As the vote to raise the debt ceiling approached, the pressure from establishment interests intensified.

On one side were conservatives who backed a plan originated by principled limited-government constitutional conservative senator Jim DeMint of South Carolina, calling for an increase in the debt ceiling as part of a plan to "Cut, Cap, and Balance" the budget.

On the other side were those, such as Senate minority leader Mitch McConnell, who were prepared to do pretty much anything to avoid a fight over the debt ceiling. They were prepared to even give

Obama and the Democrats an extension beyond the 2012 election—and of course the Democrats just wanted more money without any conditions, a so-called clean increase in the debt ceiling.

Conservative leaders were holding regular meetings and conference calls to coordinate support for Cut, Cap, and Balance, much as we New Right leaders had done in the late 1970s and early 1980s to rally support and coordinate action on our agenda—and it seemed to be working. Thousands of calls, e-mails, and letters poured into Congress, and getting the federal budget under control was the dominant issue on talk radio, the evening news, and the top opinion-leading websites.

In what was to become a hallmark of his Speakership, Boehner held a vote on a House version of Cut, Cap, and Balance. The House passed the bill 234 to 190 (112th Congress, first session, roll call vote 606) to much brave talk from the Speaker about the president abandoning his veto threat and Senate Democrats quickly passing the bill.

> House Republicans are the only ones to put forward and pass a real plan that will create a better environment for private-sector job growth by stopping Washington from spending money it doesn't have and preventing tax hikes on families and small businesses. The White House hasn't said what it will cut. And Senate Democrats haven't passed a budget in more than two years. The President should abandon his veto threat, and urge Senate Democrats to quickly pass the "Cut, Cap, and Balance" plan to help get our economy back to creating jobs.[8]

And just as quickly as the House passed the bill, Boehner began to backtrack and back down.

As soon as the Senate Democrats, under the iron fist of Majority Leader Harry Reid, voted down Cut, Cap, and Balance, Boehner put up another bill that, as FreedomWorks said in its analysis, "not only violates the Cut, Cap and Balance Pledge, it doesn't even reflect the 'spirit' of Cut, Cap and Balance, as House leaders claim, because it neither cuts nor caps nor balances federal spending. And it creates an opening for Washington to raise taxes next year."[9]

Many conservatives, including me, couldn't understand why Boehner was backing down. It seemed clear to us that conservatives were winning when we stood on principle and our opponents offered nothing but threats.

What's more, all of the self-appointed financial arbiters who were issuing the threats had one thing in common: they had all benefited from the trillions of dollars the American taxpayers had shoveled into the maw of Big Government over the past four decades. For example, Tom Donohue of the US Chamber and managing director of the International Monetary Fund demanded the United States raise the debt ceiling or face some ill-defined consequences. Similarly, Moody's Investors Service (the same outfit that missed the causes of the meltdown of 2008) raised the pressure on US lawmakers to increase the debt limit by placing the nation's credit rating "under review" for a downgrade.

The threats confirmed what I'd been saying for two years—the Tea Party could succeed in changing Washington; all that was required was for the members of Congress who were backed by the Tea Party movement to hold fast to their principles.

And if Republicans couldn't or wouldn't fight to the bitter end for Cut, Cap, and Balance, it seemed to me that the next best solution to our spending, debt, and deficit crisis might be found in a bill to make immediate spending cuts in exchange for raising the debt ceiling for six to nine months.

After fifty-plus years in conservative politics at the national level, it was clear to me that great issues like those are decided by voters, not politicians. I didn't think establishment politicians should be allowed to kick the spending, debt, and deficit can past the next election. A six- to nine-month increase in the debt ceiling would put the next debate squarely in the middle of the 2012 presidential election campaign. As long as the Republicans didn't cave in, Obama, Pelosi, and Reid were doing a great job of solidifying the Democratic Party's image as the party of Big Government and taxes; that could

Forsyth County Public Library

Sharon Forks Branch

Thank you for using   *Express* Check!

Telephone : 770-781-9840

Telephone Renewal : 770-781-9865, Option 2

www.forsythpl.org

Date : 8/9/2014 Time : 12:15:21 PM

Name : RILEY, JOSHUA DEAN

Fines/Fees Owed : $3.40

Items checked out this session : 2

Title : Takeover : the 100-Year war for the soul of the
GOP and how conservatives can finally win it
Barcode : 1002559948
Due Date : 08/23/2014 23:59:59

Title : The next America : boomers, millennials , and
the looming generational showdown
Barcode : 1002558899
Due Date : 08/23/2014 23:59:59

---

only help conservatives.

An increase in the debt ceiling good for six to nine months would empower the Tea Party and mean the next election would be nationalized. The coming election would be focused on who will cut spending to solve the debt-and-deficit crisis. Conservatives would welcome the opportunity to put the issues in that debate before the people and to make the next campaign a referendum on exactly which members of Congress caved in to Obama's request for a blank check.

However, instead of solidifying the new four-part coalition of economic conservatives, national defense conservatives, social conservatives, and the constitutional conservatives of the Tea Party movement by nationalizing the 2012 election and making it a referendum on spending, deficits, and the debt, the stage was set for a near-fatal rupture between the new conservative coalition and the Republican Party.

Rather than stand for conservative principles—or at least play hardball politics—by making Democrats defend their indefensible spending, deficits, and debt, there was a complete cave-in by the House Republican leadership, and the passage of a deal long in the works between Senate leaders Democrat Harry Reid and establishment Republican Mitch McConnell: the Budget Control Act of 2011.

In a gross breach of the promise Boehner made to give Members and the public three days to review legislation, fewer than twenty-four hours after the legislation was first posted online, with no review by a legislative committee, the bill was rushed to the floor. The House then voted 269 to 161 (112th Congress, first session, roll call vote 677) to approve the Budget Control Act of 2011.[10]

Conservatives had many objections to the Budget Control Act of 2011, from the substantive constitutional issues engendered by the creation of an extra-constitutional "Super Committee," to the political, in that it gave Obama and the Democrats a free pass on the spending, deficit, and debt issue until after the 2012 election.

On passage of the Budget Control Act of 2011, twenty-two

principled conservatives voted against the Speaker's cave-in. This included two freshmen Tea Party–backed representatives, Justin Amash of Michigan and Tim Huelskamp of Kansas, whom the Speaker would later strip of their committee assignments for trying to hold him and the House Republican Conference to conservative principles, and for rallying conservatives to oppose the House leadership when it strayed.

There would be many more cave-ins and much more backtracking by the establishment Republican leadership of the House, but the debt ceiling battle and the debate over Cut, Cap, and Balance set the pattern that establishment Republicans would follow throughout the Obama presidency.

The grassroots, limited-government constitutional conservatives of the Tea Party were outraged, and Senator Jim DeMint's prediction that "the establishment is much more likely to try to buy off your votes than to buy into your limited-government philosophy" was proven correct.

Less than eight months into the addition of the Tea Party movement as the "fourth leg" of Republican coalition, the Republican Party's Capitol Hill establishment threw away any pretense of adopting the goals and values of the Tea Party (and the potential to realign American politics for a generation or more) and opted instead for business as usual in Washington, DC.

When Republican leaders wouldn't fight for Cut, Cap, and Balance and passed the Reid–McConnell deal embodied in the Budget Control Act of 2011, conservatives were outraged and many were demanding that heads roll—particularly those of the Tea Party–backed freshmen who had caved in and gone along with the establishment leadership to pass the bill.

My counsel was that there should be no recriminations and no witch hunt.

It was inevitable that some Tea Party–backed members of Congress were going to waiver or be won over by the blandishments of the DC establishment. At that point the Tea Party movement was barely two years old and it had achieved an amazing victory in the 2010 congressional elections. Through this grassroots, limited-government constitutional conservative movement, the old go-along-get-along GOP establishment was being challenged in the halls of Congress, in the news media, and at coffee shops and water coolers across the country.

Some will look at the 112th Congress and see a failure of the Tea Party agenda. To me the important thing was—and is— that the Tea Party movement and those candidates it backed changed the debate in Washington, and just as the New Right did in the late 1970s in the lead-up to Reagan's 1980 victory, supplanted the Republican establishment to provide the real opposition to the Democrats.

18

THE PARTY of STUPID PUTS the MEDIA IN CHARGE of THEIR DEBATES

I f the definition of insanity is doing the same thing over and over while expecting a different result, welcome to the nut house of the establishment media-sponsored Republican presidential debates.

What would you call a political party that hands the power to set the agenda during its presidential primaries to its sworn enemies in the liberal media, then doubles down to give the power to set the agenda in the waning days of the general election to a self-perpetuating "commission" of Washington, DC, progressive insiders?

Some people might call that the national Republican Party— I call it the Party of Stupid.

I'm not going to dissect every one of the twenty-plus debates held during the 2012 Republican primary season or the details of the three general election debates between Mitt Romney and Barack Obama. However, a few examples from the 2012 election will illustrate how the primary debates helped launch the Democrasts' "war on women" narrative they use against Republicans to this day, how their questions helped solidify Mitt Romney as the Republican nominee, and how the media then turned on Romney to help resuscitate Obama after his abysmal performance in the first general election debate.

On January 7, 2012, ABC News, Internet giant Yahoo! and WMUR-TV hosted a New Hampshire Republican presidential primary debate; the media panel consisted of Diane Sawyer of ABC News, Josh McElveen of WMUR-TV, and former Clinton campaign operative and White House press secretary George Stephanopoulos, now of ABC News.[1]

Not long into the debate, George Stephanopoulos bizarrely pressed former governor Mitt Romney on whether he believed the US Supreme Court should overturn a 1965 ruling that a constitutional right to privacy bars states from banning contraception—the *Griswald v. Connecticut* case. Here's the exchange according to the transcript of the debate:

> GEORGE STEPHANOPOULOS: Governor Romney, I want to go straight to you. Senator Santorum has been very clear in his belief that the Supreme Court was wrong when it decided that a right to privacy was embedded in the Constitution. And following from that, he believes that states have the right to ban contraception. Now, I should add that he's said that he's not recommending that states do that. [*Santorum tries to jump in but is inaudible*] Well, I'll, I'll, absolutely, I'm giving you your due.[2]

Persisting, Stephanopoulos later said: "But I do want to get that core question. Governor Romney, do you believe that states have the right to ban contraception? Or is that trumped by a constitutional right to privacy?"

As Brad Wilmouth of the Media Research Center so accurately characterized it, Romney was "befuddled by the off the wall nature of the question on such an issue that is not on any state's legislative agenda, eventually observed that it was a 'silly thing' for the ABC co-moderator to ask such an irrelevant question."

But Stephanopoulos was not to be deterred and kept after Romney with an odd persistence that prolonged the discussion with Romney for more than three and a half minutes. Only after Stephanopoulos's hectoring of Romney inspired a number of boos from the audience were Ron Paul and Rick Santorum allowed an opportunity to speak.[3]

Although former senator Santorum made it clear that he would be *opposed* to banning contraception, as contraception merely violates his religious beliefs without entering into his public policy agenda, Stephanopoulos began the question to Romney by referring to what he claimed was Santorum's position in favor of allowing states to ban contraception.

So not only did Stephanopoulos make the headline story on the New Hampshire debate about a nonexistent issue—he set up the question by mischaracterizing Senator Santorum's position on *Griswald*, delivering a "twofer" to President Obama and his radical liberal feminist allies.

This was all part of the plan, claimed Rush Limbaugh:

> "The design was they hoped Romney would say, 'Well, if the states want to,' they could then allude to the Republican front-runner suggesting that contraception be banned. Then they went out and they found an interview with Santorum where they can take him out of context and say that this is what he intends to do when he has not and did not say that."[4]

Limbaugh later noted that this was all about exciting the radical feminist base of the Democratic Party. As Rush put it, "All you have to do to get their attention is to dredge it back up that the Republicans want to get rid of their birth control pills and deny them abortion, and that will bring 'em back, and that's what they're trying to do. It's a total move of feint and distraction."[5]

And by allowing President Clinton's former press secretary George Stephanopoulos on the media panel, the Republican Party played right into their hands. The liberal message that feminists must rise up to protect women's rights from hostile, paternalistic Republicans was pushed hard by the liberal talking heads on TV and was all over the opinion pages of the nation's newspapers for the next few days.

What would make Republican candidates for President agree to a debate moderated by George Stephanopoulos, the former press secretary of a Democratic president, or the likes of CNN's notoriously liberal host Anderson Cooper? Besides rank stupidity, it is hard to think of a reason.

And here is what Republicans get when they act like the Party of Stupid and agree to a debate moderated by the same Anderson Cooper whose vulgar jocularity with David Gergen resulted in this crass comment about the Tea Party during a 2009 broadcast, "It's hard to talk when you're tea-bagging."[6]

If you'd never heard about "tea bagging" (as I hadn't) before this, take my word for that it refers to a homosexual activity.

During the 2011 debt ceiling debate, CNN conducted a poll that Cooper reported as showing 64 percent of the public supported raising taxes, making Republicans appear to be dishonest for claiming most Americans were opposed to a tax increase.

What Cooper failed to report was that the same CNN poll showed that two-thirds of those polled favored the Cut, Cap, and Balance plan advocated by conservatives and passed by House Republicans.[7]

Likewise, during the CNN-sponsored Republican primary debate in Tampa before the crucial Florida Republican primary election, the question of Social Security being a "Ponzi scheme," as Texas governor Rick Perry had called it in his book, was thoroughly aired.

However, a question from a member of the audience that went right to the heart of Republican voters' concerns about the growth of government: "Out of every dollar that I earn, how much do you think that I deserve to keep?" was referred to only one of the candidates, with no follow-up.[8]

Republicans who agreed to this debate on the theory that Cooper and CNN would be on their good behavior and dispense with the junior high school vulgarity need to wake up and take a look at just how liberals like Anderson Cooper make Republicans look bad.

It isn't by fabricating news or outright lying; it is by selecting questions that set the agenda on liberal terms and presuppose the outcome favored by liberals—or by editing out the conservative viewpoint or facts that tend to support the conservative viewpoint.

The result in the general election debates is that Republican presidential candidates are always outnumbered two or three to one in a fight that pits them against a liberal debate moderator and their liberal Democratic opponent.

After the first 2012 debate between Mitt Romney and Barack Obama, moderator and PBS host, James Lehrer was roundly criticized by his fellow liberals for not wading in and helping Obama.

Still, he slipped several interesting "tells" of his liberal bias, such as referring to Romney's economic plans as "trickle-down" and breaking up Romney's train of thought by calling time when he was prosecuting especially effective attacks on Obama, while letting Obama go well past his deadline to finish his thoughts.

But these were fairly minor things compared to how Lehrer handled the 2000 debate between George W. Bush and Al Gore.

In 2000, Lehrer moderated all three presidential debates. In the third one, as the Media Research Center pointed out, "a town hall debate, Lehrer approved mostly liberal questions from the 'uncommitted' audience. Eight questions came from the Left, only two could be counted as conservative, and five were requests for information without an ideological tone."

And that's the key to how liberal bias at the debates, and in the media at large, works. It is not so much that reporters will lie or make up things to make conservatives look bad—it is the premises of the questions and even the questions themselves that accept an underlying belief in liberal policy choices.

It is the old joke about asking a candidate, "When did you stop beating your spouse?" turned into "Why do you want to starve poor people by sending food stamp programs back to the states?"

Democrats never buy into the idea that a "debate" is a nonpartisan affair.

In 2008, under pressure from liberal groups and blogs, Nevada Democrats decided to cancel a debate to be hosted in part by Fox News.

Liberal bloggers and groups, as well as some Nevada Democrats, had demanded that Fox be removed as a sponsor, arguing that its coverage was slanted toward Republicans.

Markos Moulitsas, the founder of Daily Kos, one of the most popular liberal blogs, began polling the Democratic 2008 presidential field to see who would attend the debate, and of course to intimidate them into not attending. Additionally, liberal activist group MoveOn.org collected more than 250,000 signatures, demanding that Fox be dropped as a sponsor.

According to the *New York Times*, "In response to the query from Mr. Moulitsas, John Edwards said he would not participate. His campaign cited Fox as a factor, as well as a heavy schedule." Moulitsas later reported that Gov. Bill Richardson of New Mexico, who previously said he would attend, had decided against it. Nevada Democratic leaders, attempting to salvage what they hoped would be a good opportunity to reach a new group of voters, offered a compromise in which an affiliate of liberal (and now defunct) radio network Air America would also broadcast the debate and promised a "progressive" voice would be added to the panel of moderators.

All to no avail; the pressure from the liberal activists was too strong and the debate was canceled.

Any Republican candidate who is smart enough to be president ought to be smart enough to see that the way to defeat the Democrats is to stop letting liberals like George Stephanopoulos, Anderson Cooper, James Lehrer, Martha Raddatz, Candy Crowley, and Robert Schieffer set the agenda through these debates, and instead only participate in debates with fair, objective journalists as moderators.

But the problem isn't so much the Republican presidential candidates as it is the establishment Republicans on the Commission on Presidential Debates and the leadership of the Republican National Committee who are not innocent bystanders.

More reflective of the establishment Republican Party of 1987 when the commission was set up, and the DC Republican establishment, than it is of today's more conservative GOP, the Republicans on the Commission are all too ready to cede the role of debate moderator and agenda setter to the establishment media elite they meet at Georgetown salons.

That's how, even in the face of decades of proof that establishment journalism has a hard Left tilt, we always end up with liberal debate moderators like 2012's group: Lehrer, Stephanopoulos, Martha Raddatz, Anderson Cooper, Candy Crowley, and Robert Schieffer.

The bad news for future Republican candidates who go along with playing the Party of Stupid is that since Lehrer was hammered by his fellow liberals for not being an aggressive moderator, they can expect the moderators of the 2016 debates to avoid the pounding Lehrer took by doing their best to help the Democratic candidate—particularly if that candidate is Hillary Clinton.

Martha Raddatz, who moderated the vice presidential debate in 2012, is a fawning member of the Washington liberal sisterhood that has promoted and supported Hillary Clinton since the day she arrived in DC back in 1993. Raddatz has deep ties to the old-line liberal media and to Washington's Democratic establishment, having been married to the son of Washington's ultimate establishment liberal, longtime *Washington Post* editor Ben Bradlee, and later to Obama's FCC chairman, Julius Genachowski.

Candy Crowley, chief political correspondent for CNN, is likewise a longtime member of Washington's liberal sisterhood, who said during the 2008 campaign cycle she brought her daughter to see Hillary Clinton, "you know, because I think this might be history."

But this is the treatment the equally historic candidacy of Republican Michele Bachmann received from Crowley:

> We have a poll where the majority of Americans said you all need to compromise on this debt ceiling, you all need to raise the debt ceiling, and the deal ought to include a combination of

tax increases and spending cuts. You are opposed to both raising the debt ceiling and that kind of compromise. So doesn't that put you outside the mainstream?[9]

CBS News anchor and *Face the Nation* host Bob Schieffer may not be quite equal to Lehrer in stature among the old-time Washington journalism establishment, but he is second to none in promoting the liberal agenda in the media—especially the liberal fable that Republicans must "move to the center" to win a national election. At least twice in the month leading up to the 2012 debate he moderated, Schieffer called upon Mitt Romney to renounce the conservative agenda and to say he was a moderate.

"Do you think that Mitt Romney's got to move a little bit more toward the center here as we come toward the election?" Schieffer asked a guest on *Face the Nation*. Fortunately for Romney, that guest was Newt Gingrich, who forcefully rebuffed the suggestion by saying, "No, I think Mitt Romney has to move to clarity in drawing the contrast between the two futures."[10]

But it doesn't have to be that way.

Herman Cain and Newt Gingrich participated in a Lincoln-Douglas–style debate hosted by the Texas Patriots PAC. There was no moderator, and the two candidates discussed and responded to each other's positions on domestic policy during an event in The Woodlands, Texas.[11]

The Cain–Gingrich Debate 2011 showed that, without the interference of the establishment media, the candidates can have an interesting and instructive discussion on the issues and that Republicans have a host of thoughtful ideas about how to deal with the challenges facing America. The best thing Republican candidates could do to get those ideas out is to stop participating in the TV ratings games that pass for presidential debates—especially during Republican primaries.

The one 2012 Republican presidential candidate who seemed to actually be helped by the debate format was Newt Gingrich—and

Newt worked the debates to his advantage by confronting the media, not his fellow Republican candidates, for the nomination.

Were one to judge the debates strictly on "applause-ometer" results, Newt Gingrich was usually the runaway winner when he took the moderators to task for highlighting petty differences between the candidates in lieu of focusing on the real issues facing the country.

During the debate at the Reagan Library, Gingrich said to moderator John Harris of *Politico*, "I for one . . . hope that all of my friends up here are going to repudiate every effort of the news media to get Republicans to fight each other, to protect Barack Obama, who deserves to be defeated. And all of us are committed as a team. Whoever the nominee is, we are all for defeating Barack Obama." He got most of the audience out of their chairs.

To many Tea Party and conservative activists, Gingrich was the winner of the 2012 Republican primary season debate marathon because he was the candidate who best challenged the conventional wisdom of the liberals asking the questions.

So, note to future Republican candidates for president: the liberals on the media panel of the presidential debates during the primary and general elections think they are the smartest people in the room, and that it is their job to make you look like an idiot or a woman-hating Neanderthal.

Imagine a debate between the Democratic candidates for president in which Britt Hume, Megyn Kelly, George F. Will, Steven Hayes, and Michael Barone asked the questions.

Such a debate will never happen because the Democrats don't feel the need to pretend that conservative journalists and commentators are "nonpartisan" or to pander to the conservative media the way establishment Republicans feel compelled to pander to the national media.

National Republicans are all too willing to be the Party of Stupid when it comes to dealing with the establishment media. They rarely challenge the conventional wisdom behind media policy questions and are all too willing to let themselves be boxed in to answer questions solely intended to drive a wedge between voters and Republican candidates. These so-called journalists want to drive voters away from Republican candidates, not actually conduct a "debate" about conservative principles.

The result in 2012 was, they let the liberal media all but choose Mitt Romney as their presidential nominee, with predictably disastrous results.

If there's one lesson even the Party of Stupid could take away from the 2012 Republican primary debates, it is that media will look favorably on, promote, and highlight the most liberal or most progressive Republican capable of winning the nomination, then turn on that candidate in the general election.

If conservatives are to win and govern America, one of the things the GOP needs to do is to walk away from the self-perpetuating Commission on Presidential Debates. This undemocratic organization won't even identify its sources of funding, and its staff is dominated by liberal Washington insiders, such as executive director Janet Brown. The next Republican presidential candidate should deal directly with his or her Democratic counterpart and cut out the Commission, which has been putting its thumb on the scale in favor of DC insiders for more than twenty-five years.

19

CONSULTANTS MAKE MILLIONS WRECKING the GOP

t says a lot about the caliber of advice Mitt Romney was getting in 2012 that in the midst of the worst economy since the Great Depression of the 1930s, with unemployment at 7.9 percent in October 2012, and 12.3 million people unemployed (40.6 percent of whom were unemployed for more than six months), Romney ended up losing the presidential campaign by almost five million votes.

The same goes for the establishment Big Government Republican Senate candidates who lost in 2012. Heather Wilson in New Mexico, Rick Berg in North Dakota, Denny Rehberg in Montana, Tommy Thompson in Wisconsin, George Allen in Virginia, Connie Mack in Florida, and Linda Lingle in Hawaii—were all defeated in a year when the Senate, under the leadership of Democrat Harry Reid, hadn't passed a budget in over three years.

A big part of the problem was and is, in a word, consultants, especially the small coterie of Washington, DC–based Republican insiders that have come to dominate Republican political strategy and ad making over the past two decades.

The great strength of the Republican Party has always been its grassroots conservative base—the entrepreneurs, small business people, farmers, and working families of Main Street America who donate to candidates, volunteer to knock on doors, make phone calls, and stamp envelopes every election cycle to elect conservatives to office.

These individuals aren't involved in politics for personal gain—they are involved out of a sense of patriotism and because they want to, as Ronald Reagan said, "preserve for our children this, the last best hope of man on earth."

This growing class of professional political consultants and self-anointed political "strategists" that has come to dominate the management of Republican political campaigns over the past two decades generally opts for content-free campaigns instead of campaigns based on conservative ideas and ideology—naturally they want their clients to win, but in their hands politics is all too often reduced to a business, not a clash of ideas.

One of my first negative experiences with so-called professional political strategists came during a campaign that led to the defeat of California's liberal Republican US senator Tommy Kuchel, the US Senate's Republican minority whip, by the relatively unknown conservative Max Rafferty.

As I noted earlier, Max Rafferty chose my firm, and our expertise in the new and alternative media of direct mail, to get his conservative message out to California's Republican primary voters.

We mailed twice to two million registered Republican voter households in California. I'm confident that the over four million letters we mailed to reach about seven million people in California was the major reason a relatively unknown state superintendent of public instruction with little campaign money was able to beat one of California's best known and most powerful politicians by sixty-seven thousand votes.

However, when the November general election came around, Rafferty's consultants decided they didn't want a big direct-mail effort; they asked us to mail only to sixty thousand Rafferty contributors and probably used the money our letters raised mostly to buy TV advertisements.

While that wasn't the only reason Rafferty lost badly in November, I think it certainly was one of the principal reasons. I'm sure the fact that consultants receive a hefty commission for placing TV advertising had nothing to do with the decision to use expensive, and largely ineffective, TV ads instead of the new and alternative media and grassroots voter contact techniques to promote Rafferty's insurgent campaign.

These professional political operatives (particularly the inside-the-Beltway crowd) aren't interested in building a great grassroots conservative movement to back Republican candidates who will reduce the size of government and govern America according to conservative principles—the economic incentives being what they are, they concentrate on those techniques that pay rather than build the grassroots base of the Republican Party.

Think this assessment is too harsh?

Morton Blackwell, the principled conservative Republican national committeeman from Virginia, founder of the Leadership Institute and an expert in campaign management, made these observations in a column for the *Daily Caller* a few weeks after the 2012 election.

> Most consultants take a 15 percent commission (over and above client-paid production costs and his retainer) from media vendors for all placements.
>
> The consultant knows he gets no commission for campaign funds spent on people-intensive activity, such as:
>
> • precinct organization
>
> • voter ID phone banks
>
> • voter registration drives
>
> • youth effort
>
> • the Election Day process to get out the vote

With their budgets warped toward media spending, candidates and in-state organizations are led to measure the progress of campaigns by dollars raised and tracking polls.

He [the consultant] decides to branch out into lobbying, where his influence enables him to pull down some really fat fees from major corporations, trade associations, and even foreign governments which have major financial interests in the decisions of elected and appointed government officials.[1]

In Morton Blackwell's view this situation has led to a general decline in citizen participation as activists and, often, even as voters.

Blackwell believes volunteer participation in elections has been the greatest preparation for competent campaign management, and when campaigns focus on paid media and neglect grassroots organization, the supply of good candidates and new activists dries up.

What's more, a small group of DC consultants have become a virtually closed guild of "you scratch my back, I'll scratch yours" favor traders who have burrowed into the fabric of the Republican National Committee and the Congressional and Senatorial Committees like parasites.

If you think that assessment is too harsh, consider these facts gleaned from the 2012 election disclosures and an interview *Breitbart*'s Michael Patrick Leahy conducted at C-PAC 2013 with Pat Caddell, the Fox News contributor and Democrat pollster who engineered Jimmy Carter's 1976 presidential victory:

When you have the Chief of Staff of the Republican National Committee and the political director of the Romney campaign, and their two companies get $150 million at the end of the campaign for the "fantastic" get-out-the-vote program . . . some of this borders on RICO [the 1970 Racketeer Influenced and Corrupt Organizations Act] violations. . . . It's all self-dealing going on. I think it works on the RICO thing. They're in the business of lining their pockets.[2]

"The Republican Party," Caddell continued, "is in the grips of what I call the CLEC—the consultant, lobbyist, and establishment complex." Caddell described CLEC as a self-serving, interconnected network of individuals and organizations interested in preserving their own power far more than they're interested in winning elections.

"Just follow the money," Caddell told a rapt audience:

> It's all there in the newspaper. The way it works is this—ever since we centralized politics in Washington, the House campaign committee and the Senate campaign committee, they decide who they think should run. You hire these people on the accredited list [they say to candidates] otherwise we won't give you money. You hire my friend or else.[3]

Financial corruption is a key component of the current process, according to Caddell. "There's money passing under the table on both parties. Don't kid yourself. . . . If you can't see racketeering in front of you, God save you."[4]

Leahy further documented how Federal Election Commission reports filed by the Republican National Committee show that one-third of the $59.3 million it spent directly with vendors in the last five weeks of the 2012 election was paid to one telemarketing firm, FLS Connect, LLC.

FLS Connect, LLC, was paid $19.6 million by the RNC between October 18, 2012, and November 26, 2012, for telemarketing services. Republican National Committee chief of staff Jeff Larson cofounded FLS Connect, LLC, in 1999 along with Tony Feather and Tom Synhorst, who now serves as the chairman and managing partner of the DCI Group, a powerful Washington lobbying and public relations firm. Larson was a partner in the firm until November 2010. In February 2011, incoming RNC chairman Reince Priebus named Larson as his chief of staff.

All in all, two consulting firms with close ties to key staffers at the Romney campaign and the Republican National Committee were paid more than $152 million by the three organizations that funded Mitt Romney's unsuccessful 2012 presidential campaign.[5]

Erick Erickson at *RedState* also did an excellent job of detailing the relationships between the various people and entities involved in just this one scheme to bleed the Republican Party in a column entitled "The Incestuous Bleeding of the Republican Party."[6]

Given that politicians are focused on winning elections, the leadership of the Republican Party might overlook these financial shenanigans if these consultants actually won campaigns, but they don't.

As Erickson put it:

> Strip away the candidate and coalition and it is on the fifth floor of 66 Canal Center Plaza (home to a dozen or more interconnected consulting firms, including FLS Connect and Black Rock Group) where the seeds of Mitt Romney's ruin and the RNC's get out the vote (GOTV) effort collapsed—bled to death by charlatan consultants making millions off the Party, its donors, and the grassroots.
>
> The fifth floor of 66 Canal Center Plaza reveals a tangled web of incestuous relationships among Republican consultants who have made millions all while the GOP went down the tubes. Here the top party consultants waged war with conservative activists and here they waged war with the Democrats. On both fronts, they raked in millions along the way with a more fractured, minority party in their wake. And they show no signs of recognizing just how much a part of the problem they are.[7]

But this financial conflict of interest isn't limited to TV ad placements. During the Bush era, the Republican National Committee developed Voter Vault, a database used to identify and mobilize voters to the polls. It was light-years ahead of anything the Democrats had.

At some point, a partner at FLS Connect, Rich Beeson, went to work at the RNC as political director. Also, the RNC sold its Voter Vault data to FLS Connect and then leased that data back from FLS

Connect. By the end of 2008, activists and others were complaining that the voter vault data was no longer very good.

To most of these highly paid political "strategists," the campaigns of Ronald Reagan are a grade school memory, and growing up in the rarified atmosphere of Capitol Hill, where most of them got their start in politics, they know only one way of winning—raise a lot of money from special interests and buy a lot of negative ads on TV—and earn themselves millions in ad placement commissions in the process.

And most important, don't run as a conservative or take any socially conservative positions that might be at odds with those of the urban elites who dominate the mainstream media.

This advice derives from two sources—one grounded in ignorance and the other in greed.

Most of the Washington insiders who make up the Republican establishment have a warped view of history that seems to end on Election Day 1964 and the defeat of the modern conservative movement's first Republican presidential nominee, Barry Goldwater.

In this warped view of history, a conservative candidate can't win, because Goldwater lost in a landslide. However, since 1964, when Americans were presented with a clear choice between the conservative Republican agenda, and the liberal Democrat agenda, the voters always chose the conservative agenda.

I have previously quoted my old friend, conservative author and former Reagan official Jeff Bell's insight: "Social issues were nonexistent in the period 1932 to 1964," Bell observed. "The Republican Party won two presidential elections out of nine, and they had the Congress for all of four years in that entire period . . . When social issues came into the mix—I would date it from the 1968 election . . . the Republican Party won seven out of 11 [now 12] presidential elections."

The Democrats who have won since 1968—even Barack Obama in 2008—did not play up social liberalism in their campaigns.

In the past twelve presidential elections, the Republican Party ran seven unabashedly conservative campaigns and won seven times.

Every time we run as moderate establishment insiders—think: 1976, 1992, 1996, 2008, and 2012—we lose.

The same can be said of congressional elections which saw Republicans as a permanent and powerless minority until Newt Gingrich crafted the Contract with America in 1994 and Tea Party–backed candidates pushed the establishment GOP off the front page and the TV screen in 2010, running on an unabashedly conservative agenda.

While the ignorance and establishment bias of Washington's Republican insiders is damaging, what is truly destructive is their greed and the conflicts of interest that have become so commonplace among this elite fraternity.

Many of DC's elite Republican consultants actively oppose the platform of the Republican Party and advocate positions at complete odds with the grassroots voters on issues such as same-sex marriage and amnesty for illegal aliens.

Ever wonder why the outcry against Washington's crony capitalism that is heard every day on Main Street rarely finds its way into Republican political campaigns?

Simple—the same consultants who run Republican political campaigns also advise and run ad campaigns for special interests who feed off the largesse of the federal budget—and running an advocacy campaign for Wall Street pays a lot better than your average congressional campaign too.

Constitutional conservative candidates do face a dilemma, though, since the consultants with expertise are overwhelmingly from the GOP establishment. Constitutional conservative candidates have said that they'd like to hire consultants who share their beliefs, but cannot find ones with the level of experience and skills of the establishment GOP consultants.

Here is where one of my Four Horsemen of Marketing would certainly apply. There is a huge hole in the market for constitutional conservative campaign consultants. That hole won't be filled overnight, but conservatives who see this opportunity can "cut their teeth" in local campaigns, then move to state-level candidates. Under sound free-market principles, the cream will rise to the top, and we'll end up with consultants who have our principles and the experience to manage campaigns at the federal level.

Until Republicans throw off the influence of these self-serving insiders, and actually run as principled, limited government, constitutional conservatives, they risk suffering the same fate they suffered in 1976, 1992, 1996, 2008, and 2012, while in the process making millions of dollars for the architects of their defeat.

20

KARL ROVE AND REINCE PRIEBUS GIVE AWAY KEY ELECTIONS IN 2012 AND 2013

T o gain the majority in the United States Senate in 2012, Republicans needed to win a net of four seats in the Senate elections. In the aftermath of the Republican Party's disastrous conduct of the 2012 campaign, it became an accepted fact among the inside-the-Beltway crowd that "the Tea Party cost Republicans control of the Senate."

That is pure hogwash, to put it politely.

The Republican establishment has a long history of opposing primary elections in favor of the kind of backroom deals that allow them to field candidates "anointed by the string-pullers inside the Beltway," as Frisco, Texas, Tea Party organizer Lorie Medina put it, rather than put candidates to the test of a campaign of ideas that requires them to compete with conservatives to earn the Republican nomination for office.

In 2012, the Republican establishment was particularly anxious to manipulate the results of the Republican Senate primaries to avoid what it saw as a dangerous repeat of the nominations of candidates like Christine O'Donnell and Sharron Angle, two Tea Party–backed candidates who lost in spectacular fashion in 2010.

To that end they pulled out all the stops to make sure that

establishment Republicans, such as Texas lieutenant governor David Dewhurst, Florida congressman Connie Mack III, Wisconsin's former governor and Bush cabinet official Tommy Thompson, and Virginia's former Republican governor and senator George Allen, became the Party's Senate nominees.

They also pumped millions into the campaigns of Republican establishment incumbents, such as Indiana's six-term incumbent Richard Lugar, who were perceived to be on the bubble and subject to strong primary challenges from Tea Party–backed candidates.

The result of this attempted manipulation was a virtual wipeout of the Republican establishment's candidates that deprived the GOP of control of the upper house of Congress for the second election in a row.

The three bright spots on the GOP's 2012 Senate election scorecard: Texas senator Ted Cruz, Arizona senator Jeff Flake, and Nebraska senator Deb Fischer all won their races running as limited-government constitutional conservative Tea Party candidates.

They ran against business as usual in Washington; and even if one senator, specifically Senator Jeff Flake, proved to be a disappointment once he got to the Senate, that doesn't negate the fact that what elected all three of them to the Senate in 2012 was a promise to pursue the limited government, constitutional conservative values and legislative goals of the Tea Party.

The charge that the Tea Party cost Republicans control of the Senate rests entirely on the implosion of two conservative Senate candidates—Todd Akin of Missouri and Richard Mourdock of Indiana.

But Akin and Mourdock were not "outsider," first-time Tea Party candidates; both were experienced Republican politicians.

Akin was an incumbent Republican member of Congress who had served six terms in the House and emerged from a tough three-way Republican primary to claim the Missouri Republican Senate nomination.

Mourdock was the sitting Indiana State treasurer who ran for office several times before winning a tough statewide campaign to become Indiana's chief financial officer. He made a name for himself opposing Obama's Chrysler bailout for taking extra-legal action that favored the United Auto Workers union over the Indiana State Employees' Pension Fund. Mourdock defeated incumbent Republican senator Richard Lugar in a hard-fought Republican primary that saw a majority of Indiana's Republican county chairs oppose Senator Lugar's renomination.

What's more, the blunders of Akin and Mourdock had nothing to do with the Tea Party's limited government, constitutional conservative agenda—they each put their foot in their mouths dealing with the Democrats' "war on women" campaign gambit—a line of attack that Republicans still have not realized can be countered by attacking the extreme liberal positions of the Democrats on partial-birth abortion, taxpayer funded abortions, and the Democrats' opposition to "born alive" laws.

In the course of a radio interview, Todd Akin, a good and decent man known for his effective advocacy of the right to life, came forth with the astonishing claim:

> Well you know, people always want to try to make that as one of those things, well how do you, how do you slice this particularly tough sort of ethical question. First of all, from what I understand from doctors, that's really rare. If it's a legitimate rape, the female body has ways to try to shut that whole thing down. But let's assume that maybe that didn't work or something. I think there should be some punishment, but the punishment ought to be on the rapist and not attacking the child.[1]

Akin immediately apologized and clarified what he characterized as a "misstatement," but that wasn't enough for Reince Preibus, Karl Rove, and the National Republican Senatorial Committee—they wanted Akin out of the race, to be replaced by the candidate of their choosing, or they would pull all funding from Akin's campaign.

When Todd Akin stumbled, the establishment GOP power brokers immediately caved in to Democrat-driven liberal media pressure and demanded that Akin relinquish the Republican senate nomination he had just won in a hard-fought Republican primary— a primary, we might add, that he won in large measure because he ran as a principled, pro-life candidate, in opposition to a Chamber of Commerce–type, Big Government establishment Republican.

Akin refused to quit and doggedly worked and campaigned his way to make it a real horse race with McCaskill, despite being outspent by millions of dollars in liberal interest group and union money.

The GOP power brokers pulled all support for Akin's campaign, worked to discourage other donors from helping him, and attacked him relentlessly—even though his Democratic opponent, Senator Claire McCaskill, remained extremely unpopular, and Akin, despite the heavy handicap of establishment GOP opposition, remained competitive to the very end.

A month out from Election Day, Akin was in a statistical tie with McCaskill, yet Republican National Committee chairman Reince Priebus and the barons of the establishment GOP announced that they would not give a penny to their Missouri GOP Senate candidate, even if he were *tied* in the polls.

That's right; the chairman of the Republican National Committee, Reince Priebus, said, "He [Akin] could be tied. We're not going to send him a penny."

Senator John Cornyn, chairman of the National Republican Senatorial Committee, said that the group did not plan to help Todd Akin.

Karl Rove even said, "We should sink Todd Akin. If he's found mysteriously murdered, don't look for my whereabouts!"

Their stated reason: political correctness–driven paranoia about Akin's foot-in-mouth comments on abortion.

One would think that after Todd Akin's difficulties the Republican National Senatorial Committee would have had an "all hands" to help Republican candidates navigate the Democrats' "war on women" campaign and polish their answers to the inevitable questions about abortion as it relates to rape.

Apparently not. In Richard Mourdock's case, the actions—or inaction—of the Republican national leadership, was even more egregious.

Mourdock—Indiana's GOP Senate candidate—was presented with a pivotal question from a reporter during a "debate." The question set up the Democratic "war on women" line of attack by asking about his stance that abortions should be illegal in all instances, except those where the mother's life is in danger. Here's what Mourdock said: "I struggled with it myself for a long time, but I came to realize life is that gift from God. And I think even when life begins in that horrible situation of rape, that it is something that God intended to happen."[2]

Mourdock's Democratic opponent Congressman Tom Donnelly was behind at that point in the campaign and was quick to pounce on Mourdock's apparent misstep. "I think rape is a heinous and violent crime in every instance. The God I believe in and the God I know most Hoosiers believe in, does not intend for rape to happen—ever. What Mr. Mourdock said is shocking, and it is stunning that he would be so disrespectful to survivors of rape."[3]

Mourdock quickly clarified his remarks, saying: "God creates life, and that was my point. God does not want rape, and by no means was I suggesting that he does. Rape is a horrible thing, and for anyone to twist my words otherwise is absurd and sick."

But the comments were already going viral and played straight into the Democrats' "war on women" narrative, which, of course, was exactly what the reporter asking the question intended.[4]

Democratic National Committee chair Debbie Wasserman Schultz quickly got into the act with a statement saying:

> Richard Mourdock's rape comments are outrageous and demeaning to women. Unfortunately, they've become part and parcel of the modern Republican Party's platform toward women's health, as Congressional Republicans like Paul Ryan have worked to outlaw all abortions and even narrow the defini-

tion of rape. As Mourdock's most prominent booster and the star of Mourdock's current campaign ads, Mitt Romney should immediately denounce these comments.[5]

The Romney campaign promptly obliged Ms. Wasserman Schultz through a statement issued by campaign spokeswoman Andrea Saul, stating, "Gov. Romney disagrees with Richard Mourdock's comments, and they do not reflect his views." Saul did not respond when asked whether Romney still supported Mourdock.

Notice a pattern here?

When conservatives put their foot in their mouth, establishment Republicans run for the hills, or worse yet, join the Democrats in attacking them. In this case Mourdock was fatally wounded, perhaps as much by Romney's prompt disavowal as by his own inartful words.

Yet, when George Allen made his race-tinged comments referring to a heckler of Indian heritage as a "Macaca," or monkey, in 2006, no one tried to drum him out of the Republican Party—the GOP establishment demanded conservatives close ranks with the damaged candidate. In 2012, far from disavowing the damaged Allen, the establishment showered him with money and buried the other contenders in the Virginia Republican Senate primary in a mountain of cash.

Why the double standard?

Establishment Republicans are consumed with being accepted by the establishment elite. They don't want to be seen as right-wingers or social conservatives; they want to get invited to all the nice parties in Georgetown more than they wanted to win the majority in the Senate.

And frankly, they wanted to teach conservatives a lesson. They want us to do what we are told, rather than to do whatever it took to win the Missouri and Indiana Senate seats.

Had the shoe been on the other foot, as it was when establishment Republican senator George Allen made a racially charged comment that sank his 2006 campaign, had Mourdock or Akin been the establishment's first choice, the inside-the-Beltway Republican leadership would have been all over conservatives to shore up their faltering candidate.

So the two conservatives, both decent and honorable men, who put their foot in their mouths, were quickly abandoned by the leaders of the national Republican establishment and lost two winnable Senate seats.

If the Republican Party's failure to capture the Senate majority rests on the failure of Akin and Mourdock, that must mean that most of the Republican establishment's favored Senate candidates all won.

So, how did all the candidates that were handpicked by the Republican National Senatorial Committee, the Republican National Committee, and Karl Rove's American Crossroads PAC fare?

First Lady of the conservative movement Phyllis Schlafly summed up the results nicely in a post-election column:

> Of the 31 races in which Rove aired TV ads, Republicans won only 9, so his donors got little return on their investment. . . . Rove's Establishment losers included Rick Berg who lost in North Dakota and Denny Rehberg who lost in Montana, even while Romney was carrying both those states. Other Establishment losers were George Allen in Virginia, Tommy Thompson in Wisconsin, Connie Mack in Florida and Heather Wilson in New Mexico.[6]

Phyllis Schlafly also made this point: "There are two reasons why Rove and his rich donors don't like grass-roots Republicans and Tea Partiers. The Establishment can't order them how to vote, and the Establishment wants candidates to talk only about economic issues, never about social, moral, or national-security issues."

Club for Growth president Chris Chocola had it pretty well right when he told *NewsMax*: "The question isn't why Todd Akin and Richard Mourdock lost—we know why they lost," said Chocola. "The question is really why did Heather Wilson in New Mexico,

Rick Berg in North Dakota, Denny Rehberg in Montana, Tommy Thompson in Wisconsin, George Allen in Virginia and Linda Lingle in Hawaii—why did they lose?"[7]

Or perhaps more precisely, why did establishment Republican Senate candidates lose—even in several states Mitt Romney won—while Ted Cruz bucked the establishment through a hard-fought primary where he was outspent, and seemingly outgunned, to win the primary runoff and the general election?

Throughout 2011 and 2012 I said repeatedly that the battle to be the Texas GOP Senate nominee was the most important Senate election of 2012.

Through a grassroots campaign based on the clear and unafraid advocacy of limited-government constitutional conservative principles, Tea Party–backed Texas Senate candidate Ted Cruz overcame long odds and forced establishment favorite Lt. Gov. David Dewhurst into a runoff in the race for the open Texas US Senate seat.

"Dewhurst failed to get a majority because he failed to fight for conservative principles. His false attacks backfired," Senator Jim DeMint, a Cruz supporter, tweeted the night of the first primary.

According to the *Dallas Morning News*, Dewhurst, who spent more than $20 million in personal funds to get elected lieutenant governor in 2002, had already spent $10 million from his own pocket on the Senate primary.

Third-place-finisher former Dallas mayor Tom Leppert endorsed Dewhurst in the runoff, even after his campaign lashed out at Dewhurst, calling him "a career politician who is willing to lie in order to win at any cost."

Cruz, who was endorsed by the Tea Party Express, Freedom-Works, the Club for Growth, the Constitutional Conservatives Fund, the Senate Conservatives Fund, Sarah Palin, and others connected to the Tea Party, was one of three key US Senate candidates to advance with backing from the Tea Party movement.

As a Hispanic, limited-government constitutional lawyer, Ted Cruz was seen as a game changer for conservatives—and he hasn't disappointed. Cruz's youthful energy, intellect, and constitutional scholarship have been like adding an entire division to the small, but rapidly growing army of conservatives in the US Senate.

Cruz was exactly the kind of conservative "boat rocker" conservatives want to send the Senate to change how Washington works.

On the other hand, to borrow a phrase from David Grant, the *Christian Science Monitor*'s congressional correspondent, Dewhurst's endorsement page "read more like the RSVPs for an A-list Austin lobbying shindig."

"What we need in the Senate is a fighter," Cruz told town hall meetings around Texas. "We don't need another establishment, career politician that's going to put his arm around the Democrats and keep compromising in growing the size and spending and power of the federal government."

While Cruz and his supporters were entitled to a night to celebrate and a morning to recuperate after forcing the runoff with Dewhurst, Cruz's path to the nomination was by no means clear.

As Rachel Rose Hartman of ABC News observed, Dewhurst remained "experienced, personally wealthy, well-connected and will continue to enjoy support from Gov. Rick Perry and other prominent politicians."

Once Cruz forced Dewhurst into a runoff, the real campaign began. Dewhurst, the establishment candidate, appeared ready to spend whatever he thought it would take to win. Ted Cruz could only win the run off if Tea Partiers and grassroots conservatives kept the momentum going and got to work to match Dewhurst's money and inside connections with grassroots enthusiasm and organization.

Dewhurst had the money, including his own wealth, but what he lacked was the grassroots support that Cruz was solidifying, and Dewhurst ran a typical establishment Republican consultant-driven campaign: one negative ad after another.

As one reporter noted, Dewhurst's campaign only succeeded in raising name recognition for Cruz. According to Texas GOP Vote:

[I]n the original primary, both men received nearly equal percentage of Tea Party members, but this changed in the runoff as Cruz captured three quarters of Tea Party voters. Dewhurst's negative ads not only backfired and gave Cruz a lifeline, it also showed that Dewhurst had little to offer the voters. You would have figured that the Lt. Governor of a job-creating state would be able to give the voters positive reasons to vote for him. He didn't.[8]

Dewhurst actually lost votes from the first primary to the runoff election. In the end it was really no contest; Cruz won the runoff with 57 percent of the vote, while Dewhurst collected 43 percent. More than 1 million Texans voted in the runoff, a surprisingly strong turnout for balloting that came during the dog days of summer.

Even though Dewhurst outspent Cruz 3–1, and blasted him with negative television ads—they apparently did not stick.[9]

How did Cruz do it?

According to Frisco Texas Tea Party leader Lorie Medina, one of the key Tea Party organizers for Cruz, it was because local grassroots conservatives out organized, out hustled, and out worked the establishment candidate.

The Cruz campaign removed the political consultant class and replaced it with "a new political infrastructure powered with low cost, state-of-the-art, voter contact technologies."

Still, the Cruz campaign was not an "everyone do their own thing" operation—it was disciplined, and kept focused on the message of change in Washington and electing a "boat-rocker" who would follow limited-government constitutional conservative principles as the next senator from Texas.

But could the Ted Cruz campaign that Lorie Medina and other Texas Tea Party movement activists organized work elsewhere?

Former *New York Times* election guru Nate Silver showed it can, and it did. Silver analyzed Republican insurgent campaigns in 2012 and found that the grassroots challengers were able to win nearly half of the primary races against the GOP establishment candidates despite being massively outspent five to one or even ten to one.[10]

Ted Cruz's 2012 nomination and election sent a strong signal that a new, limited-government constitutional conservative Republican Party is being born. It is up to us to rear it and nurture it to adulthood.

You would think that after the 2012 election the national Republican leadership would be out looking for candidates that could replicate the grassroots victories of candidates like Ted Cruz and Deb Fischer, but quite the reverse occurred. Rather than nurture conservative candidates in tight races, the Republican Party's national leadership all but abandoned one of their rising stars— Virginia's candidate for governor Ken Cuccinelli.

Cuccinelli, who had risen to national prominence as an outspoken advocate of the right to life and the first state attorney general to file suit against Obamacare, was in a tough race against Democrat and Clinton confidant Terry McAuliffe.

Cuccinelli was facing a huge fund-raising deficit. However, instead of offering help to make up the fund-raising deficit he was facing, even as President Obama and Bill and Hillary Clinton pulled out all the stops, and the checkbooks of their Hollywood friends, to fund a savage media campaign against Cuccinelli, the RNC actually cut back on the funds committed to the Virginia governor's race as compared to the funds committed to Bob McDonnell's campaign of just four years earlier.

Defeating Ken Cuccinelli was the top priority of a motley coalition of secular liberals and self-interested establishment types who want to continue to loot the state treasury for special favors and benefits at the expense of Virginia's hard-pressed working families.

Unless you were closely paying attention to the Virginia governor's race, you might not know that Terry McAuliffe received enormous help from national unions, abortion interests, and a Texas billionaire environmentalist who began his involvement in Virginia politics by spending $400,000 per week on TV ads on climate change to defeat Ken Cuccinelli.

That national liberal interest groups would go all in for McAuliffe was a given, and to be expected.

That the national Republican leadership would actually starve Cuccinelli's campaign for funds in the crucial final weeks of the campaign was unprecedented.

Sean Davis, cofounder of thefederalist.com and a former advisor to conservative senator Tom Coburn and Texas governor Rick Perry, claimed in an election night tweet that the RNC spent more than three times more in the 2009 race in Virginia than in the 2013 Virginia governor's race. Principled limited-government constitutional conservative author and talk show host Mark Levin claims the RNC didn't even spend $3 million compared to the $9 million spent in 2009.

Even worse than the lack of financial support was the fact that the national leadership of the Republican Party engaged in a summer-long whispering campaign against Ken Cuccinelli that more or less mirrored the Democrats' charge that Cuccinelli was an "extremist," and the organizations controlled by national Republicans gave only nominal support to Cuccinelli.

In 1964, the attacks against Goldwater as a scary "extremist" did not start with the Democrats in the general election campaign—the attacks started with the "Stop Goldwater" campaign organized by establishment Republicans, such as Michigan governor George Romney, father of 2012 establishment Republican presidential nominee Mitt Romney.

The attacks on Goldwater from the Republican establishment didn't stop when he became the official presidential nominee of the Republican Party. Romney and others in the "Stop Goldwater" gang never endorsed Barry Goldwater, did nothing to help him and much to hurt his already uphill campaign.

The conduct of the Republican leadership and many of Virginia's nominally Republican business community leaders and the national Republican organizations is reflective of the precedent the Republican establishment set in the treatment of Barry Goldwater.

When an establishment Republican—such as Mitt Romney—

gains a nomination for office, the Republican leadership demands that conservatives close ranks with establishment Republicans and support the nominee, even if that nominee refuses to campaign as a conservative and has an anti-conservative record. But when a conservative gains a nomination, establishment Republicans are free to criticize the nominee and to do everything they can to undercut the conservative's campaign.

Ken Cuccinelli did not lose because he is a principled limited-government constitutional conservative. Cuccinelli lost because he was all but abandoned by the national leadership of his own party, who allowed him to be drowned in a sea of money and then hit from behind by a Republican establishment that would rather see a Democrat in the governor's mansion than end the "good ol' boy" politics in the Virginia State House and allow a real conservative anywhere near the levers of power, where he might actually make good on his promises to govern as a limited-government constitutional conservative.

21

IT'S THE PRIMARIES, STUPID!

Why do I keep repeating, "It's the primaries, stupid!"? Simple, because for more than a hundred years, we conservatives have had our political guns trained on the wrong target. We've been focused on defeating the liberal, Big Government Democrats, when the first, and most important, roadblock to our goal of governing America according to conservative principles is the progressive, Big Government Republicans.

During the entire centuries-long civil war in the Republican Party, the progressive establishment leadership of the GOP has been selling the notion that the Democrats and the liberals are the problem, and that if conservatives would only line up behind establishment Republicans and put them in charge of the federal government, the growth of government and America's slide toward socialism would stop.

Nothing could be further from the truth.

Democrats have purged conservatives from their party. At the national level there are no conservative Democrats, but there is a small group of smart politicians, like West Virginia Democrat Joe Manchin, who talk like moderates or conservatives on some issues.

The Democratic party is the party of secular liberals, and they present a coherent worldview of government, and growing government, as the solution to every problem—and the means by which to impose those solutions on the rest of society.

Establishment Republicans, on the other hand, are not the conservative party. Establishment Republicans do not offer a coherent conservative worldview as an alternative to the Democrats' secular liberal worldview; they pursue policies that are "Democrats-lite," and they govern as "dime store Democrats," simply growing government at a slightly slower pace. Consequently, the abusive bureaucracies and extra-constitutional rules and regulations, which establishment Republicans either support or to which they offer little or no opposition, have continued to grow.

Moreover, the GOP establishment has been complicit in one of the worst abuses Washington's insiders have perpetrated on America's taxpayers—the Democrats' decades-long program that has wasted tens of billions of taxpayer dollars on slush funds for left-wing causes such as NPR, Public TV, Legal Services Corp., Planned Parenthood, radical environmentalism, homosexual and ethnic advocacy groups such as La Raza, and the various ACORN clones of the Left, that so offend conservatives and are committed to defeating Republicans and advancing a far Left agenda.

Far from shrinking government, whenever they have been in power establishment Republicans have contributed to the growth of government. The GOP leadership can't hide behind the excuse that they only control one-half of one branch of government—when Republicans had the White House, House of Representatives, and Senate, funding for Planned Parenthood still increased because they were simply not prepared to go to war to defund it.

Until we conservatives control the Republican Party and nominate conservative candidates who will actually fight for and govern according to the conservative principles the party stands for, there will be no coherent alternative to the Democrats' Big Government worldview presented to the voters, and little likelihood that we conservatives will achieve our goal of governing America according to conservative principles.

The Republican establishment loves to promote what they call the "Buckley Rule." To paraphrase comments William F. Buckley Jr. made regarding Richard Nixon: "The wisest choice would be the one who would win. No sense running Mona Lisa in a beauty contest. I'd be for the most right, viable candidate who could win. If you could convince me that Barry Goldwater could win, I'd vote for him." Richard Nixon, he said, would be the strongest GOP candidate.[1]

The problem is, people who like to cite the "Buckley Rule" forget that a very few years later William F. Buckley Jr. was leading a group of conservatives who publicly announced they were pulling their support for Nixon and his re-election because he had betrayed conservative principles. Nixon was no conservative and neither are most of the candidates who cite the "Buckley Rule" as a reason for conservatives to back them.

It is also worth noting that Buckley supported the idea of defeating liberal Republicans as a matter of principle or party discipline. To that end he later formed a PAC and organized opposition to liberal Republican senator Lowell Weicker that in 1988 helped elect Joe Liebermann to the US Senate, saying, "We want to pass the word that it's okay to vote for the other guy or stay at home."[2]

Merely having an *R* next to your name on the ballot does not mean you will hold fast to limited-government constitutional conservative principles. As I've documented elsewhere here and in my previous book *Conservatives Betrayed*, the time that President George W. Bush occupied the White House, and the Republican establishment led a Republican majority in Congress certainly demonstrates such a claim is false.

As I noted in the early chapters of this book, during the New Deal and Democrat Franklin D. Roosevelt's three campaigns for reelection, Republicans never nominated a conservative. Alf Landon, the 1936 GOP presidential candidate who had supported Theodore Roosevelt's Progressive third party in 1912; Wendell L. Wilkie (a former Democrat who had been a pro-Roosevelt delegate at the 1932 Democratic National Convention), who was the GOP candidate in 1940; and, Thomas E. Dewey, governor of New York, and the GOP presidential candidate in 1944 and 1948 were the candidates of Big Business and the Big Government Republican establishment.

What's more, we can go back through election after election and discern a pattern where Big Government progressive Republicans fought conservatives as hard as or harder in the primaries than they fought the Democrats in the general election.

Goldwater was savaged as an "extremist" by the establishment of the Republican Party in his 1964 campaign, from the earliest primaries and state conventions right through the November election—there was no establishment effort to unify the party behind Goldwater, such as establishment Republicans demanded of conservatives when Nixon, George H. W. Bush, Dole, McCain, and Romney were the nominees.

Indeed, when conservative Ronald Reagan ran and won the Republican nomination for governor of California in 1966 by defeating establishment Republican George Christopher, the former mayor of San Francisco, several prominent establishment Republican organizations pointedly refused to endorse him—even in the general election!

Christopher had been doing exactly what big-city Democratic mayors were doing at the time—like bringing the New York Giants to San Francisco, developing Candlestick Park, and engaging in an expansive program of "urban renewal," freeway building, and other massive government-funded public works projects.

Imagine for a moment what history might be like if the GOP's progressive establishment had prevailed and Ronald Reagan had been defeated in his 1966 campaign for the Republican nomination for governor of California by the now virtually forgotten Christopher.

Or let's look at Republican primaries another way—what if a limited-government constitutional conservative had run in and won another important 1966 election—that for the US House of

Representatives for Texas's Seventh district. Arguably, George H. W. Bush's political career would have been stopped before it got started, and there likely would have never been a President George H. W. Bush, or a President George W. Bush, or a Governor Jeb Bush.

Or what if a conservative had run against Oregon's establishment Republican senator Mark Hatfield in the 1990 Oregon Republican primary and won? A conservative could have been on the floor of the Senate in 1995 to cast the deciding vote in favor of the Balanced Budget Amendment, instead of killing it by voting against it as Hatfield did—the lone Republican senator to do so.

The fact of the matter is, policies that have grown the federal government and grown spending have advanced regardless of whether Democrats or Big Government progressive establishment Republicans are in power. The only time government has not grown is when there were enough conservatives in Washington who were willing to stand and fight for limited government, constitutional conservative principles.

When Ronald Reagan was president, discretionary domestic spending went down by 1.4 percent, the only time it has done so in over sixty years. When conservatives held sway in the House of Representatives, spending was curtailed, the deficit went to zero, and the federal government actually had budget surpluses—with Democratic president Bill Clinton in the White House.

How did those conservatives get to Washington?

It's the primaries, stupid!

What would today's political narrative be if limited-government constitutional conservatives had not won the 2010 Republican Senate primary in Kentucky and Utah, and the 2012 Texas Republican Senate primary?

The old-line establishment Republican–affiliated power brokers would have been happy to have Utah Senator Robert Bennett back, instead of his replacement, boat-rocking Senator Mike Lee, and with Mitch McConnell's acolyte Trey Grayson in the Senate, instead of Rand Paul, there would be no pushback against the

Obama administration's shredding of our right to privacy and the Fourth and Ninth Amendments to the Constitution.

And with establishment Texas lieutenant governor David Dewhurst in the Senate, instead of boat-rocking, limited-government constitutional conservative Ted Cruz, all the special interests that contributed to Dewhurst's campaign would by now have had their fill of pork funded by hard-pressed federal taxpayers. Increasing the debt ceiling would be just another routine vote in Congress, and Obamacare would be just another bad law Americans have to live with, instead of the existential battles over the unlimited growth of government that Ted Cruz has made them.

In the 1950s and 1960s, the conservative movement was a coalition built around two issues: economic conservatism and anti-communist national defense conservatism. This gave us a base to occasionally win an election, but was not enough to build a successful national conservative party.

That all changed in the latter part of the 1970s when social conservatives added their strength to the movement and Ronald Reagan came forward as the standard-bearer for conservative ideas.

We won three landslide presidential elections in the 1980s, but we were still only slowing the erosion of our freedoms because we were still burdened by the dead wood of the business-as-usual wing of the Republican Party, and its addiction to Democrat-lite policy and spending.

For fifty years I have been saying that to change things and stop the slide to socialism, two things needed to happen: first, things need to get really bad really fast; and second, there needs to be some political vehicle, some means for the people to channel their anger, and to translate their outrage into political action. Guess what: we're there.

The failure of Republican president George W. Bush to deliver on his promise of conservative governance, coupled with the excesses and corruption of the Republican Congress, have so alienated conservative voters that they began to look outside the Republican establishment for new leaders and for a new vehicle to translate their anger and outrage into political action.

And when Barack Obama was elected president, with a Democratic majority in Congress, things got real bad, real fast.

Once, twice, three times a day, Obama is going to do something to make you angry—that's okay. Take thirty or forty seconds maximum to let off some steam, and then fall down on your knees and thank the good Lord for the excesses of Obama, Harry Reid in the Senate, and Nancy Pelosi as Speaker of the House.

Within thirty days of Obama's inauguration, the Tea Party movement rose from nothing, but the concern of ordinary Americans for the future of their country, to challenge Big Government Republicans and create a vehicle that translated conservative outrage into a fifty-seat turnover in the US House of Representatives.

And with the rise of the Tea Party came the opportunity—no guarantee, just the opportunity—to end the erosion of our liberties and return us to the constitutional principles our Founders envisioned.

The Tea Party has added a fourth leg to the three-legged stool that supported the conservative movement for the past thirty-five years, to create a large and stable table upon which to build a real conservative governing coalition.

And in addition to sheer numbers at the ballot box, the Tea Party—unfettered by old ties and old relationships with Washington's Republican establishment—has brought a new willingness to engage in the primary election battles necessary to prune away the dead wood of the Republican establishment and make way for the growth of a new Republican Party committed to limited-government constitutional conservatism.

Tea Party influence in Republican primaries will ensure that voters have a stark choice between Big Government Republicans, who have been complicit in the Democrats' decades-long campaign to recast America into a collective-centered society built around an intrusive central government, and limited-government constitutional conservative candidates who stand for American exceptionalism based on individualism, liberty, and the sanctity of the human spirit.

The turnaround we've been working for isn't going to happen with one election. We will have much work to do to find and support candidates who are prepared to fend off the inevitable calls to return to the old ways of compromise instead of principle. As we enter the 2014 and 2016 election cycles, I'm more optimistic about the future of this great country than I've ever been, because Tea Partiers and other liberty loving voters are finally beginning to understand—*it's the primaries, stupid!*

22

THE LIBERTY PRIZE: PRACTICAL IDEAS
TO TAKE OVER THE GOP

The focus of this book is one of the most important political battles in American history—and this battle is not between Republicans and Democrats or between Liberals and Conservatives. It is inside the Republican Party.

It is the battle for control of the Republican Party between establishment Big Government Republicans and limited-government constitutional conservatives.

For the one hundred–plus years this battle for the soul of the Republican Party has been raging, conservatives have often been blamed for Republican defeats, including the 2012 debacle, despite the fact that, while substantial majorities of Americans back conservative positions on the growth of government, balancing the budget, and traditional values, conservatives have been excluded consistently from the leadership of the Republican Party.

As the second decade of the twenty-first-century advances, it has become clear that establishment Republican and Democratic politicians have failed America because they have both accepted Big Government. as the solution to every problem.

Far from making "progress" in the sense of advancing liberty and unleashing the potential in every human being, these "progressive" Big Government policies have taken us backwards to a time when people were ruled by the decrees of kings, and a small, self-perpetuating elite made all the decisions.

If we are to save what makes America exceptional, *we the people*—grassroots conservatives—must lead.

As the Bible tells us in Proverbs 11:14, "For lack of guidance a nation falls, but many advisers make victory sure."

That is the same concept upon which *New Yorker* business columnist James Surowiecki based his best-selling book *The Wisdom of Crowds*. Large groups of people are smarter than an elite few, no matter how brilliant—better at solving problems, fostering innovation, coming to wise decisions, even predicting the future.

What could be in tune more with the ethos of the Tea Party movement and its grassroots, bottom-up approach to politics and government than "crowdsourcing" a plan for conservatives to take over the Republican Party and govern America according to conservative principles by 2017?

On February 15, 2013, I announced on the Conservative HQ website "The Liberty Prize," a $10,000 prize to generate ideas and plans for the limited-government constitutional conservative takeover of the Republican Party, and urged grassroots conservatives to organize teams to brainstorm ideas or submit a plan for publication in a book.

To facilitate the process I suggested that entrants gather their Tea Party, Republican Club, or friends and neighbors around a table and work through the Vision-Goal-Strategy-Projects/Tactics process that Newt Gingrich had used to help the leaders of the New Right plan our opposition to progressive policies and politicians in the late 1970s and 1980s.

I was overwhelmed by the response—the announcement of the Liberty Prize generated more than a thousand submissions of plans and ideas to guide conservatives to take over the Republican Party and govern America in 2017.

The vast majority of the comments and submissions dwelt upon the sad state of the establishment Republican Party. If there was one theme that ran through the Liberty Prize submissions, it was that Republicans lose elections when they fail to run on, and deliver on, their promises of conservative governance.

Naturally, I agreed with that analysis. While those submissions provided a useful commentary on why conservatives must devote their energies to taking over the GOP, they did not help us find a path forward.

The question was, and is, how do we change things and take over the GOP to make the Republican Party the political home of limited-government constitutional conservatives, and govern America according to conservative principles in 2017?

Two submissions to the Liberty Prize contest stood out as offering practical—but very different—paths forward to accomplish that goal.

One, submitted by longtime Tea Party leaders Michael Patrick Leahy and Lorie Medina of the Real Conservatives National Committee, focused on identifying, recruiting, and, through effective grassroots campaign techniques, nominating and electing limited-government constitutional conservatives to office—particularly to the US House and Senate.

The other was submitted by Republican precinct committeeman and attorney Daniel J. Schultz of Tempe, Arizona, author of *Taking Back Your Government: The Neighborhood Precinct Committeeman Strategy*, and it focused on getting conservatives elected to Republican Party office—starting with precinct committeeman.

Dan Schultz's great insight was that the best tool for defeating the Democrat Party at the polls is the Republican Party, but it is weak and ideologically split because not enough conservatives engage in the real ball game of politics—party politics—at the grassroots level as precinct committeemen.

Dan's submission focused on getting limited-government constitutional conservatives to become involved in their local Republican Party organization and, ultimately, to become the leaders of the Republican Party at the local, state, and national levels.

We had two solid ideas about how to take over the GOP, but

which one was right and which one offered the best path to accomplishing the goal set forth in the Liberty Prize announcement?

Conservatives have indeed begun to master the tools of grassroots politics and campaigning.

As Lorie Medina and Michael Patrick Leahy have demonstrated in the formation of the Real Conservatives National Committee, and their well-focused campaign to defeat incumbent Tennessee establishment Republican senator Lamar Alexander, this includes "RINO hunting." Defeating establishment Republican incumbents is an important part of accomplishing our goal of governing America according to conservative principles in 2017.

However, electing limited-government constitutional conservatives to office, and especially defeating Big Government Republican incumbents, is substantially more difficult if the Republican Party apparatus remains in the hands of the establishment.

As I have documented throughout this book, the greatest impediment to conservative governance is not the Democrats and liberals—it is the progressive leadership of the Big Government Republican establishment in the halls of Congress, state houses, and at Republican Headquarters, especially at the Republican National Committee.

Just look at the record of the manipulation of the party rules at the Republican National Convention to rob Taft of the presidential nomination in 1952; the attacks on Goldwater as an "extremist" in 1964; the party rules changes in 2012 designed to freeze out Ron Paul supporters at the Republican National Convention; and in 2013 the financial starvation of Ken Cuccinelli's campaign for governor of Virginia.

All of the grassroots commitment and shoe leather conservatives put into nominating their candidates is wasted if, after we win the nomination, our conservative candidates are undercut and defeated by the opposition of their own party leadership.

Did that mean Dan Schultz was right and fielding candidates for precinct committeeman, county chairman, and state committeeman and state committeewoman should be our top priorities?

The answer is, they were both right. I split the $10,000 Liberty Prize between the two submissions and have included summaries of their ideas and plans to provide you with practical ideas on how to take over your Republican Party.

THE REAL CONSERVATIVES NATIONAL COMMITTEE PLAN

In the analysis of Michael Patrick Leahy and Lorie Medina, the Republican establishment—as led by the Republican National Committee and its associated organizations—is unduly influenced by a tight-knit and corrupt cabal whose primary purpose is not to win elections for Republicans but to ensure that a small group of well-connected consultants will remain in power and control the lucrative donations that generous (but uninformed) Republican donors continually provide them.

The Republican establishment and its consultants continue to campaign with the tools of past eras while the Democratic Party and the left wing have for over a decade been operating an innovative, technology-driven, highly market-segmented operation that relies heavily on person-to-person, door-to-door, and digital communications.

The results have been predictable. Democrats won the Senate and the House in 2006, and the presidency in 2008 and 2012. The technology advantage the Democrats have continues to widen. The Republican establishment is bringing a toothpick to a gunfight.

The Republican National Committee and its associated organizations are totally incapable of competing technologically with the Democrats. Nor do they show any inclination to change their strategy.

In Leahy and Medina's analysis, the Republican establishment consultants who currently control the RNC are not conservatives, competent campaign practitioners, or honest and reliable people. Their primary function is to drain the bank accounts of Republican donors, transfer that wealth to themselves, and deliver inferior campaign management services to Republican candidates through a tightly controlled crony system.

These services are so outdated that the candidates who receive them are at a competitive disadvantage. While doing all this, the elite GOP "crony consultants" minimize and deny the value of grassroots campaign technology, and marginalize candidates and activists that really want a conservative America.

Leahy and Medina predict that left to their own devices, it is highly likely the Republican establishment will not be able to maintain control of the House in 2014. With a Democratic-controlled House and Senate in the last two years of a Democratic president's final term, there will be no constitutional constraint on President Obama's unconstitutional actions that will destroy the free-market country we know and love.

When Obama won in 2012, he did not have an overwhelming national mandate. Obama won because he successfully and brilliantly won hundreds of micro campaigns all across America. Only through advanced technology can conservatives compete in any significant way. For example, we must master the science and execution of micro-targeting church-attending home school families through meaningful communication.

The way for conservatives to do that, and to win in the primary and general elections, is to mount aggressive get-out-the-vote campaigns that focus on person-to-person communication, using what voters tell them on the doorstep to craft personalized messages of encouragement and support delivered through a state-of-the-art, analytics-driven data base and communication system.

To accomplish this vision, conservatives must change the way the Republican primary election game is played so as to give qualified, boat-rocking conservative candidates like Ted Cruz and Rand Paul far better chances of defeating establishment Republicans.

Medina and Leahy said that grassroots conservatives can do so by first removing the political consultant class from the process of selecting and managing conservative candidates. Then replacing them with a new political infrastructure powered with low-cost, state-of-the-art, voter contact technologies that draws its manpower from the largely volunteer conservative grassroots army that has sprung to life over the past four years and is now awaiting a path to victory.

What's more, this new political infrastructure can be created at a fraction of the cost of the stodgy, tired, expensive television advertising–driven campaigns of establishment Republicans managed by the political consultant class.

The Real Conservatives National Committee plan started with these simple propositions:

- Do not hire Washington-based consultants to drive your messaging and fund-raising.

- Do not spend most of your money on wasteful television commercials.

- Do not focus on needless and ineffective rallies and petitions.

- Do give local control to local groups.

- Do be respectful to local organizations and groups.

- Do provide local groups needed resources, unlike Washington-based groups, which take resources from them.

Leahy and Medina point out that to begin the process, volunteers must be taught how to use the voter contact system by participating in a fun day of door-to-door political canvassing. Their activities consisted of door-to-door canvassing of Republican primary voters, using state-of-the- art smartphone technology that integrates with sophisticated databases, as well as old-style paper-and-clipboard data collection. For the volunteers who do not have smartphones, walk lists from the database management system can be printed, and the results of the door-to-door canvass can be inputted the old-fashioned way.

The Real Conservatives National Committee conducted a "National Ground Game Day" on May 25, 2013—Memorial Day weekend—that was a smashing success.

Obviously, key to making the Real Conservatives National Committee plan work is finding an inexpensive, tested, reliable, robust, easy-to-use database that tracks voter behavior at the individualized level. The Real Conservatives National Committee has tested and recommends Moonshadow Mobile's Ground Game mobile application.[1]

Leahy and Medina researched numerous other technologies, and say none compare from a tech or finance standpoint; accordingly, they selected Moonshadow Mobile as the Real Conservatives National Committee's exclusive voter canvassing technology partner. Ground Game was used by a number of political campaigns during the 2010 and 2012 election cycles. During the 2012 election cycle, former Reagan administration official Tom McCabe's Associated Strategies used Ground Game in four campaigns. Three of the four races in which it was deployed resulted in conservative victories:

- Two State of Washington State Senate Races

- One congressional race—Keith Rothfus, (R-PA)

In the fourth race, an incumbent congressional candidate, Ann Marie Buerkle (R-NY), was defeated, a result due in large part to redistricting by the Democratic Party–controlled state legislature.

These past election results show that the most effective way to influence undecided voters, or to confirm committed voters, is to deliver six "communication touches" between the initial canvass and Election Day.

To be most effective the grassroots campaign must deliver these follow-up contacts or "communication touches" in four ways:

1. E-mail communications

2. Text messages

3. Follow-up personal visits at the voter's residence, with a brief conversation and literature drop

4. The alternative media of direct mail

These were used by Tom McCabe and Associated Strategies in the four campaigns they worked on in the 2012 election cycle.

In addition to the focus on using effective grassroots campaign tactics and tools to defeat the Republican establishment's typical advantage in money and fatal addiction to consultant-run TV campaigns, Leahy and Medina offered two other important insights.

First, the grassroots campaign to Republican primary voters must focus on the three core values of the Tea Party movement: constitutionally limited government, free markets, and fiscal responsibility. They must demonstrate how those values support public policies that influence the key issues identified for each voter in the door-to-door canvassing.

Second, conservatives should strive to avoid splitting the conservative vote in the primary, and establish a "vetting" process or some means of coalescing grassroots constitutional conservatives around one candidate. This is the key to fielding the best challenger to an incumbent establishment Republican, or to an establishment Republican who has been, as Lorie Medina once said, "anointed by the string-pullers inside the Beltway" as the favored candidate in an open seat.

TAKING BACK YOUR GOVERNMENT: THE NEIGHBORHOOD PRECINCT COMMITTEEMAN STRATEGY

Dan Schultz's plan took an entirely different tack from the elective office–focused approach of Lorie Medina, Michael Patrick Leahy, and their Real Conservatives National Committee strategy. What

Dan says is, "Calling talk radio stations does not really DO much. Twittering and ranting in chat rooms about what's happening does not really *do* much." If you want to save your country, then "you MUST become a ballplayer in the real ballgame of politics: It is your civic duty to become involved in Party politics."

Schultz goes on to point out that conservatives have the power and the numbers to take back their government from the current crop of officeholders who seem hell-bent on ignoring the strictures of the United States Constitution and foisting socialism upon Americans, but to do so we conservatives have to do more than complain or read a book—we have to invest a few hours a month in attending the meetings of our local Republican Party.

Every square inch of the United States is within a "political neighborhood," a precinct. When you vote, your polling place is your precinct's polling place. Your precinct has a number and, probably, a name. Dan Schultz lives in precinct number 918, Tempe 59. His precinct has eight precinct committeemen. He is one of them. Each of them was elected in the primary election. To get on the ballot, each of them had to get ten signatures from Republicans or independents in the precinct. That's it. Ten signatures.

Schultz says it took him about forty minutes to get the signatures—the Party gave him a "walking sheet" for his precinct that told him in which houses Republicans and independents lived. In some precincts, the precinct committeemen only had to get three signatures. Every state has a different system. Some, like Arizona and Ohio, elect the leaders in their precincts. Other states require meeting attendance and dues. None of the requirements are onerous. Schultz has compiled links on his website to some of the states' rules relating to how to become a leader in your precinct.

Encouraging conservatives to run for precinct committeeman has been a longtime goal of the First Lady of the conservative movement, Phyllis Schlafly. Her e-pamphlet *The Most Powerful Office in The World Is NOT The President of the United States!* is a great starting point and primer on the importance of the precinct committeeman in Republican politics.

How is this a strategy for taking over the Republican Party and governing America according to conservative principles in 2017?

It is simple. We have a two-party political system. One group of Americans has hijacked the Democrat Party and has been able to fool enough Americans to vote for their candidates, who usually run as "moderates." Another group of Americans has hijacked the Republican Party, which claims to represent conservatives, but all too often governs from the same Big Government progressive perspective as the so-called moderate Democrats.

Phyllis Schlafly calls precinct committeeman and women "the most powerful political office in the world," because they determine who gets the chance to be elected to office at every level of government. Schlafly sagely observes:

- To change things, we must change the laws.

- To change the laws, we must change the people who make them.

- To get elected, your candidate must be on the ballot.

- To get on the November ballot you must win the Primary.

- To win the Primary, you must get the support of people who make endorsements in the Primary, who reliably vote in the Primary, and who get out the vote of others in the Primary.

Those people are the precinct committeemen.

Now, here is the open secret establishment Republicans don't want you to know: *half* of the Republican precinct committeeman slots, on average, in 2008, in every state, were *vacant*. (In Arizona, where Dan Schultz is from, he says it was worse—over *two-thirds* of the slots were vacant; now, they are almost up to half strength.)

And the currently filled slots are split about fifty-fifty between conservatives and "Republicans In Name Only" (RINOs). What if conservatives could fill up all the vacant slots?

As Dan Schultz said: Do the math.

The Republican Party would be transformed from a half-strength, ideologically split party into a full-strength, 75 percent majority conservative political juggernaut.

Why have I never heard about this? you are probably wondering. And more important, why have you never heard about this before from your local Republican Party?

Dan Schultz says that it is because virtually all Republican incumbents, including many who profess to be conservative, are terrified that you and other conservative Americans will figure this out and replace them, too, because they have not fought hard enough to preserve your liberties.

They are terrified a more principled conservative adversary might get the backing of a majority of precinct committeemen in their district and state and throw out the incumbents. Like the new, conservative grassroots Tea Partiers and 9.12-ers did in Utah in 2010, denying incumbent senator Robert Bennett the primary nomination by keeping him off the ballot and endorsing boat-rocking senator Mike Lee at the Utah GOP state convention. In 2012 Indiana incumbent establishment Republican Richard Lugar was opposed by over half the Republican county chairs in the state, and likewise lost the primary.

What's more, precinct committeemen—and only precinct committeemen—get to vote in the party elections that determine the leadership of the party.

Think of it. The more conservatives who become precinct committeemen, the more conservative the party, and its candidates, will become. The Party again might appear to the voters to offer a clear choice from the Democrat Party, rather than an echo of it.

Precinct committeeman is a volunteer position. You put into it the effort you can and want. Some will do more, some less. But, even if you put in only two or so hours a month, you will be making a real difference, especially in light of the fact that you will be eligible to vote for your local party leaders.

As a precinct committeeman, you will also be eligible to attend your county committee meetings and elect your county leaders. You will be eligible to attend the party nominating convention (assuming you can get elected as a delegate). You could even become your state party chairperson or one of the two Republican National Committee members from your state.

If you want to see establishment Republican Reince Priebus replaced as Republican National Committee chairman with a principled, limited-government constitutional conservative, then you have to start in your neighborhood by running for precinct committeeman or woman.

Dan Schultz says you can't blame the incumbent elected officials and the existing party leaders for keeping the large number of vacancies a secret—their goal is to hold on to their power.

He blames us.

There are thousands and thousands, probably hundreds of thousands, of Americans who are now active in the Tea Party movement and other conservative grassroots organizations, who want the Constitution to be followed, who by their mere existence demonstrate we have the *numbers* to take back the Republican Party.

This strategy is not rocket science. Just good, old-fashioned, basic American civics. What Tea Partiers and limited-government constitutional conservatives seem to lack is the basic civics information on how to become precinct committeemen and women—and the curiosity to dig it out.

Start by asking around. If you don't know who your Republican precinct committeeman is, chances are the office is vacant or he or she is a do-nothing RINO who is holding down the job merely for the "honor" of the title, not to restore constitutional government to America.

If you can't find the Republican Party rules for your state online, which should set forth the rules for electing precinct committeemen, you should be able to get the necessary forms from your local election official, such as the county clerk or supervisor of elections.

In some counties your interest will be welcome—in others, not so much.

You may be seen as a threat to the establishment, so you need to be the judge of how public you want to make your efforts. If you get the cold shoulder from your local Republican organization, don't be surprised, but don't be dissuaded—in most states precinct committeeman is an elected office, and you have just as much right to run as any other person who meets the qualifications.

You can go to our website at www.goptakeover.org for information to supplement what Dan Schultz and Phyllis Schlafly have compiled.

What's Dan Schultz's plan for conservatives to take over the Republican Party and govern America according to conservative principles by 2017?

In its simplest form it is this: *Elect a majority of Republican precinct committeemen who subscribe to limited-government constitutional conservative principles in every county in America.*

Can such an audacious plan be accomplished?

Yes, if YOU file and run for precinct committeeman or woman in your precinct.

23

VIGUERIE'S PLAN FOR CONSERVATIVES TO TAKE OVER THE GOP AND GOVERN AMERICA BY 2017

arlier in this book I told you about "Viguerie's Four Horsemen of Marketing," which are:

- Position (a hole in the marketplace)

- Differentiation

- Benefit

- Brand (what makes you singular or unique)

The Republican establishment is losing elections because they have failed utterly to apply my four principles to politics.

POSITION

As Democrats-lite they occupy no unique position or hole in the marketplace of ideas; Democrats own the position of the party that delivers ever-increasing services and "benefits" of Big Government to "clients," and Republicans are never going to be able to outbid the Democrats for those votes, nor should they want to.

DIFFERENTIATION

As progressives, "me too" Big Government Republicans have little or no way of positively differentiating themselves from Big Government Democrats. They long ago surrendered any claim to being the party of good government and joined, and then exceeded, the Democrats in their pay-to-play cronyism and special interest–driven corruption.

BENEFIT

The benefit of electing an establishment Republican eludes most voters, but it appears to be framed by the GOP's Capitol Hill establishment as something along the lines of "vote for us, and socialism will creep over America a little slower," and we run a more efficient Big Government.

BRAND

Brand is really defined by a combination of the other three elements; it is what makes Republicans unique and stand apart from Democrats. So it is little wonder that in the hands of the current Republican establishment leadership, the Republican Party's brand has been diluted to the point that it is seen by conservatives and conservative-leaning independents as little better, and maybe, because it is so hypocritical, even worse than the Democrats.

To help you understand how to apply my Four Horsemen of Marketing, I've selected an organization and a politician to illustrate by example how to apply these marketing concepts to you or your organization.

Rand Paul, Kentucky's junior senator, elected to the United States Senate in 2010.

Position (hole in the marketplace)
Limited government, constitutional conservative with significant libertarian leanings.

Differentiation
Rand Paul consistently approaches public policy from a strongly libertarian perspective, making him the only libertarian-leaning US senator. That, combined with his close association with his libertarian father, differentiates Rand Paul from all other US senators.

Benefits
Paul appeals to important parts of the voting public that Republicans need and have trouble reaching—Libertarians and young people. He inherits much of his father's political base (supporters and donors), but not the negatives.

Brand (what makes Rand Paul singular/unique)
Articulate, attractive, and ambitious libertarian leaning in domestic, foreign policy, and social issues, popular with the Tea Party movement, but still remains in the mainstream of Republican and independent voters.

Students for Life (SFL) Is a large pro-life organization, headquartered in Manassas, Virginia, led by a dynamic young wife and mother, Kristan Hawkins.

There are numerous good pro-life organizations, but it's hard to tell how most differ from the others. And if you want to be effective, you'll need lots of members, money, and media attention. But it will be difficult for this to happen unless you positively separate your organization from your competition in the public's mind.

Position (hole in the marketplace)

SFL starts with a strong advantage because their name separates them from all other pro-life groups.

Differentiation

SFL differs from all other pro-life organizations because their leadership is young and their audience is exclusively students, and a youth organization is seen as being best equipped to communicate with other youth.

Benefit

Supporters, and potential supporters of the pro-life cause, as well as the media, can easily and quickly grasp the importance and effectiveness of young people counseling other young people.

Brand (what makes SFL singular/unique)

This is a combination of the other three, plus what SFL has done with the stories they tell, graphics, social media, website, etc., to stand apart from all the other pro-life groups.

In the words of America's best-known marketer, Seth Godin, in a field of cows that all look alike, you can't tell one from another; however, if one is a purple cow, it stands out. Students for Life is a purple cow standing apart from all other pro-life groups.

But the establishment Republican Party is no purple cow—like the Democratic Party, it is merely another vehicle for advancing Big Government and the spending, deficit, debt, and loss of liberty that goes with Big Government.

The only way for the Republican Party to reestablish its brand, and start governing America is for it to become differentiated from the Democrats. And the only way for Republicans to do that is for the GOP to become the political home of limited-government constitutional conservatives, and then to field candidates who will actually articulate, campaign on, and govern according to those principles.

Too often we conservatives have gone to bed after a hard-fought campaign, such as the 2010 congressional elections, thinking our candidates had won and conservative governance was just over the horizon. However, even though our candidates defeated both the Democrats and Republican establishment candidates, the push for conservative governance stalled because the leadership of the Republican Party remained firmly in the hands of establishment insiders.

That means limited-government constitutional conservatives must not only run in and win Republican primary elections; they must also run for and win Republican Party leadership positions.

Or to put it in a way that even teenage kids can understand; we need to (politically) walk and chew gum at the same time.

I wish I could hand you a plan that was guaranteed to accomplish that goal, but I can't. Formulating such a plan, given the vast number of precincts and counties in this country and the state-specific rules and regulations governing elections for public and Republican Party office, is beyond the scope of any book or the powers of any individual.

What I can do is give you a plan for a plan, a road map of how to formulate your own specific plan for winning your local precinct committeeman campaign or your campaign for public office, be it city council or United States Senate, and for rebuilding the Republican Party's brand in the process.

Don't be intimidated by the notion that you have to go through the process of planning to accomplish your vision and goals—you do the same thing every day. For example:

Vision: enjoy quality time this evening with the family

Goals: eat together and play a game after

Strategy: have everyone participate either by cooking, setting the table, or cleaning-up

Tactic: fix family's favorite food and choose a board game that the children will enjoy

See, it's not so hard after all.

So, I invite you to gather your friends, family, Tea Partiers, and limited-government constitutional conservatives around your kitchen table or living room. Set up the whiteboard or a scratch pad, as we did at my home when the leaders of the New Right planned the strategy and tactics we used to help put the Reagan Revolution in motion.

Start by writing Vision, Goals, Strategy, and Tactics on that blank sheet of paper, and then with the wisdom and input of your team, identify the activities necessary to accomplish your vision, and the names, dates, and dollars needed to accomplish your plan.

It doesn't matter if your vision is as simple as running for precinct committeeman in your precinct or as complex as Ted Cruz's decision to run for the Senate; this model can work for you, because it worked for those of us who helped build the conservative coalition that elected Ronald Reagan.

VIGUERIE'S PLAN

VISION

For limited constitutional government, liberty, and freedom under God's laws to be the guiding principles governing America by 2017:

GOALS IN 2014

1. Elect 300+ new principled conservatives to the state legislatures

2. Elect 30+ new principled conservatives to the US House of Representatives

3. Elect 8+ new principled conservatives to the US Senate

4. Defeat 8+ establishment Republican members of the US House of Representatives

5. Defeat 2+ establishment Republican members of the US Senate (Alexander, TN; Cochran, MS; Cornyn, TX; Graham, SC; McConnell, KY, Roberts, KS)

6. Elect 100,000 principled conservative Republican precinct committeemen in the approximately 186,000 precincts in America

7. Have conservatives take control of a majority of the GOP state committees

8. Elect a majority (85+) of principled conservatives to the 162-member Republican National Committee, giving conservatives control of the RNC

9. Have conservatives' top three or four issues dominate the public policy debate

10. Celebrate for no more than one day; then get to work on 2015 goals

GOALS IN 2015

1. Continue working on any unachieved 2014 goals

2. Replace the chairman of the RNC, Reince Priebus, with a principled conservative

3. Have conservatives' top three or four issues dominate the public policy debate

GOALS IN 2016

1. Continue working on any unachieved 2014 and 2015 goals

2. By February, unite conservatives behind a principled conservative Republican candidate for president

3. Nominate a principled conservative for president

4. Nominate a vice presidential nominee who will unite the four main voting blocs of the twenty-first-century

Republican base: social conservatives, economic conservatives, Tea Partiers, and libertarians

5.   Focus the 2016 election on conservatives' top three to four issues so that when we win we will have a mandate to govern

6.   Elect a principled conservative as president

7.   Celebrate Election Night, perhaps all the following day (after all, how often do we elect a conservative president and Congress?), then get to work on 2017 goals

GOALS IN 2017

1.   Demand that in the first 100 days Congress pass major elements of the agenda we campaigned on in 2016

2.   Demand replacement of all executive branch political appointees with principled, limited-government constitutional conservatives

3.   Demand the new Congress launch government-wide investigations of abuses of the Obama administration, including, but not limited to the IRS, NSA, NLRB, ATF, EPA, and the attorney general and leadership of the Department of Justice

4.   Demand that the president and Congress repeal all unconstitutional and illegal executive orders issued by President Obama

STRATEGY

1. Before the filing date for elective office in your state, including precinct committeeman and all Republican Party offices, gather like-minded individuals together to use this model to formulate a plan to field limited-government constitutional conservative candidates and

take over the Republican Party at the level at which you operate in politics and public life. If you are involved in politics in your county, gather your Tea Party and other limited-government constitutional conservatives to develop a Vision, Goals, Strategy, and Tactics plan for your county. If you are a state leader of a conservative organization, bring together your peers to do the same.

2. Field a candidate in every public office or party race (local, state, and federal) except where an incumbent principled conservative is running.

3. Avoid having two or more conservatives in the same race if there is an establishment Republican running—unless there is a runoff requirement if no one gets a majority.

4. Qualities to look for in a candidate

    a.   Boat rocker

    b.   Walks with conservatives

    c.   Well-read on conservative philosophy

    d.   Will put the Constitution, and their conservative principles, above party leaders

    e.   Has a personal record of achievement commensurate with the level of the office being sought

    f.   Is above reproach in their personal and business life

    g.   Is committed to building the conservative movement

    h.   Will vote to replace all establishment Republican leaders: local, state, and federal

5. The first law of politics is "define or be defined." Be quick to define the following in the public's mind by applying my Four Horsemen of Marketing to:

    a. Your candidate or organization

    b. Your opponents

6. Give the voters a "tune they can whistle," such as:

    a. My opponent is a Big Government, borrow-and-spend, establishment Republican.

    b. My opponent is a crony of the failed Big Government Republican establishment.

    c. My opponent supported Obamacare by voting for the October 2013 continuing resolution and for the Ryan–Murray spending deal (not committed to abolishing Obamacare).

    d. My opponent is financed by Karl Rove–type establishment Republican crony capitalist groups—American Crossroads, US Chamber, and their stealth committees.

    e. My opponent puts earmarks above principles.

    f. My Republican opponent's campaign is being run by Big Government establishment consultants, not the conservative grass roots.

7. Run on the issues voters are talking about, such as:

    a. The failure of the Republican establishment to prevent the growth of government (Obamacare, unconstitutional NSA snooping and IRS criminal abuses; funding for left-wing groups such as Planned Parenthood, La Raza, and others)

    b. The out-of-control spending that causes debt, high taxes, inflation

c. An immoral debt being passed on to our children and grandchildren

d. America under Democratic leadership is in decline

e. Amnesty for illegal aliens

f. Term limits

g. Fairness: for example, is it fair for politicians to burden our children and grandchildren with massive debt so they can win reelection?

h. Crony capitalism: the axis between Wall Street and Washington to loot the taxpayer

i. Need for new, mostly young, effective leadership—most of the present leaders have failed us

8. Use the problems and failures of Obamacare to indict the entire Democratic Party worldview. Help the voters connect the dots to demonstrate how almost all Big Government programs are bankrupt and lead to loss of liberty, mandates, higher taxes, and almost dictatorial rule by Obama and a small elite of unaccountable Washington bureaucrats.

9. Depending on the race, develop and promote a vision for your community, town, county, state, America. We not only need to articulate what we're opposed to, but the voters need to understand that conservatives have ideas, plans, and a vision of how to make things better. Remember, every election is about the future.

10. Conservatives need to develop new, big ideas and promote solutions at every level of government. Consider:

a. Reform of health care and health insurance (tort reform, sell insurance across state lines, reduce red tape for doctors, etc.)

b. Reform of the criminal justice system (see appendix 5)

c. Reining in government abuse of property rights

d. Opposing Common Core, and support reform of failing, union dominated public schools

e. Privacy issues, such as NSA snooping, IRS, police surveillance cameras, and red-light cameras.

f. Mental health

11. Study and receive the training necessary to become proficient in grassroots campaign technology, and build the infrastructure, including training people, necessary to execute effective grassroots campaigns, be it in a city, county, state legislature, congressional district, or state.

12. Field candidates for every open precinct committee position, and every other "RINO-occupied" Republican Party position, who will campaign for the office and stress that they will actually "do the job" and work to maximize the Republican vote, not just hold down the position as an honorary title.

13. Remember, the Republican Party Rules and election laws are formulated to protect the establishment status quo. You may be attacked or have a complaint filed against you for any violation. Become proficient and well versed in the Republican Party Rules, and have experts in election law and campaign finance rules available to advise you so that you do not make "rookie mistakes" that sink your campaign or divert precious resources from getting the maximum conservative vote to the polls.

14. Don't expect or rely upon a few big donors or special-interest money. Use the new and alternative media, grassroots fund-raising

techniques, and person-to-person contacts to solicit donations and volunteers from the grass roots.

15. Always be on the attack and respond immediately if attacked. Especially in the "war on women," show Democrats as the "extremists" on abortion, parental rights, defense of traditional marriage, their other antireligious freedom positions, and other issues where they are out of step with the majority of Americans.

16. Do not make the rhetorical and strategic blunder of sounding as though you oppose a social safety net. Speak in favor of policies that support civil society, a safety net for the vulnerable, and encouraging every citizen to achieve his or her fullest potential.

17. Work to increase the minority vote for conservatives. It is a mistake to assume that minority voters are automatically opposed to the conservative agenda. Conservative positions on social issues and economic opportunity resonate well in minority communities. One of the great bastions of social conservatism is the African-American church, and many immigrant voters have first-hand experience with political oppression, corruption, and crony capitalism in their country of origin. Ronald Reagan and Jack Kemp kept to conservative principles and connected with these voters, so can you.

    a.   Perhaps the most effective way to get minority votes is to recruit and run qualified conservative minority candidates for public and party office—especially those with substantial populations in your area be they Jewish, Hispanic, Asian, African-American, South Asian, or other religious or ethnic minorities.

    b.   Campaign on issues of importance to minorities that the establishment is wrong on, including, but not limited to, traditional marriage, the right to life, and the Democrats' attacks on open displays of religious faith.

c.   Freedom is the best route to economic advancement. Be outspoken in your advocacy of economic liberty, and advocate making it easier to own and operate small businesses and climb the economic ladder. Oppose the red tape, rules, and regulations overwhelming small business owners.

d.   Attack crony capitalism where politicians and big business collude to enrich themselves and their friends and keep the ruling class in control at the expense of the rest of us.

e.   Strongly advocate for education reform, especially fixing failing left-wing Democrat, union-dominated schools. Support providing access to a quality education for all children through such innovations as charter schools and school choice programs.

f.   *Target, target, target.* Speak to new voters in language they understand and embrace the traditions they have brought to America; campaign in minority communities and at religious and cultural festivals as appropriate. Respect the cultural traditions of the new Americans whose votes you are seeking.

18. Work to increase the youth vote for conservatives. Older voters are more likely to be loyal to their party and are usually not as persuadable as younger voters. Younger voters have their own unique set of concerns that make them prime candidates to be persuaded to become limited government constitutional conservatives. Let younger voters know that conservatism is not only best for their futures, but it is "cool" to be a conservative.

a.   Recognize that young voters are not just the urban elite portrayed on TV. They are also young parents who are working hard to raise small children, buy their first home, start a business, and take the first steps up the economic ladder. Identify and advocate family friendly policies relevant to the office you seek and your community.

b. Attack the out-of-control wasteful spending that politicians use to get reelected, such as the Bridge to Nowhere, and frame your opposition as opposition to debt that will be passed on to and paid by today's young voters.

c. Attack the unfair cost burden and mandates of Obamacare for young workers.

d. Connect the dots. Explain how Obamacare, with its loss of freedom, excessive costs and bureaucratic mandates is typical of all government programs and is the inevitable result of where left-wing Democrats and Big Government Republicans are taking America.

e. Freedom is the best route to economic advancement. Be outspoken in your advocacy of economic liberty, and advocate making it easier to own and operate small businesses and climb the economic ladder. Oppose the red tape, rules, and regulations overwhelming small business owners.

f. Attack the creation of Big Government high tech surveillance programs and the limits on privacy, freedom of conscience and freedom of expression that goes with it.

g. Attack crony capitalism where politicians and big business collude to enrich themselves and their friends and keep the ruling class in control at the expense of the rest of us; especially new entrants into the marketplace and those who are just starting out.

h. *Target, target, target.* Hunt where the ducks are and where the younger voters congregate; be online and on social media; connect with church youth groups, young family organizations, and service clubs; and make your events family friendly. Take interest in what younger folks are doing and saying, listen to them, and engage them.

i. Do not judge a book by its cover. Younger voters will follow new fashion and music trends, hairstyles and ways of speaking. You are working to build your coalition, not acting as the fashion police; embrace young voters for their idealism, energy and enthusiasm for conservative politics, whether or not you share their choices in music and clothes. Remember that our parents didn't always understand our ways in our younger days, and yet we turned out alright.

TACTICS

1. Grow the human capital of the conservative movement in your area by organizing a real campaign for every candidate. Make sure every race includes a campaign manager, treasurer, volunteer coordinator, fund-raising chairperson, Internet and social media coordinators, and press or media relations coordinator. Get people involved—give them assignments and titles.

2. Invest in your human capital by having your key people attend leadership and campaign training schools, such as the Leadership Institute. Also consider hosting training by experts in grassroots campaign techniques, such as Lorie Medina and Michael Patrick Leahy of the Real Conservatives National Committee.

3. Get online! Become computer and social media literate: Use Facebook, Twitter, MySpace, Linkedin, YouTube, build your own website, etc., to expand your connections and build your online community and brand, and engage in regular and ongoing communication with conservative voters.

4. Use Vertical Response or similar e-mail management software to build a mailing list of people in your circle of influence, and communicate at least weekly via e-mail, social media, postal mail, or all three.

5. Hone your grassroots campaign techniques and grow your organization by conducting "ground game" days or other grassroots canvassing and voter contact projects.

6. *Read, read and read*: Invest in yourself. Start with the books in the appendix. If you are well grounded in the arguments and history of conservative ideas, you will be more confident and effective in leading and arguing public policy.

7. *Educate, educate, and educate*: not only yourself but others. Make sure that all of your activities include an educational component. Start book clubs, discussion groups, etc. Follow Saint Paul's example: don't be embarrassed to speak out in public, and to talk to your friends, family, and circle of influence about your political beliefs and the truths of conservatism.

8. *Attack, attack, and attack*: whether you are in a primary or general election, draw a bright line and a clear contrast between you and your opponent. Make sure voters understand, particularly on the growth of government, taxes, and the social issues, that your opponent is out of the mainstream of American opinion.

9. Stay current on events from the conservative perspective; subscribe to at least two print conservative publications.

10. Regularly visit principled conservative websites such as:

    a. ConservativeHQ.com

    b. WND.com

    c. RedState.com

    d. Breitbart.com

e. Townhall.com

f. Heritageaction.com

g. Clubforgrowth.com

h. AmericanThinker.com

11. Don't feed the opposition: only support financially those organizations, businesses, causes, and candidates that support your worldview. This includes refusing to support liberal colleges, schools, churches, charities, professional associations, and especially the GOP national committees, as long as they are led by big-government, establishment Republicans (and when solicited, tell them why you are saying no). In 2014 this includes:

a. Republican National Committee

b. Republican Congressional Campaign Committee

c. Republican Senate Campaign Committee

d. Those state GOP committees run by the Republican establishment

12. Use small dollar events to expand your base and open up the campaign to supporters of all means; not everyone can be persuaded to go door-to-door, but most everyone likes good food, and the person who buys a ticket to your barbecue or bake sale is a donor, voter, and a potential volunteer.

13. Never accept the questions or scenarios presented by the establishment media. Don't get sucked in to their warped view of reality. Be armed with the facts and ideas to push back and explain why liberty and freedom under God's laws is always preferable to the "safety" provided by Big Government and the state.

14. Develop conservative solutions to the problems facing the area in which you are seeking office. Don't accept the idea that government is the best or only solution; propose solutions to problems that empower individuals and save the taxpayers money.

15. Don't work in isolation. Connect with other limited-government constitutional conservatives and organizations to strategize, grow your base, expand your knowledge, and build your brand.

16. Go to www.goptakeover.org and review the plans submitted by Liberty Prize winners Michael Patrick Leahy and Lorie Medina of the Real Conservatives National Committee, and read *Taking Back Your Government: The Neighborhood Precinct Committeeman Strategy* by Liberty Prize winner Dan Schultz, available through Amazon for just 99 cents.

17. Learn to present your arguments with a smile. The establishment, especially the media, wants to convince others that conservatives are angry "haters." In reality we conservatives are happier than liberals according to social scientists, and the reason why should be clear; we have our families, our homes, our churches, and our faith to inspire our efforts, and we rely upon ourselves for our success. When you are out campaigning or going door-to-door, just remember you are doing this for your children and grandchildren, and smile.[1]

ACKNOWLEDGMENTS

For all of my entrepreneurial life, I've been blessed with many talented people without whose help I would have achieved very little. And that's certainly true for this book. Most published authors devote almost full time to writing their books. However, in my case, I'm engaged in dozens of important projects, including helping run a seventy-five person national direct-marketing agency. Therefore this book would not have been possible without the active involvement of many people.

My coauthor of *America's Right Turn*, David Franke, and I had dinner in the summer of 2012 at Carmelo's, an excellent Portuguese-Italian restaurant, in Old Town Manassas, Virginia. As I was outlining my ideas for the book, David said, "Takeover," and I quickly agreed that was the obvious title.

David and I worked on the first part of the book for a few months until health issues prevented him from continuing. At that point I enlisted George Rasley, the editor of Conservative HQ.com, to help me with the book, and George and I spent most of 2013 writing *TAKEOVER*.

As a veteran of over three hundred political campaigns, who served in elected and appointed positions from city hall to the White

House, George's experience and advice were invaluable to me in translating the history of the over one hundred years of civil war in the Republican Party (and my fifty-plus years of experience on the front lines of it) into a practical guide for conservatives to finally win that civil war and take over the GOP.

David and George weighed in with excellent ideas and advice; however, I alone am responsible for the contents of *TAKEOVER*.

In addition to David and George, I received invaluable help from Mark Fitzgibbons, my friend, attorney, and president of legal affairs at American Target Advertising, Inc. In addition to being an outstanding constitutional lawyer, Mark volunteers many hours of his time and talent to local and national Tea Party leaders and individuals fighting for their property rights.

Others who have helped prepare and promote this book include Joseph and Elizabeth Farah, Geoff Stone, and the highly professional support team at WND.

Diana Banister and Craig Shirley at Shirley and Banister Public Affairs are heavily involved in the marketing of *TAKEOVER*, and finally, a big shout-out to my executive assistant, Bob Sturm, and the rest of my talented team at ATA, and to Art Kelly and Rick Buchanan.

APPENDIX 1

THE SHARON STATEMENT

Adopted by the Young Americans for Freedom Conference at Sharon, Conn., September 11, 1960

IN THIS TIME of moral and political crises, it is the responsibility of the youth of America to affirm certain eternal truths

WE, as young conservatives believe:

THAT foremost among the transcendent values is the individual's use of his God-given free will, whence derives his right to be free from the restrictions of arbitrary force;

THAT liberty is indivisible, and that political freedom cannot long exist without economic freedom;

THAT the purpose of government is to protect those freedoms through the preservation of internal order, the provision of national defense, and the administration of justice;

THAT when government ventures beyond these rightful functions, it accumulates power, which tends to diminish order and liberty;

THAT the Constitution of the United States is the best arrangement yet devised for empowering government to fulfill its proper role, while restraining it from the concentration and abuse of power;

THAT the genius of the Constitution—the division of powers—is summed up in the clause that reserves primacy to the several states, or to the people in those spheres not specifically delegated to the Federal government;

THAT the market economy, allocating resources by the free play of supply and demand, is the single economic system compatible with the requirements of personal freedom and constitutional government, and that it is at the same time the most productive supplier of human needs;

THAT when government interferes with the work of the market economy, it tends to reduce the moral and physical strength of the nation, that when it takes from one to bestow on another, it diminishes the incentive of the first, the integrity of the second, and the moral autonomy of both;

THAT we will be free only so long as the national sovereignty of the United States is secure; that history shows periods of freedom are rare, and can exist only when free citizens concertedly defend their rights against all enemies;

THAT the forces of international Communism are, at present, the greatest single threat to these liberties;

THAT the United States should stress victory over, rather than coexistence with this menace; and

THAT American foreign policy must be judged by this criterion: does it serve the just interests of the United States?"

APPENDIX 2

A TIME FOR CHOOSING

"The Speech" on behalf of Republican presidential candidate Barry Goldwater delivered to a national television audience by Ronald Reagan on October 27, 1964

Thank you. Thank you very much. Thank you and good evening. The sponsor has been identified, but unlike most television programs, the performer hasn't been provided with a script. As a matter of fact, I have been permitted to choose my own words and discuss my own ideas regarding the choice that we face in the next few weeks.

I have spent most of my life as a Democrat. I recently have seen fit to follow another course. I believe that the issues confronting us cross party lines. Now, one side in this campaign has been telling us that the issues of this election are the maintenance of peace and prosperity. The line has been used, "We've never had it so good."

But I have an uncomfortable feeling that this prosperity isn't something on which we can base our hopes for the future. No nation in history has ever survived a tax burden that reached a third of its national income. Today, 37 cents out of every dollar earned in this country is the tax collector's share, and yet our government continues to spend 17 million dollars a day more than the government takes in. We haven't balanced our budget 28 out of the last 34 years. We've raised our debt limit three times in the last twelve months, and now our national debt is one and a half times bigger than all the combined debts of all the nations of the world. We have 15 billion dollars in gold in our treasury; we don't own an ounce. Foreign dollar claims are 27.3 billion dollars.

And we've just had announced that the dollar of 1939 will now purchase 45 cents in its total value.

As for the peace that we would preserve, I wonder who among us would like to approach the wife or mother whose husband or son has died in South Vietnam and ask them if they think this is a peace that should be maintained indefinitely. Do they mean peace, or do they mean we just want to be left in peace? There can be no real peace while one American is dying some place in the world for the rest of us. We're at war with the most dangerous enemy that has ever faced mankind in his long climb from the swamp to the stars, and it's been said if we lose that war, and in so doing lose this way of freedom of ours, history will record with the greatest astonishment that those who had the most to lose did the least to prevent its happening. Well I think it's time we ask ourselves if we still know the freedoms that were intended for us by the Founding Fathers.

Not too long ago, two friends of mine were talking to a Cuban refugee, a businessman who had escaped from Castro, and in the midst of his story one of my friends turned to the other and said, "We don't know how lucky we are." And the Cuban stopped and said, "How lucky you are? I had someplace to escape to." And in that sentence he told us the entire story. If we lose freedom here, there's no place to escape to. This is the last stand on earth.

And this idea that government is beholden to the people, that it has no other source of power except the sovereign people, is still the newest and the most unique idea in all the long history of man's relation to man.

This is the issue of this election: whether we believe in our capacity for self-government or whether we abandon the American revolution and confess that a little intellectual elite in a far-distant capitol can plan our lives for us better than we can plan them ourselves.

You and I are told increasingly we have to choose between a left or right. Well I'd like to suggest there is no such thing as a left or right. There's only an up or down: [up] man's old -- old-aged dream, the ultimate in individual freedom consistent with law and order, or down to the ant heap of totalitarianism. And regardless of their sincerity, their humanitarian motives, those who would trade our freedom for security have embarked on this downward course.

In this vote-harvesting time, they use terms like the "Great Society," or as we were told a few days ago by the President, we must accept a greater government activity in the affairs of the people. But they've been a little more explicit in the past and among themselves; and all of the things I now will quote have appeared in print. These are not Republican accusations. For example, they have voices that say, "The cold war will end through our acceptance of a not undemocratic socialism." Another voice says, "The profit motive has become outmoded. It must be replaced by the incentives of the welfare state." Or, "Our traditional system of individual freedom is incapable of solving the complex problems of the 20th century." Senator Fulbright has said at Stanford University that the Constitution is out-moded. He referred to the President as "our moral teacher and our leader," and he says he is "hobbled in his task by the restrictions of power imposed on him by this antiquated document." He must "be freed," so that he "can do for us" what he knows "is best." And Senator Clark of Pennsylvania, another articulate spokesman, defines liberalism as "meeting the material needs of the masses through the full power of centralized government."

Well, I, for one, resent it when a representative of the people refers to you and me, the free men and women of this country, as "the masses." This is a term we haven't applied to ourselves in America. But beyond that, "the full power of centralized government"—this was the very thing the Founding Fathers sought to minimize. They knew that governments don't control things. A government can't control the economy without controlling people. And they know when a government sets out to do that, it must use force and coercion to achieve its purpose. They also knew, those Founding Fathers, that outside of its legitimate functions, government does nothing as well or as economically as the private sector of the economy.

Now, we have no better example of this than government's involve-ment in the farm economy over the last 30 years. Since 1955, the cost of this program has nearly doubled. One-fourth of farming in America is responsible for 85 percent of the farm surplus. Three-fourths of farming is out on the free market and has known a 21 percent increase in the per capita consumption of all its produce. You see, that one-fourth of farming -- that's regulated and controlled by the federal government. In the last three years we've spent 43 dollars in the feed grain program for every dollar bushel of corn we don't grow.

Senator Humphrey last week charged that Barry Goldwater, as

President, would seek to eliminate farmers. He should do his homework a little better, because he'll find out that we've had a decline of 5 million in the farm population under these government programs. He'll also find that the Democratic administration has sought to get from Congress [an] extension of the farm program to include that three-fourths that is now free. He'll find that they've also asked for the right to imprison farmers who wouldn't keep books as prescribed by the federal government. The Secretary of Agriculture asked for the right to seize farms through condemnation and resell them to other individuals. And contained in that same program was a provision that would have allowed the federal government to remove 2 million farmers from the soil.

At the same time, there's been an increase in the Department of Agriculture employees. There's now one for every 30 farms in the United States, and still they can't tell us how 66 shiploads of grain headed for Austria disappeared without a trace and Billie Sol Estes never left shore.

Every responsible farmer and farm organization has repeatedly asked the government to free the farm economy, but how—who are farmers to know what's best for them? The wheat farmers voted against a wheat program. The government passed it anyway. Now the price of bread goes up; the price of wheat to the farmer goes down.

Meanwhile, back in the city, under urban renewal the assault on freedom carries on. Private property rights [are] so diluted that public interest is almost anything a few government planners decide it should be. In a program that takes from the needy and gives to the greedy, we see such spectacles as in Cleveland, Ohio, a million-and-a-half-dollar building completed only three years ago must be destroyed to make way for what government officials call a "more compatible use of the land." The President tells us he's now going to start building public housing units in the thousands, where heretofore we've only built them in the hundreds. But FHA [Federal Housing Authority] and the Veterans Administration tell us they have 120,000 housing units they've taken back through mortgage foreclosure. For three decades, we've sought to solve the problems of unemployment through government planning, and the more the plans fail, the more the planners plan. The latest is the Area Redevelopment Agency.

They've just declared Rice County, Kansas, a depressed area. Rice County, Kansas, has two hundred oil wells, and the 14,000 people there have over 30 million dollars on deposit in personal savings in their banks. And when the government tells you you're depressed, lie down and be depressed.

We have so many people who can't see a fat man standing beside a thin one without coming to the conclusion the fat man got that way by taking advantage of the thin one. So they're going to solve all the problems of human misery through government and government planning. Well, now, if government planning and welfare had the answer—and they've had almost 30 years of it—shouldn't we expect government to read the score to us once in a while? Shouldn't they be telling us about the decline each year in the number of people needing help? The reduction in the need for public housing?

But the reverse is true. Each year the need grows greater; the program grows greater. We were told four years ago that 17 million people went to bed hungry each night. Well that was probably true. They were all on a diet. But now we're told that 9.3 million families in this country are poverty-stricken on the basis of earning less than 3,000 dollars a year. Welfare spending [is] 10 times greater than in the dark depths of the Depression. We're spending 45 billion dollars on welfare. Now do a little arithmetic, and you'll find that if we divided the 45 billion dollars up equally among those 9 million poor families, we'd be able to give each family 4,600 dollars a year. And this added to their present income should eliminate poverty. Direct aid to the poor, however, is only running only about 600 dollars per family. It would seem that someplace there must be some overhead.

Now—so now we declare "war on poverty," or "You, too, can be a Bobby Baker." Now do they honestly expect us to believe that if we add 1 billion dollars to the 45 billion we're spending, one more program to the 30-odd we have—and remember, this new program doesn't replace any, it just duplicates existing programs—do they believe that poverty is suddenly going to disappear by magic? Well, in all fairness I should explain there is one part of the new program that isn't duplicated. This is the youth feature. We're now going to solve the dropout problem, juvenile delinquency, by reinstituting something like the old CCC camps [Civilian Conservation Corps], and we're going to put our young people in these camps. But again we do some arithmetic, and we find that we're going to spend each year just on room and board for each young person we help 4,700 dollars a year. We can send them to Harvard for 2,700! Course, don't get me wrong. I'm not suggesting Harvard is the answer to juvenile delinquency.

But seriously, what are we doing to those we seek to help? Not too long ago, a judge called me here in Los Angeles. He told me of a young woman who'd come before him for a divorce. She had six children, was pregnant with her seventh. Under his questioning, she revealed her husband was a laborer earning 250 dollars a month. She wanted a divorce to get an 80 dollar raise. She's eligible for 330 dollars a month in the Aid to Dependent Children Program. She got the idea from two women in her neighborhood who'd already done that very thing.

Yet anytime you and I question the schemes of the do-gooders, we're denounced as being against their humanitarian goals. They say we're always "against" things—we're never "for" anything.

Well, the trouble with our liberal friends is not that they're ignorant; it's just that they know so much that isn't so.

Now—we're for a provision that destitution should not follow unemployment by reason of old age, and to that end we've accepted Social Security as a step toward meeting the problem.

But we're against those entrusted with this program when they practice deception regarding its fiscal shortcomings, when they charge that any criticism of the program means that we want to end payments to those people who depend on them for a livelihood. They've called it "insurance" to us in a hundred million pieces of literature. But then they appeared before the Supreme Court and they testified it was a welfare program. They only use the term "insurance" to sell it to the people. And they said Social Security dues are a tax for the general use of the government, and the government has used that tax. There is no fund, because Robert Byers, the actuarial head, appeared before a congressional committee and admitted that Social Security as of this moment is 298 billion dollars in the hole. But he said there should be no cause for worry because as long as they have the power to tax, they could always take away from the people whatever they needed to bail them out of trouble. And they're doing just that.

A young man, 21 years of age, working at an average salary—his Social Security contribution would, in the open market, buy him an insurance policy that would guarantee 220 dollars a month at age 65. The government promises 127. He could live it up until he's 31 and then take out a policy that would pay more than Social Security. Now are we so lacking in business sense that we can't put this program on a sound basis, so that people who do require those payments will find they can get them when they're due—that the cupboard isn't bare?

Barry Goldwater thinks we can.

At the same time, can't we introduce voluntary features that would permit a citizen who can do better on his own to be excused upon presentation of evidence that he had made provision for the non-earning years? Should we not allow a widow with children to work, and not lose the benefits supposedly paid for by her deceased husband? Shouldn't you and I be allowed to declare who our beneficiaries will be under this program, which we cannot do? I think we're for telling our senior citizens that no one in this country should be denied medical care because of a lack of funds. But I think we're against forcing all citizens, regardless of need, into a compulsory government program, especially when we have such examples, as was announced last week, when France admitted that their Medicare program is now bankrupt. They've come to the end of the road.

In addition, was Barry Goldwater so irresponsible when he suggested that our government give up its program of deliberate, planned inflation, so that when you do get your Social Security pension, a dollar will buy a dollar's worth, and not 45 cents worth?

I think we're for an international organization, where the nations of the world can seek peace. But I think we're against subordinating American interests to an organization that has become so structurally unsound that today you can muster a two-thirds vote on the floor of the General Assembly among nations that represent less than 10 percent of the world's population. I think we're against the hypocrisy of assailing our allies because here and there they cling to a colony, while we engage in a conspiracy of silence and never open our mouths about the millions of people enslaved in the Soviet colonies in the satellite nations.

I think we're for aiding our allies by sharing of our material blessings with those nations which share in our fundamental beliefs, but we're against doling out money government to government, creating bureaucracy, if not socialism, all over the world. We set out to help 19 countries. We're helping 107. We've spent 146 billion dollars. With that money, we bought a 2 million dollar yacht for Haile Selassie. We bought dress suits for Greek undertakers, extra wives for Kenya[n] government officials. We bought a thousand TV sets for a place where they have no electricity. In the last six years, 52 nations have bought 7 billion dollars worth of our gold, and all 52 are receiving foreign aid from this country.

No government ever voluntarily reduces itself in size. So, governments' programs, once launched, never disappear.

Actually, a government bureau is the nearest thing to eternal life we'll ever see on this earth.

Federal employees—federal employees number two and a half million; and federal, state, and local, one out of six of the nation's work force employed by government. These proliferating bureaus with their thousands of regulations have cost us many of our constitutional safeguards. How many of us realize that today federal agents can invade a man's property without a warrant? They can impose a fine without a formal hearing, let alone a trial by jury? And they can seize and sell his property at auction to enforce the payment of that fine. In Chico County, Arkansas, James Wier over-planted his rice allotment. The government obtained a 17,000 dollar judgment. And a U.S. marshal sold his 960-acre farm at auction. The government said it was necessary as a warning to others to make the system work.

Last February 19th at the University of Minnesota, Norman Thomas, six-times candidate for President on the Socialist Party ticket, said, "If Barry Goldwater became President, he would stop the advance of socialism in the United States." I think that's exactly what he will do.

But as a former Democrat, I can tell you Norman Thomas isn't the only man who has drawn this parallel to socialism with the present administration, because back in 1936, Mr. Democrat himself, Al Smith, the great American, came before the American people and charged that the leadership of his Party was taking the Party of Jefferson, Jackson, and Cleveland down the road under the banners of Marx, Lenin, and Stalin. And he walked away from his Party, and he never returned til the day he died—because to this day, the leadership of that Party has been taking that Party, that honorable Party, down the road in the image of the labor Socialist Party of England.

Now it doesn't require expropriation or confiscation of private property or business to impose socialism on a people. What does it mean whether you hold the deed to the—or the title to your business or property if the government holds the power of life and death over that business or property? And such machinery already exists. The government can find some charge to bring against any concern it chooses to prosecute. Every businessman has his own tale of harassment. Somewhere a perversion has taken place. Our natural, unalienable rights are now considered to be a dispensation of government, and freedom has never been so fragile, so close to slipping from our grasp as it is at this moment.

Our Democratic opponents seem unwilling to debate these issues. They want to make you and I believe that this is a contest between two men—that we're to choose just between two personalities.

Well what of this man that they would destroy—and in destroying, they would destroy that which he represents, the ideas that you and I hold dear? Is he the brash and shallow and triggerhappy man they say he is? Well I've been privileged to know him "when." I knew him long before he ever dreamed of trying for high office, and I can tell you personally I've never known a man in my life I believed so incapable of doing a dishonest or dishonorable thing.

This is a man who, in his own business before he entered politics, instituted a profit-sharing plan before unions had ever thought of it. He put in health and medical insurance for all his employees. He took 50 percent of the profits before taxes and set up a retirement program, a pension plan for all his employees. He sent monthly checks for life to an employee who was ill and couldn't work. He provides nursing care for the children of mothers who work in the stores. When Mexico was ravaged by the floods in the Rio Grande, he climbed in his airplane and flew medicine and supplies down there.

An ex-GI told me how he met him. It was the week before Christmas during the Korean War, and he was at the Los Angeles airport trying to get a ride home to Arizona for Christmas. And he said that [there were] a lot of servicemen there and no seats available on the planes. And then a voice came over the loudspeaker and said, "Any men in uniform wanting a ride to Arizona, go to runway such-and-such," and they went down there, and there was a fellow named Barry Goldwater sitting in his plane. Every day in those weeks before Christmas, all day long, he'd load up the plane, fly it to Arizona, fly them to their homes, fly back over to get another load.

During the hectic split-second timing of a campaign, this is a man who took time out to sit beside an old friend who was dying of cancer. His campaign managers were understandably impatient, but he said, "There aren't many left who care what happens to her. I'd like her to know I care." This is a man who said to his 19-year-old son, "There is no foundation like the rock of honesty and fairness, and when you begin to build your life on that rock, with the cement of the faith in God that you have, then you have a real start." This is not a man who could carelessly send other people's sons to war. And that is the issue of this campaign that makes all the other problems I've discussed academic, unless we realize we're in a war that must be won.

Those who would trade our freedom for the soup kitchen of the welfare state have told us they have a utopian solution of peace without victory. They call their policy "accommodation." And they say if we'll only avoid any direct confrontation with the enemy, he'll forget his evil ways and learn to love us. All who oppose them are indicted as warmongers. They say we offer simple answers to complex problems. Well, perhaps there is a simple answer—not an easy answer—but simple: If you and I have the courage to tell our elected officials that we want our national policy based on what we know in our hearts is morally right.

We cannot buy our security, our freedom from the threat of the bomb by committing an immorality so great as saying to a billion human beings now enslaved behind the Iron Curtain, "Give up your dreams of freedom because to save our own skins, we're willing to make a deal with your slave masters." Alexander Hamilton said, "A nation which can prefer disgrace to danger is prepared for a master, and deserves one." Now let's set the record straight. There's no argument over the choice between peace and war, but there's only one guaranteed way you can have peace—and you can have it in the next second—surrender.

Admittedly, there's a risk in any course we follow other than this, but every lesson of history tells us that the greater risk lies in appeasement, and this is the specter our well-meaning liberal friends refuse to face—that their policy of accommodation is appeasement, and it gives no choice between peace and war, only between fight or surrender. If we continue to accommodate, continue to back and retreat, eventually we have to face the final demand—the ultimatum. And what then—when Nikita Khrushchev has told his people he knows what our answer will be? He has told them that we're retreating under the pressure of the Cold War, and someday when the time comes to deliver the final ultimatum, our surrender will be voluntary, because by that time we will have been weakened from within spiritually, morally, and economically. He believes this because from our side he's heard voices pleading for "peace at any price" or "better Red than dead," or as one commentator put it, he'd rather "live on his knees than die on his feet." And therein lies the road to war, because those voices don't speak for the rest of us.

You and I know and do not believe that life is so dear and peace so sweet as to be purchased at the price of chains and slavery. If nothing in life is worth dying for, when did this begin—just in the face of this enemy? Or should Moses have told the children of Israel to live in slavery under the pharaohs? Should Christ have refused the cross? Should the patriots at Concord Bridge have thrown down their guns and refused to fire the shot heard 'round the world? The martyrs of history were not fools, and our honored dead who gave their lives to stop the advance of the Nazis didn't die in vain. Where, then, is the road to peace? Well it's a simple answer after all.

You and I have the courage to say to our enemies, "There is a price we will not pay." "There is a point beyond which they must not advance." And this—this is the meaning in the phrase of Barry Goldwater's "peace through strength." Winston Churchill said, "The destiny of man is not measured by material computations. When great forces are on the move in the world, we learn we're spirits—not animals." And he said, "There's something going on in time and space, and beyond time and space, which, whether we like it or not, spells duty."

You and I have a rendezvous with destiny.

We'll preserve for our children this, the last best hope of man on earth, or we'll sentence them to take the last step into a thousand years of darkness.

We will keep in mind and remember that Barry Goldwater has faith in us. He has faith that you and I have the ability and the dignity and the right to make our own decisions and determine our own destiny. Thank you very much.

APPENDIX 3

MORTON BLACKWELL'S LAWS OF THE PUBLIC POLICY PROCESS

1. Never give a bureaucrat a chance to say no.

2. Don't fire all your ammunition at once.

3. Don't get mad except on purpose.

4. Effort is admirable. Achievement is valuable.

5. Make the steal more expensive than it's worth.

6. Give 'em a title, and get 'em involved.

7. Expand the leadership.

8. You can't beat a plan with no plan.

9. Political technology determines political success.

10. Sound doctrine is sound politics.

11. In politics, you have your word and your friends; go back on either and you're dead.

12. Keep your eye on the main chance, and don't stop to kick every barking dog.

13. Don't make the perfect the enemy of the good.

14. Remember the other side has troubles too.

15. Don't treat good guys like you treat bad guys.

16. A well-run movement takes care of its own.

17. Hire at least as many to the right of you as to the left of you.

18. You can't save the world if you can't pay the rent.

19. All gains are incremental; some increments aren't gains.

20. A stable movement requires a healthy, reciprocal I.O.U. flow among its participants. Don't keep a careful tally.

21. An ounce of loyalty is worth a pound of cleverness.

22. Never miss a political meeting if you think there's the slightest chance you'll wish you'd been there.

23. In volunteer politics, a builder can build faster than a destroyer can destroy.

24. Actions have consequences.

25. The mind can absorb no more than the seat can endure.

26. Personnel is policy.

27. Remember it's a long ball game.

28. The test of moral ideas is moral results.

29. You can't beat somebody with nobody.

30. Better a snake in the grass than a viper in your bosom.

31. Don't fully trust anyone until he has stuck with a good cause which he saw was losing.

32. A prompt, generous letter of thanks can seal a commitment which otherwise might disappear when the going gets rough.

33. Governing is campaigning by different means.

34. You cannot make friends of your enemies by making enemies of your friends.

35. Choose your enemies as carefully as you choose your friends.

36. Keep a secure home base.

37. Don't rely on being given anything you don't ask for.

38. In politics, nothing moves unless pushed.

39. Winners aren't perfect. They made fewer mistakes than their rivals.

40. One big reason is better than many little reasons.

41. In moments of crisis, the initiative passes to those who are best prepared.

42. Politics is of the heart as well as of the mind. Many people don't care how much you know until they know how much you care.

43. Promptly report your action to the one who requested it.

44. Moral outrage is the most powerful motivating force in politics.

45. Pray as if it all depended on God; work as if it all depended on you.

APPENDIX 4

THE REPUBLICAN "CONTRACT WITH AMERICA" (1994)

As Republican Members of the House of Representatives and as citizens seeking to join that body we propose not just to change its policies, but even more important, to restore the bonds of trust between the people and their elected representatives.

That is why, in this era of official evasion and posturing, we offer instead a detailed agenda for national renewal, a written commitment with no fine print.

This year's election offers the chance, after four decades of one-party control, to bring to the House a new majority that will transform the way Congress works. That historic change would be the end of government that is too big, too intrusive, and too easy with the public's money. It can be the beginning of a Congress that respects the values and shares the faith of the American family.

Like Lincoln, our first Republican president, we intend to act "with firmness in the right, as God gives us to see the right." To restore accountability to Congress. To end its cycle of scandal and disgrace. To make us all proud again of the way free people govern themselves.

On the first day of the 104th Congress, the new Republican majority will immediately pass the following major reforms, aimed at restoring the faith and trust of the American people in their government:

FIRST, require all laws that apply to the rest of the country also apply equally to the Congress;

SECOND, select a major, independent auditing firm to conduct a comprehensive audit of Congress for waste, fraud or abuse;

THIRD, cut the number of House committees, and cut committee staff by one-third;

FOURTH, limit the terms of all committee chairs;

FIFTH, ban the casting of proxy votes in committee;

SIXTH, require committee meetings to be open to the public;

SEVENTH, require a three-fifths majority vote to pass a tax increase;

EIGHTH, guarantee an honest accounting of our Federal Budget by implementing zero base-line budgeting.

Thereafter, within the first 100 days of the 104th Congress, we shall bring to the House Floor the following bills, each to be given full and open debate, each to be given a clear and fair vote and each to be immediately available this day for public inspection and scrutiny.

1. THE FISCAL RESPONSIBILITY ACT: A balanced budget/tax limitation amendment and a legislative line-item veto to restore fiscal responsibility to an out-of-control Congress, requiring them to live under the same budget constraints as families and businesses.

2. THE TAKING BACK OUR STREETS ACT: An anti-crime package including stronger truth-in-sentencing, "good faith" exclusionary rule exemptions, effective death penalty provisions, and cuts in social spending from this summer's "crime" bill to fund prison construction and additional law enforcement to keep people secure in their neighborhoods and kids safe in their schools.

3. THE PERSONAL RESPONSIBILITY ACT: Discourage illegitimacy and teen pregnancy by prohibiting welfare to minor mothers and denying increased AFDC for additional children while on welfare, cut spending for welfare programs, and enact a tough two-years-and-out provision with work requirements to promote individual responsibility.

4. THE FAMILY REINFORCEMENT ACT: Child support enforcement, tax incentives for adoption, strengthening rights of parents in their children's education, stronger child pornography laws, and an elderly dependent care tax credit to reinforce the central role of families in American society.

5. THE AMERICAN DREAM RESTORATION ACT: A $500 per child tax credit, begin repeal of the marriage tax penalty, and creation of American Dream Savings Accounts to provide middle class tax relief.

6. THE NATIONAL SECURITY RESTORATION ACT: No U.S. troops under U.N. command and restoration of the essential parts of our national security funding to strengthen our national defense and maintain our credibility around the world.

7. THE SENIOR CITIZENS FAIRNESS ACT: Raise the Social Security earnings limit which currently forces seniors out of the work force, repeal the 1993 tax hikes on Social Security benefits and provide tax incentives for private long-term care insurance to let Older Americans keep more of what they have earned over the years.

8. THE JOB CREATION AND WAGE ENHANCEMENT ACT: Small business incentives, capital gains cut and indexation, neutral cost recovery, risk assessment/cost-benefit analysis, strengthening the Regulatory Flexibility Act and unfunded mandate reform to create jobs and raise worker wages.

9. THE COMMON SENSE LEGAL REFORM ACT: "Loser pays" laws, reasonable limits on punitive damages and reform of product liability laws to stem the endless tide of litigation.

10. THE CITIZEN LEGISLATURE ACT: A first-ever vote on term limits to replace career politicians with citizen legislators.

Further, we will instruct the House Budget Committee to report to the floor and we will work to enact additional budget savings, beyond the budget cuts specifically included in the legislation described above, to ensure that the Federal budget deficit will be less than it would have been without the enactment of these bills.

Respecting the judgment of our fellow citizens as we seek their mandate for reform, we hereby pledge our names to this Contract with America.

APPENDIX 5

A CONSERVATIVE CASE FOR PRISON REFORM

By *RICHARD A. VIGUERIE*
The New York Times: June 9, 2013

MANASSAS, Va. — CONSERVATIVES should recognize that the entire criminal justice system is another government spending program fraught with the issues that plague all government programs. Criminal justice should be subject to the same level of skepticism and scrutiny that we apply to any other government program.

But it's not just the excessive and unwise spending that offends conservative values. Prisons, for example, are harmful to prisoners and their families. Reform is therefore also an issue of compassion. The current system often turns out prisoners who are more harmful to society than when they went in, so prison and re-entry reform are issues of public safety as well.

These three principles – public safety, compassion and controlled government spending – lie at the core of conservative philosophy. Politically speaking, conservatives will have more credibility than liberals in addressing prison reform.

The United States now has 5 percent of the world's population, yet 25 percent of its prisoners. Nearly one in every 33 American adults is in some form of correctional control. When Ronald Reagan was president, the total correctional control rate – everyone in prison or jail or on probation or parole – was less than half that: 1 in every 77 adults.

The prison system now costs states more than $50 billion a year, up from about $9 billion in 1985. It's the second-fastest growing area of state budgets, trailing only Medicaid. Conservatives should be leading the way by asking tough questions about the expansion in prison spending over the past three decades.

Increased spending has not improved effectiveness. More than 40 percent of ex-convicts return to prison within three years of release; in some states, recidivism rates are closer to 60 percent.

Too many offenders leave prisons unprepared to re-enter society. They don't get and keep jobs. The solution lies not only inside prisons but also with more effective community supervision systems using new technologies, drug tests and counseling programs. We should also require ex-convicts to either hold a job or perform community service. This approach works to turn offenders from tax burdens into taxpayers who can pay restitution to their victims and are capable of contributing child support.

The good news is that a national conservative movement to reform our criminal justice system, including volunteer pastoral counseling for prisoners and encouraging frequent contacts with family members, has been growing.

This Right on Crime campaign supports constitutionally limited government, individual liberty, personal responsibility and free enterprise. Conservatives known for being tough on crime should now be equally tough on failed, too-expensive criminal programs. They should demand more cost-effective approaches that enhance public safety and the well-being of all Americans.

Some prominent national Republican leaders who have joined this effort include Jeb Bush, Newt Gingrich, the anti-tax activist Grover Norquist, the National Rifle Association leader David Keene and the former attorney general Edwin Meese III.

Right on Crime exemplifies the big-picture conservative approach to this issue. It focuses on community-based programs rather than excessive mandatory minimum sentencing policies and prison expansion. Using free-market and Christian principles, conservatives have an opportunity to put their beliefs into practice as an alternative to government-knows-best pro-grams that are failing prisoners and the society into which they are released.

These principles work. In the past several years, there has been a dra-matic shift on crime and punishment policy across the country. It really started in Texas in 2007. The state said no to building eight more prisons and began to shift nonviolent offenders from state prison into alternatives, by strengthening probation and parole supervision and treatment. Texas was able to avert nearly $2 billion in projected corrections spending increases, and its crime rate is declining. At the same time, the state's parole failures have dropped by 39 percent.

Since then more than a dozen states have made significant changes to their sentencing and corrections laws, including Georgia, South Carolina, Vermont, New Hampshire and Ohio. Much of the focus has been on shortening or even eliminating prison time for the lowest-risk, nonviolent offenders and reinvesting the savings in more effective options.

With strong leadership from conservatives, South Dakota lawmakers passed a reform package in January that is expected to reduce costs by holding nonviolent offenders accountable through parole, probation, drug courts and other cost-effective programs.

By confronting this issue head on, conservatives are showing that our principles lead to practical solutions that make government less costly and more effective. We need to do more of that. Conservatives can show the way by impressing on more of our allies and political leaders that criminal justice reform is part of a conservative agenda.

A version of this op-ed appeared in print on June 10, 2013, on page A23 of the New York edition with the headline: A Conservative Case for Prison Reform.

APPENDIX 6

RICHARD VIGUERIE'S CANDIDATE ANALYSIS

A good candidate should answer YES to most of these questions
A potential great candidate can answer YES to all 10 questions

1. Have you read three or more of the following conservative books (listed in alphabetical order)?

    Capitalism and Freedom by Milton Friedman

    Economics in One Lesson by Henry Hazlitt

    Free to Choose by Milton and Rose Friedman

    God and Man at Yale by William F. Buckley, Jr.

    Ideas Have Consequences by Richard M. Weaver

    Liberty and Tyranny by Mark Levin

    The Conscience of a Conservative by Barry Goldwater

    The Conservative Mind by Russell Kirk

    The Law by Frederic Bastiat

    The Mainspring of Human Progress by Henry Grady Weaver

    The Road to Serfdom by F.A. Hayek

    The Ruling Class by Angelo M. Codevilla

    Up From Liberalism by William F. Buckley, Jr.

    Witness by Whittaker Chambers

These are some of the most important conservative books of the last sixty years. Be wary of a candidate who has not read at least three of them.

2. Do you subscribe or have in the last five years subscribed to two or more of these print publications?

    Claremont Review of Books

    Human Events

    Imprimis

    National Review

    Newsmax Magazine

    The American Spectator

    The Washington Times

    The Weekly Standard

    Townhall Magazine

    Whistleblower

3. Do you visit two or more of these Web sites every week?

    ConservativeHQ.com

    Breitbart.com

    cato.org (CATO Institute)

    dailycaller.com (Daily Caller)

    humanevents.com (Human Events)

    nationalreview.com (*National Review* Online)

    NewsMax.com

    RedState.com

    americanthinker.com (*The American Thinker*)

    heritage.org (The Heritage Foundation)

    washingtonexaminer.com (*The Washington Examiner*)

    washingtontimes.com (*The Washington Times*)

    townhall.com (Town Hall)

    WND.com (World Net Daily)

4. Do you listen to one or more of the following at least once a week?

    Sean Hannity

    Laura Ingram

    Mark Levin

    Rush Limbaugh

    Michael Medved

    Michael Savage

5. Do you attend services at a house of worship at least once a week?

6. Do you consider yourself a boat-rocker conservative in the model of Ronald Reagan, Mike Lee, Rand Paul, Ted Cruz, Scott Walker, and Jim DeMint?

7. Do you pledge to vote to replace any current Big-Government establishment Republican (congressional, state legislative, local legislative, and party) leaders with articulate, effective, principled boat-rocking limited-government constitutional conservatives?

8. In the past year, have you financially contributed to two or more limited-government constitutional conservative organizations or candidates?

9. Do you pledge to not request or support any earmarks?

10. Do you pledge to consider the constitutionality of each official action I take or vote I cast, and to vote no on any legislation that appears to be unconstitutional?

APPENDIX 7

ROGUE'S GALLERY

Leading Big Government Republicans Whose Defeat Would Advance the Cause of Conservative Governance

1. KARL ROVE

The Architect of George W. Bush's strategy of trying to buy votes with legal plunder (Frédéric Bastiat's term) and making the corrupt, but legal, bargain with the establishment Republicans in Congress to almost double the federal budget during his first six years as President. Rove has grown wealthy by promoting the idea that content-free campaigns, rather than conservative principles, are the path to victory for the Republican Party. His record of 22 losses to 9 wins in 2012 shows the folly of the Republican establishment in following Rove's advice.

2. REINCE PRIEBUS

Priebus was elected chairman of the Republican National Committee in January 2011. Since that time he has actively worked to dilute the power of grassroots Republican activists and put more power in the hands of the inside-the-Beltway Washington elite. Unlike the wise Republican leaders who built the Reagan coalition by welcoming new voters into the Republican Party, Priebus has done all he can to drive limited-government constitutional conservatives out of the GOP.

3. JOHN BOEHNER

Ohio establishment Republican representative Boehner was handed the Speaker's gavel in 2011 by the hard work and commitment of millions of Tea Party movement voters who turned out to elect Tea Party members to Congress in 2010. Since that time Boehner has caved in on every confrontation with Obama and the Democrats and done everything in his considerable power to dilute the power of Tea Party–leaning members of Congress. Referring to limited-government constitutional conservatives as "knuckle draggers" and telling principled conservatives to "get their ass in line," abandon their principles, and support the Republican establishment, Boehner epitomizes everything that is wrong with the principle-free Capitol Hill Republican leadership.

4. CHRIS CHRISTIE

New Jersey establishment Republican governor Chris Christie may be a brawler or a bully but he is no conservative. From gun control to campaigning for liberals like Mike Castle to embracing Obamacare's expansion of Medicaid, Christie has shown that he is ready to join Democrats and liberals to expand government and limit liberty. Perhaps that is why even after his staff was caught engaging in political payback worthy of Mayor Daley's Chicago politics, Christie remains one of the favored presidential candidates of the Republican establishment.

5. MITCH MCCONNELL

Kentucky's establishment Republican senator Mitch McConnell rose from Senate staffer to being one of the most powerful Republican politicians in America without any real experience in the private sector. McConnell follows in the tradition of other Senate Republican leaders, such as Howard Baker and Bob Dole, who rose to power by cutting deals with the Democrats rather than standing for conservative principles. McConnell's total lack of conservative principles was confirmed in November of 2013 when he convinced Republicans to compromise their principles and raise the debt ceiling and increase spending while he walked away with a $2.9 billion locks and dam project in the deal he brokered with Obama and the Democrats.

6. PAUL RYAN

While Wisconsin establishment Republican representative Paul Ryan talks a good game on some conservative principles, such as the right to life, he has risen to power by playing along with John Boehner, Eric Cantor, and the rest of Capitol Hill's Republican establishment. As the 2012 Republican vice presidential nominee Ryan failed to be an active advocate for conservative principles and his much-vaunted "Ryan Plan" to balance the budget would take almost thirty years to accomplish. Ryan burned his last bridges with limited-government constitutional conservatives when he announced his support for amnesty for illegal aliens and joined with Democratic Senator Patty Murray to break the spending limits in the sequester and ram through the Ryan–Murray budget to increase spending by $63 billion more than the budget caps set by the Budget Control Act of 2011.

7. KEVIN MCCARTHY

California establishment Republican representative Kevin McCarthy is one of the primary reasons the Capitol Hill Republicans and Democrats are virtually indistinguishable. One of the once-vaunted "young guns" of the House Republican Conference, McCarthy has used his formidable powers of persuasion to strong-arm reluctant Republican House members into betraying conservative principles and backing the lobbyists of K Street over the interests of the grassroots conservatives on Main Street. Perhaps McCarthy's greatest betrayal of conservative principles is his plan to help Boehner ram through an "amnesty for illegal aliens" bill which will make House Republicans the moving force behind the number one legislative priority of Obama's second term.

8. ERIC CANTOR

Once thought of as a somewhat more conservative alternative to establishment Republican Speaker John Boehner, Virginia establishment Republican and House majority leader Eric Cantor has become fully invested in Boehner's lobbyist-driven legislative agenda. From breaking the spending caps in the sequester to voting for the Wall Street bailout through the Troubled Asset Relief Program (TARP), when faced with a choice between business as usual and fighting for limited-government constitutional conservative principles, Cantor always sides with big business and the Capitol Hill establishment. Amnesty for illegal aliens is just the latest in a long list of betrayals conservatives have suffered at the hands of Eric Cantor.

9. LAMAR ALEXANDER

Tennessee's establishment Republican senator Lamar Alexander as Republican Conference Chairman was once the number three Republican leader in the Senate, but he resigned his post before his term was up in order to, as he put it, "foster consensus." It says a lot—and not in a good way—about the current state of the Senate Republican Conference that Alexander prefers Washington deal-making to foster consensus over staying in a leadership role where he could have advanced conservative principles. But that's par for the course for Senator Alexander. Be it the Gang of Eight amnesty bill or busting the budget with spending, Alexander votes Obama's position on the issues more often than practically any other Republican in the Senate.

10. THAD COCHRAN

"Why are you mad at Thad Cochran, he hasn't done anything?" you might be asking. Well, that's just the point. Mississippi establishment Republican senator Cochran, one of the least distinguished members of the Senate, has spent a thirty-six year career grasping for pork-barrel projects and feeding at the taxpayer-funded trough instead of fighting for conservative principles. In 2010 Citizens Against Government Waste named Cochran the leading pork-seeker in the Senate because he had his name on 240 earmarked projects worth $490.2 million of your hard-earned dollars.

11. PAT ROBERTS

Over the decades Kansas establishment Republican senator Pat Roberts has unfortunately become the quintessential career politician. He talks a good game, but when push comes to shove and conservative policy needs a strong and active advocate, he's not there. Roberts's 86 percent lifetime American Conservative Union rating doesn't put him that far ahead of progressive Republicans like John McCain and Lindsey Graham. Roberts's recent surge to the right reminds us all too much of Utah's senator Orrin Hatch, who adopted more conservative positions in the lead up to the 2012 campaign only to abandon conservatives and rejoin the Capitol Hill Republican establishment the day after the election.

12. JOHN CORNYN

Texas establishment Republican senator John Cornyn is the number two leader of the Senate Republican Conference. In this position he could be a strong voice for conservative policy and a counterweight to Senate Republican leader Mitch McConnell's deal-making ways. Instead Cornyn has succumbed to the fatal Washington "go along to get along" disease. When his fellow Texan senator, Ted Cruz, circulated a letter calling on Senate Republicans to defund Obamacare, Cornyn first put his name on the letter and then, when he realized Cruz, Mike Lee, and others were serious, he quickly took his name off the letter. Cornyn's tendency to cut and run in the face of opposition is the very opposite of the political ethos that raised the "come and take it" flag and won Texans their liberty.

13. JOHN MCCAIN

Arizona establishment Republican senator John McCain seems to relish antagonizing conservatives. From criticizing conservative leaders to attacking the principles millions of conservative voters live by to calling members of his own party who subscribe to limited-government constitutional conservative principles "whacko birds," McCain readily trains his guns on his fellow Republicans while giving the Democrats a pass. McCain's frequent sallies against his fellow Republicans earned him in January 2014 an unprecedented rebuke from the Arizona Republican State Committee for his "long and terrible" record of voting with liberal Democrats.

14. LINDSEY GRAHAM

South Carolina's establishment Republican senator Lindsey Graham rose to prominence as John McCain's reliable "wingman," ever ready to criticize conservatives for standing on principle. One of the first to blame the Tea Party for the GOP's failure to win the Senate majority in 2010, Graham was an outspoken advocate for unilateral military action in Syria and for supporting the ousted radical Islamist Muslim Brotherhood government in Egypt. Rather than embrace the Founder's wise counsel against foreign entanglements, Graham has rarely met a military spending bill or foreign adventure that he won't support.

15. THOMAS J. DONOHUE

As President of the US Chamber of Commerce, Tom Donohue knows none of his member companies would run their business the way the Washington establishment runs the federal government. But his job isn't to advocate for fiscal sanity or pro-growth economic policies, it is to protect the Wall Street–Washington–Silicon Valley axis that pays his salary. That is why when limited-government constitutional conservatives stood against raising the debt ceiling without spending cuts, Donohue told Tea Partiers that they must raise the debt ceiling or "we will get rid of you." Now Donohue is the leading advocate for amnesty for illegal aliens and has promised to spend $50 million raised from the cheap-labor wing of the business community to advance amnesty, the number one goal of Obama's second term.

16. JEB BUSH

No matter who else gets in the Republican presidential primaries, Jeb Bush will remain the "great white hope" of the Republican establishment. In addition to supporting all of their major policy goals from Common Core to amnesty for illegal aliens, a Bush candidacy also holds out the hope of millions of dollars in consulting business and lucrative lobbying contracts for a small but powerful coterie of Bush family supporters and acolytes. No one else in America, save Hillary Clinton, starts the 2016 political season with a larger Rolodex of Washington insider supporters than does Jeb Bush. A Jeb Bush election as president would ensure that the Republican establishment stays in power for at least another decade, and it would also ensure that, no matter if Jeb or the Democrat wins, Big Government will prevail.

APPENDIX 8

STRAW POLL SURVEY

GET IN THE FIGHT:
TAKE OUR SURVEY ON THE FUTURE OF AMERICA

Now that you have read *TAKEOVER*, I invite you to go to goptakeover.org and tell Americans how you feel on two important questions: NSA spying and your favorite Republican presidential candidate for 2016.

You can see your results immediately online. We will be sending the results to the national media (TV, radio, newspapers, bloggers, an d more). Tell your friends and family that if they want their opinion heard too, they should take the survey at goptakeover.org today.

QUESTION #1
Where do you stand on privacy and the Fourth Amendment? Please select the answer that most closely reflects your opinion.

❑ NSA eavesdropping on e-mail and telephone communications is necessary for our national security.

❑ The NSA needs complete top-to-bottom reform to stop the unconstitutional actions in which its out-of-control bureaucrats have engaged.

❑ Undecided, not sure

QUESTION #2

TAKEOVER 2016 Presidential Straw Poll—Who is your preferred
Republican candidate for President?

(Listed in alphabetical order)

- ❑ Jeb Bush
- ❑ Chris Christie
- ❑ Ted Cruz
- ❑ Mike Huckabee
- ❑ Rand Paul
- ❑ Sarah Palin
- ❑ Mike Pence
- ❑ Rick Perry
- ❑ Paul Ryan
- ❑ Marco Rubio
- ❑ Rick Santorum
- ❑ Scott Walker
- ❑ Other_____

NOTES

INTRODUCTION

1. "The Sharon Statement," September 11, 1960, accessed January 27, 2014, http://www
    .heritage.org/initiatives/first-principles/primary-sources/the-sharon-statement.
2. Joy Wilke, "Americans' Belief That Gov't Is Too Powerful at Record Level," Gallup Politics *,
    September 23, 2013, accessed January 27, 2014, http://www.gallup.com/poll/164591/
    americans-belief-gov-powerful-record-level.aspx.
3. Elizabeth Mendes, "In U.S., Fear of Big Government at Near-Record Level," Gallup Politics®,
    December 12, 2011, accessed January 27, 2014, http://www.gallup.com/poll/151490/Fear
    -Big-Government-Near-Record-level.aspx?utm_source=alert&utm_medium=email&utm
    _campaign=syndication&utm_content=morelink&utm_term=Business%20-%20Politics.

1: TEDDY ROOSEVELT THROUGH BARRY GOLDWATER

1. Medford Evans, "The 1952 Republican Convention," *American Opinion*, October 1976,
    accessed January 27, 2014, http://www.scribd.com/doc/54824285/1952-Republican
    -Convention.
2. Matthew Dallek, "The Conservative 1960s," review of *Turning Right in the Sixties: The
    Conservative Capture of the GOP* by Mary C. Brennan, *The Atlantic Monthly Digital Edi-
    tion*, December 1995, accessed January 27, 2014, http://www.theatlantic.com/past/docs
    /issues/95dec/conbook/conbook.htm.
3. Bart Barnes, "Barry Goldwater, GOP Hero, Dies," *The Washington Post*, Saturday, May 30,
    1998, accessed January 27, 2014, http://www.washingtonpost.com/wp-srv/politics/daily
    /may98/goldwater30.htm.
4. Dallek, "The Conservative 1960s."
5. Barnes, "Barry Goldwater, GOP Hero, Dies."
6. "YAF Awards Rally Planned for March; Goldwater to Speak," *Harvard Crimson*, January 17,
    1962, http://www.thecrimson.com/article/1962/1/17/yaf-awards-rally-planned-for-march/.
7. Dallek, "The Conservative 1960s."
8. Barnes, "Barry Goldwater, GOP Hero, Dies."

9. Michael Kenney, "The Goldwater Disaster and the Rise of Conservatism," review of *A Glorious Disaster: Barry Goldwater's Presidential Campaign and the Origins of the Conservative Movement* by J. William Middendorf II, *Chicago Tribune*, January 7, 2007, accessed January 27, 2014, http://articles.chicagotribune.com/2007-01-07/entertainment/0701060162_1_middendorf -conservative-movement-glorious-disaster.

10. Barnes, "Barry Goldwater, GOP Hero, Dies."

11. Dallek, "The Conservative 1960s."

12. Ibid.

13. Darcy G. Richardson, *A Nation Divided: The 1968 Presidential Campaign* (Lincoln, NE: Writers Club Press, 2002), 185.

14. George F. Will, "The Cheerful Malcontent," *Washington Post*, May 31, 1998, http://www .washingtonpost.com/wp-srv/politics/daily/may98/will31.htm.

15. Larry Harnisch, "Ronald Reagan and 'A Time for Choosing'," The Daily Mirror, *Los Angeles Times*, February 10, 2011, accessed January 27, 2014, http://latimesblogs.latimes.com /thedailymirror/2011/02/ronald-reagan-and-a-time-for-choosing.html.

16. Ronald Reagan, "A Time for Choosing" (speech delivered on national television on behalf of the Goldwater for President Committee, Los Angeles, CA, October 27, 1964), https:// constitution.hillsdale.edu/document.doc?id=287.

17. Harnisch, "Ronald Reagan and 'A Time for Choosing'."

2: RICHARD NIXON AND THE RISE OF RONALD REAGAN

1. Harnisch, "Ronald Reagan and 'A Time for Choosing'."

2. Ibid.

3. Rick Perlstein, "The Marriage that Ended a Political Career," George Mason University History News Network, undated, accessed January 25, 2014, http://hnn.us/article/203.

4. Stephen F. Knott, "Interview with Robert Tuttle and Maureen Molloy," *Ronald Reagan Oral History Project*, Miller Center, University of Virginia, December 12, 2003, http://millercenter .org/president/reagan/oralhistory/robert-tuttle.

5. Jeffery Lord, "The 1966 Election's Warning To Obama," *The American Spectator*, March 24, 2009, accessed January 28, 2014, http://spectator.org/articles/41919/1966-elections-warning-obama.

6. David R. Stokes, "The Forgotten Lesson of 1964," *The New Nixon* (blog), Nixon Foundation, October 8, 2010, accessed January 28, 2014, http://blog.nixonfoundation.org/2010/10/the -forgotten-lesson-of-1964/.

7. Stokes, "The Forgotten Lesson of 1964."

8. Andrew E. Busch, "Ronald Reagan's Electoral Career," The Heritage Foundation, undated, accessed January 28, 2014 http://www.reagansheritage.org/html/reagan_career_busch.shtml.

9. Larry J. Sabato, "George Romney's 'Brainwashing' – 1967," Feeding Frenzy, *Washington Post*, undated, accessed January 28, 2014, http://www.washingtonpost.com/wp-srv/politics/special /clinton/frenzy/romney.htm.

10. Jeff T. Wattrick, "How an Interview with Detroit Talk Show Host Lou Gordon Effectively Ended Mitt Romney's Father's Presidential Hopes," MLive Media Group, February 24, 2012, accessed January 28, 2014, http://www.mlive.com/news/detroit/index.ssf/2012/02 /how_an_interview_with_local_ta.html.

11. Peter Schweizer, *Reagan's War* (New York: Doubleday, 2002), 48.

12. Busch, "Ronald Reagan's Electoral Career."

13. Jack Doyle, "1968 Presidential Race," Hollywood & Politics, The Pop History Dig, undated, accessed January 28, 2014, http://www.pophistorydig.com/?tag=1968-democratic-primaries.

14. Lee Edwards, "Standing Athwart History: The Political Thought of William F. Buckley Jr.," *First Principles Series Report #29 on Political Thought*, The Heritage Foundation, May 5, 2010, accessed January 28, 2014, http://www.heritage.org/research/reports/2010/05 /standing-athwart-history-the-political-thought-of-william-f-buckley-jr.

15. Edwards, "Standing Athwart History."

16. Peter W. Schramm, "Who was John Ashbrook?" *American National Biography*, ed. John A. Garraty and Mark C. Carnes, vol. 1, (New York: Oxford University Press, 1999), accessed January 28, 2014, http://ashbrook.org/about/john-ashbrook/.
17. Schweizer, *Reagan's War*, 89.
18. Ibid., 90.
19. Busch, "Ronald Reagan's Electoral Career."
20. Ronald W. Reagan, *An American Life* (New York: Simon and Schuster, 1990), 202.

3: THE NEW RIGHT AND REAGAN'S 1980 VICTORY

1. Reagan, *An American Life*, 203.
2. "American President: A Reference Resource, Gerald Rudolph Ford," Miller Center, University of Virginia, undated, accessed January 28, 2014, http://millercenter.org/president/ford/essays/biography/4.
3. Reagan, *An American Life*, 206.
4. James Taranto, "Social Issues and the Santorum Surge," *Wall Street Journal*, February 18, 2012, accessed January 28, 2014, http://online.wsj.com/news/articles/SB10001424052970204880404577227694132901090.
5. Jon Margolis, "Reagan Finds Help In Mainstream," *Chicago Tribune*, February 28, 1987, accessed January 28, 2014, http://articles.chicagotribune.com/1987-02-28/news/8701160700_1_sen-baker-howard-baker-riverboat-gamble

4: THWARTING THE REAGAN REVOLUTION

1. Reagan, *An American Life*, 314.
2. Ibid., 315.
3. Ibid., 316.
4. Ibid., 314.
5. Sara Fritz, "'Pork Barrel' Bill Reagan Opposes Tied to Contra Aid," *Los Angeles Times*, April 16, 1986, accessed January 28, 2014, http://articles.latimes.com/1986-04-16/news/mn-1_1_spending-bill.
6. Staff Report, "GOP VP Prospect Supported Nuclear Freeze, Opposed SDI," CNS News, August 14, 2008, accessed January 28, 2014, http://cnsnews.com/news/article/gop-vp-prospect-supported-nuclear-freeze-opposed-sdi.
7. Timothy Aeppel, "Scientists Lining Up for and against Reagan's 'Star Wars'. Politics Intrudes on Missile Defense Research," *Christian Science Monitor*, October 23, 1986, accessed January 28, 2014, http://www.csmonitor.com/1986/1023/adeb.html.
8. Mark W. Davis, "Reagan's Real Reason for SDI," *Policy Review*, no. 103 (October 1, 2000), Hoover Institution, Stanford University, accessed January 28, 2014, http://www.hoover.org/publications/policy-review/article/7552.
9. Aeppel, "Scientists Lining Up."

5: THE 1988 PRIMARY CAMPAIGN: THE ESTABLISHMENT STRIKES BACK

1. Reagan, *An American Life*, 321.

6: "READ MY LIPS. . . "

1. "The Republicans in New Orleans; Transcript of Bush Speech Accepting Nomination for President," *New York Times,* August 19, 1988, accessed January 28, 2014, http://www.nytimes.com/1988/08/19/us/republicans-new-orleans-transcipt-bush-speech-accepting-nomination-for-president.html?pagewanted=all&src=pm.

2. Ibid.
3. Ibid.
4. "Barry Never Was One To Beat Around The Bush, George," Philly.com, September 22, 1988, accessed January 28, 2014, http://articles.philly.com/1988-09-22/news/26231641_1_bush-dukakis-lectern-bush-people.

8: THE NEW MEDIA AND THE RISE OF THE CONTRACT WITH AMERICA CONGRESS

1. Jeffrey B. Gayner, "The Contract with America: Implementing New Ideas in the U.S.," *Political Thought*, The Heritage Foundation, October 12, 1995, accessed January 28, 2014, http://www.heritage.org/research/lecture/the-contract-with-america-implementing-new-ideas-in-the-us.
2. Edward H. Crane, "On My Mind: GOP Pussycats," *Forbes*, November 13, 2000, accessed January 28, 2014, http://www.cato.org/publications/commentary/mind-gop-pussycats.

9: BIG GOVERNMENT REPUBLICANS BACK IN CONTROL

1. Jack W. Germond & Jules Witcover, "Bob Dole, alias Ronald Reagan?" *Baltimore Sun*, June 5, 1996, accessed January 28, 2014, http://articles.baltimoresun.com/1996-06-05/news/1996157061_1_bob-dole-ronald-reagan-tax-cuts.
2. Taranto, "Social Issues and the Santorum Surge."
3. George Will, "A Squalid Presidency Vs. An Unintelligible Opponent," *Orlando Sentinel*, November 3, 1996, accessed January 28, 2014 http://articles.orlandosentinel.com/1996-11-03/news/9611011016_1_unintelligible-dole-squalid.
4. Barbara Shelly, "Commentary: Dole Changes Tune on Health Care," *Kansas City Star*, October 13, 2009, accessed January 28, 2014, http://www.mcclatchydc.com/2009/10/13/76997/commentary-dole-changes-tune-on.html.

10: CONSERVATIVES OPEN THE DOOR TO ANOTHER BUSH

1. Evan Thomas and Peter Goldman, "Victory March: The Inside Story," *Newsweek*, November 18, 1996, 124.
2. Dan Balz, "Subdued GOP Resumes Lead With Eye to Past," *Washington Post*, January 8, 1997, accessed January 28, 2014, http://www.washingtonpost.com/wp-srv/national/longterm/inaug/issues/gop.htm.
3. Balz, "Subdued GOP Resumes Lead."
4. Ibid.
5. Ann Scales, "Governors in talks on GOP agenda," *Boston Globe*, November 25, 1996, accessed January 28, 2014, http://www.highbeam.com/doc/1P2-8400793.html.
6. Thomas J. Fitzgerald, "GOP Reduces Vision For New Congress," *The Record* (Bergen County, NJ), November 26, 1996, accessed January 28, 2014, http://www.highbeam.com/doc/1P1-22524466.html.
7. Judith Havemann, "With Help, GOP Gains Kentucky Senate," *Washington Post*, January 29, 1997.
8. Robert Novak, "Donors' Hot Spot?" *Chicago Sun-Times*, March 9, 1997, accessed January 28, 2014, http://www.highbeam.com/doc/1P2-4373688.html.
9. Transcript of Remarks of Texas Governor George W. Bush to Republican Midwestern Leadership Conference, August 23, 1997, accessed January 28, 2014, http://votesmart.org/public-statement/225/delivers-remarks-at-the-republican-midwestern-leadership-conference#.UuflFhAo6M8.

11: THE SELLING OF GOVERNOR GEORGE W. BUSH AS A "CONSERVATIVE"

1. Andrew Marshall, "George W Bush Was Meant to Be a Shoe-In for the White House," *The Independent* (London, England) February 15, 2000, accessed January 28, 2014, http://www.highbeam.com/doc/1P2-5057093.html.
2. Ibid.
3. Curtis Wilke, "South Carolina's GOP Lines Up behind Bush but Senator McCain Finds Enthusiasm for Candidacy in Next Year's Primary," *Boston Globe*, March 14, 1999, accessed January 28, 2014, http://www.highbeam.com/doc/1P2-8525073.html.
4. "Profile: McCain and Bush Getting in Their Final Jabs at One Another Before the All-Important South Carolina Primary," NPR, *All Things Considered*, February 18, 2000, http://www.highbeam.com/doc/1P1-77193586.html.
5. Ibid.
6. "Governor George W. Bush Delivers Victory Speech Following Republican Primary in South Carolina," Washington Transcript Service, February 19, 2000, http://www.highbeam.com/doc/1P1-29464528.html.
7. Marshall, "George W Bush Meant to Be a Shoe-In."

12: CONSERVATIVES BETRAYED: THE PRESIDENCY OF GEORGE W. BUSH

1. Alison Acosta Fraser, "Federal Spending by the Numbers — 2012," Heritage Foundation, accessed January 28, 2014, http://www.heritage.org/research/reports/2012/10/federal-spending-by-the-numbers-2012.
2. Brendan Greeley, "Earmarks: The Reluctant Case for Ending the Ban," *Bloomberg BusinessWeek*, January 10, 2013, accessed January 28, 2014, http://www.businessweek.com/articles/2013-01-10/earmarks-the-reluctant-case-for-ending-the-ban.
3. Phil Kerpen, "Earmarks and the Executive," *National Review Online*, January 4, 2008, accessed January 28, 2014, http://www.nationalreview.com/articles/223271/earmarks-and-executive/phil-kerpen.
4. Nancy Benac, "Scandal Increases Scrutiny of K Street," AP Online, February 1, 2006, accessed January 28, 2014, http://www.highbeam.com/doc/1P1-118009935.html.
5. Veronique de Rugy, "Spending Under President George W. Bush," Mercatus Center, George Mason University, March 2009, accessed January 28, 2014, http://mercatus.org/sites/default/files/WP0904_GAP_Spending-Under-President-George-W-Bush_v2.pdf.
6. Ibid.
7. "Bush a Convert to Nation Building," *Washington Times*, April 7, 2008, accessed January 28, 2014, http://www.washingtontimes.com/news/2008/apr/7/bush-a-convert-to-nation-building/?page=all.
8. Brad Knickerbocker, "Illegal Immigrants in the US: How Many Are There?" *Christian Science Monitor*, May 16, 2006, accessed January 28, 2014, http://www.csmonitor.com/2006/0516/p01s02-ussc.html.
9. Owen S. Good, "Tancredo, Bush At Odds Again Congressman Says Visa Holders Take Americans' Jobs," *Rocky Mountain News* (Denver, CO), September 23, 2003, accessed January 28, 2014, http://www.highbeam.com/doc/1G1-108187524.html.
10. Rachel Uranga, "Immigration Report Says One Out of Every 11 Mexicans Has Emigrated to U.S.," *Daily News* (Los Angeles, CA), June 15, 2005, accessed January 28, 2014, http://www.highbeam.com/doc/1G1-133251261.html.
11. Phyllis Schlafly, "Pretending Immigration Isn't an Issue," The Phyllis Schlafly Report 36, no. 2 (September 2002), accessed January 28, 2014, http://www.eagleforum.org/psr/2002/sept02/psrsept02.shtml.
12. President Bush Delivers Remarks on Border Security and Immigration Reform, Davis-Month Air Force Base, Tucson, Arizona, Political Transcript Wire, November 28, 2005.
13. Carl Hulse and Jim Rutenberg, "Border Fence Puts Momentum into U.S. Senate Immigration Measure," *International Herald Tribune*, May 18, 2006, accessed January 28, 2014, http://www.highbeam.com/doc/1P1-123785778.html.

14. Ibid.
15. "Not Criminal, Just Hopeful," *The Economist* (US edition), April 15, 2006, accessed January 28, 2014, http://www.economist.com/node/6802645.
16. Fox News Transcript: 'Special Report with Brit Hume,' May 30, 2007, accessed January 28, 2014, http://www.foxnews.com/story/2007/05/31/transcript-special-report-with-brit-hume-may-30-2007/.
17. Ibid.
18. Ibid.

13: THE 2006 ELECTION: AMERICA REJECTS BIG GOVERNMENT REPUBLICANISM

1. L. Brent Bozell, III, "From the Right, He Looks Too Blue; Think Real Conservatives Will Vote for John McCain? Don't Count on It," *Washington Post*, March 9, 2008, accessed January 28, 2014, http://www.highbeam.com/doc/1P2-15475658.html.
2. Bill Berkowitz, "Republicans Must Lose Now To Win Later," Interpress Service, October 9, 2006, accessed January 28, 2014, http://www.highbeam.com/doc/1G1-161268648.html.
3. Melissa Block, "GOP Groundswell Stems from Party Discontent; Viguerie Interview," National Public Radio, *All Things Considered*, June 9, 2006, accessed January 28, 2014 http://www.npr.org/templates/story/story.php?storyId=5475146.
4. Richard A. Viguerie, "The Show Must Not Go On," *Washington Monthly*, October 2006, accessed January 28, 2014, http://www.washingtonmonthly.com/features/2006/0610.viguerie.html.
5. John Aloysius Farrell, "Bush Suffering Second-Term Doldrums," *Deseret News* (Salt Lake City), August 14, 2005, accessed January 28, 2014, http://www.highbeam.com/doc/1P2-7229795.html.
6. "Editorial: Republican Spendthrifts," *Chicago Tribune*, August 16, 2005, accessed January 28, 2014, http://articles.chicagotribune.com/2005-08-16/news/0508160014_1_budget-that-sets-priorities-congressional-budget-office-homeland-security.
7. Stephen Slivinski, "Cato Scholars Available to Comment on CBO's New Deficit Numbers," The Cato Institute, January 26, 2006, accessed January 28, 2014, http://www.cato.org/news-releases/2006/1/26/cato-scholars-available-comment-cbos-new-deficit-numbers.
8. Michael D. Tanner, "What If Economic Conservatives Stay Home on Election Day?" The Cato Institute, November 20, 2007, accessed January 28, 2014, http://www.cato.org/publications/commentary/what-economic-conservatives-stay-home-election-day.

14: 2007 AND 2008: GEORGE W. BUSH'S CRAVEN RETREAT AND SURRENDER

1. Juliet Eilperin and Michael Grunwald, "A New Pitchman -- and a New Pitch," *Washington Post*, May 9, 2007, accessed January 28, 2014, http://www.washingtonpost.com/wp-dyn/content/article/2007/05/08/AR2007050801924.html.
2. Gary Langer, Dalia Sussman, Peyton Craighill, Rich Morin, Brian Hartman and Bob Shapiro, "Much-Diminished GOP Absorbs the Voters' Ire," ABC News, November 8, 2006, accessed January 28, 2014, http://abcnews.go.com/Politics/Vote2006/story?id=2637650&page=1.
3. Office of Management and Budget, "Historical Tables," accessed January 28, 2014, http://www.whitehouse.gov/omb/budget/HISTORICALS.

15: MCCAIN WASTES CONSERVATIVE ENTHUSIASM FOR PALIN, OBAMA WINS

1. Stephen Dinan, "Moderates Fuel McCain Victories; Huckabee Holds off Romney in South," *Washington Times*, February 6, 2008, accessed January 28, 2014, http://www.highbeam.com/doc/1G1-174293690.html.

2. Michael Cooper, "McCain's Moment at CPAC," The Caucus Blog, *New York Times*, February 7, 2008, accessed January 28, 2014, http://thecaucus.blogs.nytimes.com/2008/02/07 /mccain-at-cpac/?_r=0.
3. "Richard Viguerie: She's Perfect," *Politics & Government Week*, September 18, 2008, accessed January 28, 2014, http://www.highbeam.com/doc/1G1-185982189.html.
4. Gallup Daily: Election 2008, Gallup Politics®, undated, accessed January 28, 2014, http:// www.gallup.com/poll/107674/gallup-daily-election-2008.aspx.
5. George Rasley, "Sarah Palin's Magic," *Politico*, November 13, 2008, accessed January 28, 2014, http://www.politico.com/news/stories/1108/15596.html.

16: THE TEA PARTY BECOMES THE OPPOSITION TO OBAMA

1. Rasley, "Sarah Palin's Magic."
2. Linda Feldmann, "After GOP Landslide of Election 2010, What Next for Obama?" *Christian Science Monitor*, November 3, 2010, accessed January 28, 2014, http://www.highbeam.com /doc/1G1-241232339.html.

17: ESTABLISHMENT REPUBLICANS THROW AWAY THE 2010 REALIGNMENT

1. Timothy P. Carney, "In Energy Race, Boehners Vote Is Enough for Upton," *Washington Examiner*, November 11, 2010, accessed January 28, 2014, http://www.highbeam.com /doc/1P2-26817721.html.
2. Ibid.
3. Ibid.
4. Ibid.
5. Statement of CAGW President Tom Schatz, "CAGW Blasts Imperial Congress: Deficit Soars While Pols Jet-Set," August 10, 2009, accessed January 28, 2014, http://cagw.org/media /press-releases/cagw-blasts-imperial-congress-deficit-soars-while-pols-jet-set.
6. Halimah Abdullah, "'Prince of Pork' Gets Key House Post," *Seattle Times*, December 8, 2010, accessed January 28, 2014, http://www.highbeam.com/doc/1G1-243838322.html.
7. Froma Harrop, "In Politics, Disapproval, of course, Is a Relative Thing," *Charleston* (WV) *Gazette*, September 14, 2011, accessed January 28, 2014, http://www.highbeam.com/doc/1P2-29625034.html.
8. Statement of Speaker John Boehner, "House Passes Boehner-Backed Cut, Cap, & Balance Act," July 20, 2011, accessed January 28, 2014, http://www.johnboehner.com/blog/house -passes-boehner-backed-cut-cap-balance-act.
9. Dean Clancy, "Instant Analysis: Boehner Debt Plan Falls Short of 'Cut Cap & Balance,'" FreedomWorks, July 26, 2011, accessed January 28, 2014, http://www.freedomworks.org /blog/dean-clancy/boehner-debt-plan-falls-short-of-cut-cap-balance.
10. Rob Bluey, "House Won't Provide 72 Hours to Review Budget Control Act," The Heritage Foundation, *Scribe: Heritage Investigates* (blog), August 1, 2011, accessed January 28, 2014, http://blog.heritage.org/2011/08/01/house-wont-provide-72-hours-to-review-budget-control -act/.

18: THE PARTY OF STUPID PUTS THE MEDIA IN CHARGE OF THEIR DEBATES

1. Dan Balz and Philip Rucker, "N.H. debate raises variety of issues, but Romney's lead is largely untouched," *Washington Post*, January 7, 2012, accessed January 28, 2014, http:// www.washingtonpost.com/politics/mitt-romney-under-other-gop-candidates-attack-ahead -of-nh-debate/2012/01/07/gIQAf3UlhP_story.html.
2. Brad Wilmouth, "In Debate, ABC's Stephanopoulos Presses Romney on 1965 Contraception Ruling," NewsBusters, January 8, 2012, accessed January 28, 2014, http://newsbusters.org /blogs/brad-wilmouth/2012/01/08/debate-abcs-stephanopoulos-presses-romney -contraception-ruling.

3. Rush Limbaugh, "Democrats Ginned Up Contraception Debate to Fire Up Their Base, Divide the GOP and Distract from the Economy," Rush Limbaugh program transcript, February 16, 2012, accessed January 28, 2014, http://www.rushlimbaugh.com/daily/2012/02/16 /democrats_ginned_up_contraception_debate_to_fire_up_their_base_divide_the_gop _and_distract_from_the_economy.
4. Ibid.
5. Ibid.
6. George Rasley transcription of Anderson Cooper audio, accessed January 28, 2014, http:// media.eyeblast.org/newsbusters/static/2009/04/2009-04-14-CNN-AC360.mp3.
7. Matt Hadro, "Anderson Cooper Cherry Picks Poll Info to Disgrace Republicans," NewsBusters, July 28, 2011, accessed January 28, 2014, http://www.newsbusters.org/blogs/matt-hadro /2011/07/28/anderson-cooper-cherry-picks-poll-info-disgrace-republicans.
8. "Part 3: 21:00-21:30, CNN-Tea Party Republican Debate Transcript," CNN, September 12, 2011, accessed January 28, 2014, http://transcripts.cnn.com/TRANSCRIPTS/1109/12/se.04 .html.
9. "State Of The Union With Candy Crowley Transcript," CNN, August 14, 2011, accessed January 28, 2014, http://transcripts.cnn.com/TRANSCRIPTS/1108/14/sotu.01.html.
10. Brent Baker, "CBS's Schieffer Pushes Romney to Move 'Toward the Center,' Urges Him to Say 'I'm a Moderate,'" NewsBusters, September 30, 2012, accessed January 28, 2014, http:// newsbusters.org/blogs/brent-baker/2012/09/30/cbs-s-schieffer-pushes-romney-move-toward -center-urges-him-say-i-m-mode.
11. "Cain, Gingrich Debate Lincoln-Douglas Style," C-SPAN®, Updated: Monday, November 7, 2011 at 10:06am (ET), accessed January 28, 2014, http://www.c-span.org/Events/Cain -Gingrich-Debate-Lincoln-Douglas-Style/10737425199/.

19: CONSULTANTS MAKE MILLIONS WRECKING THE GOP

1. Morton Blackwell, "The GOP's consultant problem," *Daily Caller*, November 26, 2012, accessed January 28, 2014, http://dailycaller.com/2012/11/26/the-gops-consultant -problem/?print=1.
2. Michael Patrick Leahy, "Caddell Unloads On 'Racketeering' GOP Consultants," *Breitbart*, March 14, 2013, accessed January 28, 2014, http://www.breitbart.com/Big-Government /2013/03/14/Caddell-Blows-the-Lid-Off-CPAC-With-Blistering-Attack-on-Racketeering -Republican-Consultants.
3. Ibid.
4. Ibid.
5. Michael Patrick Leahy, "FEC: Romney Campaign, RNC Paid Over $150M To Two Well- Connected Consulting Firms," *Breitbart*, December 7, 2012, accessed January 28, 2014, http://www.breitbart.com/Big-Government/2012/12/07/Romney-Campaign-RNC-Paid -More-Than-150-Million-to-Two-Well-Connected-Consulting-Firms.
6. Erick Erickson, "The Incestuous Bleeding of the Republican Party," *RedState*, November 28, 2012, accessed January 28, 2014, http://www.redstate.com/2012/11/28/the-incestuous -bleeding-of-the-republican-party/.
7. Ibid.

20: KARL ROVE AND REINCE PRIEBUS GIVE AWAY KEY ELECTIONS IN 2012 AND 2013

1. Terence P. Jeffrey, "Which Babies Should Get the Death Sentence?" CNS News™, August 22, 2012, accessed January 28, 2014, http://cnsnews.com/blog/terence-p-jeffrey/which-babies -should-get-death-sentence.
2. Lucy Madison, "Richard Mourdock: Even Pregnancy from Rape Something 'God Intended,'" October 24, 2012, accessed January 28, 2014, http://www.cbsnews.com/news/richard -mourdock-even-pregnancy-from-rape-something-god-intended/.

3. Josh Voorhees, "GOP Senate Candidate Suggests Pregnancy From Rape Is 'Something That God Intended,'" *Slate*, Oct. 24, 2012, accessed January 28, 2014, http://www.slate.com /blogs/the_slatest/2012/10/24/richard_mourdock_rape_comment_gop_senate_hopeful _says_rape_is_something.html.

4. Jeffrey Meyer, "NBC Demands: 'Does the Romney Campaign Believe That God Intends Rape?'" NewsBusters, October 24, 2012, accessed January 28, 2014, http://newsbusters.org /blogs/jeffrey-meyer/2012/10/24/nbc-demands-does-romney-campaign-believe-god-intends -rape.

5. Voorhees, "GOP Senate Candidate Suggests."

6. Phyllis Schlafly, "No More Karl Rove Candidates!" WND Commentary, February 11, 2013, accessed January 28, 2014, http://www.wnd.com/2013/02/no-more-karl-rove-candidates/.

7. Paul Scicchitano and Kathleen Walter, "Chocola to Rove: 'You're Not Helping the Republicans' by Targeting Candidates," *NewsMax*, February 4, 2013, accessed January 28, 2014, http://www.newsmax.com/Newsfront/Chocola-Rove-Republicans-electability/2013/02/04 /id/488853.

8. Tom Donelson, "Lessons From A Ted Cruz Victory," *Texas GOP Vote*, August 2, 2012, accessed January 28, 2014, http://www.texasgopvote.com/knowledge-topics/2012-elections /lessons-ted-cruz-victory-004403.

9. Jason Whitely, "Cruz Stuns Republican Establishment, Beats Dewhurst," WFAA television report, July 31, 2012, accessed January 28, 2014, http://www.wfaa.com/news/politics/Texas -GOP-chooses-tea-party-backed-Cruz-for-Senate-164529536.html.

10. Nate Silver, "New Rove Group Could Backfire on G.O.P.," Five Thirty Eight (blog), *New York Times*, February 11, 2013, accessed January 28, 2014, http://fivethirtyeight.blogs.nytimes .com/2013/02/11/new-rove-group-could-backfire-on-g-o-p/#more-38592.

21: IT'S THE PRIMARIES, STUPID!

1. Bill Barry, "A Trip Into Idea Land With Bill Buckley," *Miami* (FL) *News*, April 18, 1967, accessed January 28, 2014, http://news.google.com/newspapers?id=IqwyAAAAIBAJ&sj id=z-kFAAAAIBAJ&pg=646,313367&dq=buckley+rightward+viable-candidate&hl=en.

2. Ann Coulter, "William F. Buckley: R.I.P., Enfant Terrible," WND Commentary, February 27, 2008, accessed January 28, 2014, http://www.wnd.com/2008/02/57528/.

22: THE LIBERTY PRIZE: PRACTICAL IDEAS TO TAKE OVER THE GOP

1. I do not endorse the purchase of any product mentioned in this book and encourage readers of *TAKEOVER* to do their own research and to contact Lorie Medina or Michael Patrick Leahy for firsthand information on and their experience with MoonShadow Mobile's Ground Game.

23: VIGUERIE'S PLAN FOR CONSERVATIVES TO TAKE OVER THE GOP AND GOVERN AMERICA BY 2017

1. Arthur C. Brooks, "Why Conservatives Are Happier Than Liberals," *New York Times*, July 7, 2012, accessed January 28, 2014, http://www.nytimes.com/2012/07/08/opinion/sunday /conservatives-are-happier-and-extremists-are-happiest-of-all.html?_r=0.

INDEX

Thank you for choosing to read

TAKEOVER

If you enjoyed this book, we hope that you will tell your friends and family. There are many ways to spread the word:

Share your thoughts on Facebook, your blog, or Tweet "You should read #TAKEOVER by Richard Viguerie // @worldnetdaily"

Take the survey at **goptakeover.org** and tell your family and friends to take the survey too.

Send a copy to someone you know who would benefit from reading this book.

Write a review online at Amazon.com or BN.com

Subscribe to WND at www.wnd.com

Visit the WND Superstore at superstore.wnd.com

WND Books

A WND COMPANY   •   WASHINGTON DC   •   WNDBOOKS.COM

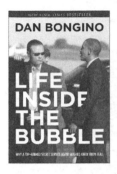
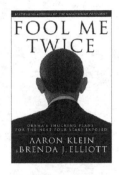

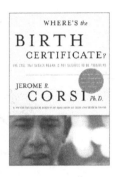

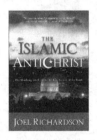

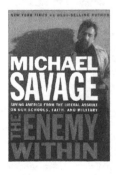
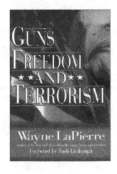
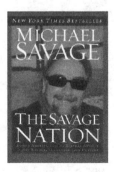
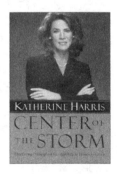

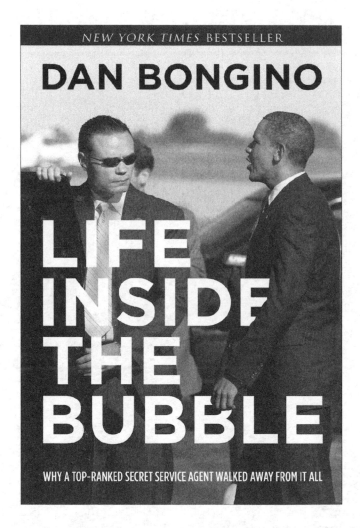

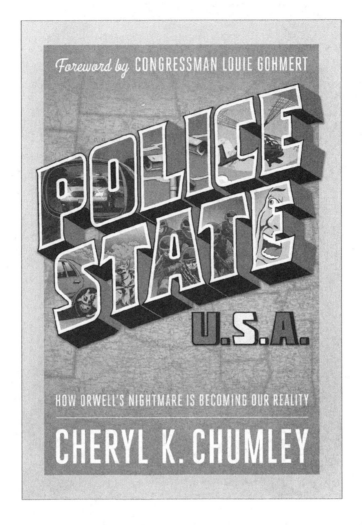

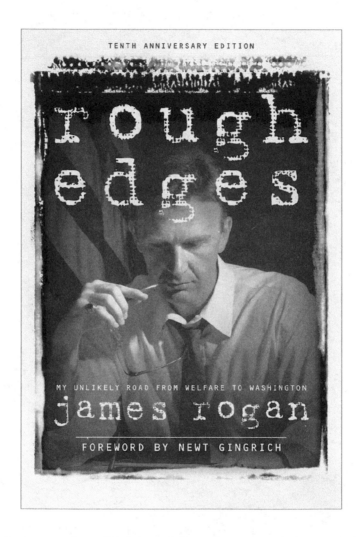

WND Books

PRESENTS

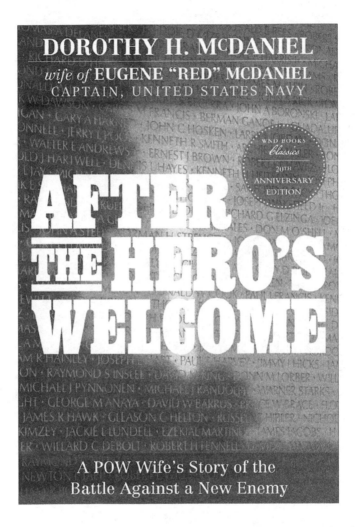

After the Hero's Welcome is the critically acclaimed war memoir that chronicles Dorothy H. McDaniel's fight to find information on her POW husband, Eugene, and his subsequent release from a North Vietnam prison that prompted them both to fight to have the United States government conduct search and rescue missions for prisoners they believed were still being held.

WND Books • A **WND** COMPANY • WASHINGTON DC • WNDBOOKS.COM